Apr 1993

PARENTS, KIDS &
COMPUTERS

An Activity Guide for Family Play and Learning

R. RASKIN & C. ELLISON

RANDOM HOUSE
ELECTRONIC PUBLISHING

New York

Parents, Kids, and Computers

Copyright © 1992 by Robin Raskin and Carol Ellison
Illustrations Copyright © 1992 by Udo Drescher

Published in the United States by Random House, Inc., New York, and simultaneously in Canada by Random House of Canada, Limited.

Manufactured in the United States of America.

Library of Congress Cataloging-in-Publication Data

Raskin, Robin, 1954–
    Parents, kids & computers / an activity guide for family fun and learning / written by Robin Raskin and Carol Ellison.
        p.   cm.
    Includes index.
    ISBN 0-679-73910-6
    1. Microcomputers. 2. Computers and children. I. Ellison, Carol. II. Title. III. Title: Parents, kids, and computers.
    QA76.5.R362   1992
    004—dc20   92-23044
                                                                          CIP

The author(s) and publisher have used their best efforts in preparing this book. However, the author(s) and publisher make no warranties of any kind, express or implied, with regard to the documentation or programs or data contained in this book, and specifically disclaim without limitation, any implied warranties of merchantability and fitness for a particular purpose with respect to programs and/or data contained therein, program listings in the book and/or the techniques described in the book. In no event shall the author or publisher be responsible or liable for any loss of profit or any other commercial damages, including but not limited to special, incidental, consequential or any other damages in connection with or arising out of furnishing, performance, or use of this book or the programs or data.

Trademarks
A number of entered words in which we have reason to believe trademark, service mark, or other proprietary rights may exist have been designated as such by use of initial capitalization. However, no attempt has been made to designate as trademarks or service marks all personal computer words or terms in which proprietary rights might exist. The inclusion, exclusion or definition of a word or term is not intended to affect, or to express any judgment on, the validity or legal status of any proprietary right which may be claimed in that word or term.

To our parents who managed to raise fine families
without any computer aided assistance.

Acknowledgments

When you're the Executive Editor of a magazine, the mother of three activity-ridden children, and you try and write a book as a labor of love, you need all the help you can get. And I got it ... in the form of encouragement and hard work from many different sources.

My first and deepest thanks go to my husband who suffered through some rotten evenings while I played with software. Second thanks go to my co-author, Carol Ellison, since co-authoring is fairly close to marriage. And my children, Kari, Arli, and Reed ... you can take a short break from the computer and get some fresh air now. Udo, my cartoonist brother-in-law, and Gayle, Bruce, Michael, Mom and Dad who rolled up their sleeves and offered everything from babysitting to legal advice. And to Heather, who keeps our house functional.

Then there's Michael Mellin, my editor at Random House, who let us share a piece of his vision of an electronic future. And Julie O'Leary, an editor who sheltered us from many storms. And Jane Mellin, Clay Andrus, and Mia McCroskey, who's specific knowledge and editorial pens enhanced these pages.

There's Bill Gross (Knowledge Adventure), Sharyn Fitzpatrick (Learning Company), Connie Connors (Connors Communications) and Karen Olmholt/Jessica Switzer (Broderbund) ... longtime friends whose belief in high-tech kids and parents fueled us.

And finally thanks to all my very special friends at PC Magazine for putting up with me as I worked double time. Special thanks to Vice President, Bill Machrone, who first encouraged me to take the plunge and to Editor in Chief, Michael Miller who indulged me as I talked about phonics and farm animals instead of spreadsheets and databases. And to Chris Evelyn, who kept the chapters coming and going.

—Robin Raskin

My deepest thanks go to Robin for the opportunity and for her friendship and the stamina that kept us both going. And to my husband Craig Ellison who supported me and our home computer network through this effort and moved a household from Massachusetts to New Jersey while his wife was chasing Carmen Sandiego across a computer screen.

Special acknowledgements go to my parents who have never been far away and never will be, to Jake Winebaum and the gang at Family Fun magazine who share the hope and vision Robin and I have of the future, to John Dickinson and Nancy Vanatt whose counsel and support was there when it was most needed, to Brandon Haverburg who is the best four-year-old editorial consultant I've ever worked with, to Kimberly Mulligan who counsels me with teen-aged wisdom and to her mother, Phyllis, who should have been with us to share this joy. We miss you, my friend.

—Carol Ellison

CONTENTS

Preface   xv

Introduction Kids and Computers: An Equation for Success   xxi
              Section I: Nuts and Bolts   xxiii
              Section II: A Plan of Action for a Computer Literate Family   xxiii
              Section III: Software Classics for Kids   xxiv
              A Little Editorializing   xxiv

Section 1   Nuts and Bolts   1

Chapter 1   What You'll Need: Hardware   3
              The Basic Box   6
              Big Macs: A Hearty Selection   13
              Inside IBM PC-Compatibles: The Chip's the Thing   16
              Disks: Electronic Filing Cabinets   19
              Memory: The Ultimate Desktop   21
              Video: Getting the Picture   23
                  Macintosh Video   24
                  Video On IBM PC-Compatible Computers   26
              Plugging in Keyboards, Mice, and Modems   29
              Printers   34
              Sound, Action   36
              CD-ROM and Multimedia PCs   37
              Putting It All Together   39
                  IBM PC-Compatible Systems   39
                  Macintosh Systems   41

Chapter 2   What You'll Need: Software   43
              Choosing Good Software   46
              Sorting through the Kids' Software Maze   49
                  Simulations   50
                  Edutainment   50
                  Arcade Games   51
                  Role-Playing and Fantasy Games   52
                  Creativity Tools   53
                  Drill and Practice   53
                  Adult Programs   54

Chapter 3   Finding the Best Buys   55
              Where to Buy   60
                  Finding the Best Buy   60

Shopping Tips **61**
Sources for Products and Information **62**
    Mailorder Companies **64**
    Discount Stores and Buyers Clubs **65**
    Homebrewers **68**
    Computer Fairs **69**
    Garage Sales and the Classifieds **69**
    Mac Simplicity **70**

Chapter 4   **Bringing Home Baby—The Perfect Setup for Your New PC 73**
Childproofing Your Computer **76**
Encouraging Independence **80**
Choosing from a Menu **81**
    Rolling Your Own PC Menu **82**
    The Pictorial Approach **84**
Windows **84**
    Readying Windows for the Older Child **85**
    Readying Windows for the Younger Child **88**

Section II   **A Plan of Action 93**

Chapter 5   **Plan I: Playing Games for All Their Worth—The Playroom 97**
Introducing .... *The Playroom* **100**
Quick Start **100**
Step-by-Step Tour **102**
    The Activities **102**
    The Exploratory Games **104**

Chapter 6   **Plan II: Where in the World is Carmen Sandiego?—Taking Carmen Beyond the Display Screen 115**
Introducing *Where in the World Is Carmen Sandiego?* **118**
    Where in the World Is Carmen Sandiego? **121**
    Where in the World Is Carmen Sandiego? Deluxe Edition **121**
    Where in Europe Is Carmen Sandiego? **122**
    Where in the USA Is Carmen Sandiego? **122**
    Where in Time Is Carmen Sandiego? **122**
    Where in America's Past Is Carmen Sandiego? **123**
Quick Tour **123**
Step-by-Step Tour **128**
Activities to Stretch the Fun **131**
    Carmen Cops and Robbers **131**

Where In the World Is My Family?   132
The International Carmen Sandiego Party   133
Let the Music Play   133
Pad the Play   134
Trivially Pursuing Carmen   134
Digging for Definitions   135
Record the World   135
Games and More Games   136

Chapter 7   Plan III: The Ultimate Electronic Canvas—Kid Pix   141
Introducing *Kid Pix*   144
Quick Tour   145
Step-by-Step Tour   148
Wacky City   148
Menus and Commands   157
A Gaggle of *Kid Pix* Activities   158
Floor Plan   158
A Matching Game for PreSchoolers   158
Rorschach for Juniors   159
Connect-The-Dots   159
Rubber Stamp   160
Illustration   161
Group Activities   162
Further Explorations   162

Chapter 8   Plan IV: Roll The Presses—Children's Writing and
Publishing Center   165
Introducing *The Children's Writing and Publishing Center/
The Writing Center*   168
Quick Tour   169
Step-by-Step Tour   173
Publishing a Short Daily Journal   174
Advanced Features   184
Activities   186
Newsletters   186
Expand the Journal   187
Create Awards and Certificates   187
Create a Comic Strip   188
Send Invitations and Well Wishes   188
Create a Treasure Hunt   188
Moving on   189

Chapter 9   Plan V: Kids Activities for Windows   191
              Introducing Windows   194
                  Moving around Windows   195
                  What Comes with Windows   198
              Quick Tour   200
              Calendar   201
              Calculator   204
              Clock   206
              Cardfile   206
              Notepad   210
              Write   212
              Paintbrush   216
              Using *Write* and *Paintbrush* Together   219

Chapter 10   Plan VI: Communicating with Others—Prodigy   223
              Introducing Prodigy E-Mail   226
              Quick Tour   229
                  The Jump Command   231
                  Your Personal Path   232
                  The Shortcut Keys   233
              Step-by-Step Tour   234

Chapter 11   Plan VII: Online Research with Online Services   241
              Introducing Prodigy's Library   244
              Quick Tour   245
              Step-by-Step Tour   245
              Homework Helpers   251

Chapter 12   Plan VIII: Logo—A Taste of Programming   257
              Introducing *LogoWriter*   260
              Quick Start   262
              Step-by-Step Tour   266

Section III   Software Classics for Kids—Previews of Your Favorite
              Products   279

Chapter 13   Reading and Writing: The Essential Skills   283
              Introduction   286
              Bank Street Writer Plus   287

Davidson's *Kid Works* **288**
Shopping for Sound for PC's **290**
The Mickey Mouse Series **291**
Midnight Rescue! **296**
Reader Rabbit and *Reader Rabbit 2* **297**
Spellbound! **300**
The StickeyBear Series: ABCs, Opposites, Shapes, Numbers **301**
Talking Once Upon A Time **302**
Treasure Mountain **303**

Chapter 14   Math Software—Adventures in Numbers   307

Stickeybear Numbers **310**
Math Rabbit **311**
New Math Blaster Plus! **312**
Math Blaster Mystery **312**
Operation Neptune **314**
Out Numbered! **315**
What's My Angle? **317**

Chapter 15   Logic Software—Sharpening the Thinking Process   319

Ancient Empires **323**
BushBuck Charms, Viking Ships and Dodo Eggs **324**
Choices, Choices **325**
Decisions, Decisions **325**
Earthquest **327**
Facemaker **328**
Headline Harry and the Great Paper Race **330**
Knowledge Adventure **332**
Mickey's Jigsaw Puzzle **335**
PC Globe **336**
SimEarth, SimCity, SimAnt and *A-Train* **338**
The Secret Island of Dr. Quandry **339**
Think Quick! **340**
The Treehouse **341**

Chapter 16   Art Software—The Electronic Canvas   345

Cartooners **349**
ColorMe: The Computer Coloring Kit **350**
MetroGnome's Music **352**
My Paint **353**

NotePlay **354**
Picture Wizard **355**
The New Print Shop **356**

Chapter 17   CD-ROM Software—The Wave of the Future is Here Now   **359**

Amanda Stories, A Silly Noisy House, and *Rodney's Wonder Window* **363**
Composer Quest **363**
Compton's Multimedia Encyclopedia **364**
Living Books: *Just Grandma and Me, Arthur's Teacher Trouble,* and *The Tortoise and the Hare* (available soon) **365**
Macmillan Dictionary for Children **366**
Mammals: A Multimedia Encyclopedia **366**
Microsoft Bookshelf **366**
Mixed-Up Mother Goose **367**
Multimedia Beethoven: The Ninth Symphony **367**
Voyager's CD Companions **368**
The 1992 Grolier Multimedia Encyclopedia **368**
Our House **369**
Playing with Language **369**

Appendix A   Hardware   **371**

Computers **372**
Mice **372**
Sound Cards **372**

Appendix B   Software   **373**

Other Software Companies **384**

Index   **387**

PREFACE

It's been ten years since I began my career with children and software. And ten years in any business, particularly the computer business, seems like a lifetime.

In 1982, when my eldest daughter Kari was two, my computer-programmer husband built us a computer. He wrote a very primitive program that put giant-sized letters on the screen. Each time my daughter pressed a letter on the keyboard, that letter appeared on our green-glowing monitor. Pressing the keys on the keyboard and waiting to see the effect of her actions on screen was an activity she enjoyed. Despite the austere display of personal computers in those days, their limited options, and the negligible reinforcement they offered to kids, Kari loved the game. Ultimately, she mastered the alphabet, though it's hard to say how much credit is owed to the computer.

A few years later, in 1984, The Learning Company introduced Reader Rabbit. By then we had an IBM PC clone with 128K of memory and the ability to create some rudimentary graphics on the screen. This new computer even had a built-in speaker good for making "bleeping" game noises.

And so, my second child Arli learned her ABCs with a bit more panache. That first edition of Reader Rabbit couldn't match what's on the market today, but it captured Arli's attention. A crude rabbit sat by a hat and watched as she chose words that matched certain letter characteristics. Did she learn to read any faster than daughter number one? No, of course not, but with the advancement of technology her computer experience was certainly a bit richer.

In the spring of 1991, I put that first edition of Rabbit to bed and installed Reader Rabbit 2 ("Rabbit Redux," as we like to call it) for my third child, son Reed. This modern version of the game takes advantage of the many advancements in technology. Its scenery is as rich as a painting with 256-color VGA graphics, and it supports a sound board that fits inside the computer to produce music as good as any we'd heard in a movie theater. The new rabbit is a fully rendered cartoon figure. He moves across the screen in a quick and fluid motion, every bit as animated as Roger Rabbit, Bugs Bunny, or any of the other famous rabbits the kids see at the movies. And, as a parent, I especially appreciate the fact that the installation of the software is, as they say, a no-brainer that requires little effort on my part.

Reader Rabbit 2 is one of the programs Reed is growing up with. And, no, he has not learned to read any earlier than my daughters did. But he gets around a computer like hellfire. And in Reed's life, the computer provides a rich and compelling place to explore. As he explores, he learns. At five years old, he can navigate his way through computer menus. He loads his own programs. And he even helps me review software at *PC Magazine*, maintaining lists of "bugs," undesirable little glitches in computer programs.

More importantly, Reed is growing up in an era when the computer has finally become a reasonable adjunct to school and home learning. When Kari was his age, my husband had to write the software. There was simply not much available for children. With Arli, we incurred the perils of crude copy-protected software, software that vendors kept kids from copying illegally. But the schemes they used to do this also made it difficult for parents to install. Early software also suffered from the limitations of early hardware. It was slow, ugly, and certainly no contest for the TV. The only way to enter a response was to type it at the keyboard. Animation was jerky, and early video systems could display no more than four colors on screen—and two of those were black and white! But Reed is the lucky child. He is growing up at a time when he gets full color, dazzling animation and sound, and a friendly computer that's easy for a child to master and control.

Now that we have fast machines, input devices like mice, monitors that can display as many colors as an artist's palette, sound boards capable of competing with the audio on Saturday morning TV, and software installation routines that don't require a Ph.D. in computer science, the computer is living up to its promise as a home appliance that can serve the entire family. Not only is it convenient for the professional who brings work home, it's the perfect playmate for young explorers who are growing up in the information age.

It's easy enough to install software, pull a chair up to the keyboard, and let the kids wile away the hours. But a bit of parental guidance and support can turn the computer into a challenging playmate, a learning tool that's easy to use and more engaging that any other device you have in your home.

All the imagination that the kids bring to fingerpaints, Play-Doh, word games, and spelling contests can be set loose on a computer.

Over the years in the Raskin household, we have found all sorts of ways to embellish the computer experience for Kari, Arli, and Reed. We involve it in many activities at our house—from writing and illustrating homemade invitations to family affairs to supplementing computerized games with fun and competitive contests that challenge the children to learn.

In 1987, I met Carol Ellison, a journalist who has studied and written about children's interactions with computers. Since then, we've often compared thoughts on how far technology has come, how well it could be used to help children learn and how few activities are available to parents to help them connect the computer experience their kids get in school with the activities they perform on the computer at home. Kids tend to learn about computers at school and play on the computer at home. But rarely are parents given any guidance or pointers on things they can do at home to expand the experience their kids get in school. We continue to be amazed at how little has been done to exploit the home computer as the effective learning tool it is.

What was needed, we agreed, was a parent guidebook to help parents make that link, a kind of cookbook of activities they could do with their kids. And so we decided to write one.

In Section I, I offer tips on how to identify good software for children. Carol offers pointers on how to find the best buy on a good computer, whether you're buying a ready-made system from a national manufacturer like Apple, IBM, Tandy, or Magnavox or "rolling your own" by choosing the components to go into the system. Carol should know. She and her husband, Craig, who is the network manager at *PC Magazine*, have a home computer network of five IBM-compatibles. The PCs and the components in them hail from such places as discount store, mailorder dealers, and "homebrewers" like the operator of a Chinese food distribution warehouse in Jersey City, New Jersey, who built their computer while they waited among sacks of dried fungi and 50-pound satchels of rice.

In Section II of this book, I share with you the many computer-based activities that my family has shared over the years. You'll read about all the ways we have found to spin off fun-filled learning experiences from computer games and educational programs on the market. And you'll learn how to extend the learning activities the kids perform at the keyboard into other forms of playful learning. You'll see how to insure that learning games like *Reader Rabbit* and *Where in the World is Carmen Sandiego?* do more to teach than entertain. And I'll tell you how to work with your child and develop all sorts of other learning activities around these educational games. Carol tells you how to put the world at your child's fingertips with online services like Prodigy, as well as how to get the most for your money when you shop for computer equipment and educational software.

By the time you've finished with this book, we think you'll agree that the personal computer is the family entertainment device of the 1990's. Much like television for those of us who grew up in the 1950's and 1960's, you'll soon see parents and children competing for time at the keyboard and you'll have to arbitrate debates over who gets to use this great device when. We have no easy advice on who takes precedence at the keyboard. At times, work brought home from the office will have to come first. At other times, it will be homework. You'll have to make judgments, just as our parents did when they had to determine whether the kids got to watch cartoons on TV or Dad got to watch the basketball game.

Together we hope to bring you a computer book like none you've read before, one that helps you milk these miraculous machines for all they're worth.

—Robin Raskin
Executive Editor
PC Magazine

INTRODUCTION

KIDS AND COMPUTERS: AN EQUATION FOR SUCCESS

If you bought this book, you probably have a kid. And you probably have a computer. Or, you're thinking of buying one. Kids and computers are a combination to behold. Kids take to keyboards like the proverbial fish to water. But it takes more than just putting them in a room together to make truly wonderful things happen. How do you go from having a kid in your house and having a computer in your house to having a "computer kid," one who can ride the wave of this new technology? How do you insure that the computer is more than just an expensive desktop decoration and that your child will use it in a way that gives him the kind of edge you hoped to provide when you bought the machine?

There are lots of ways to do it. But parents, who often don't take to computers as readily as the kids do, may require some sort of guide to avoid frustrating trial and error. Without a map, the road to computer literacy can also be expensive, requiring lots of purchases of both hardware and software before you light upon the right combination to provide your child with a worthwhile learning experience. Make the wrong purchasing decisions up front and you'll either take your child along a poorly plotted course, using software that's inappropriate, antiquated, or even unable to run on the hardware you have; or you'll go back and spend more money to correct the error.

Just like books, most software is designed for kids of certain ages and interests. And, with most software selling at list prices of $39.95 and up, it's easy to run up a big tab for software you'll never use, especially if you don't know how to properly decipher label information and determine whether the software is appropriate to your child's age and interests. And, like books, software is plentiful, and some of it is not especially worthwile. Simply buying an expensive software package and tossing it to your children is like throwing money at a problem you're not sure how to solve. However honorable your intentions may be, you won't get the most out of the dollars you spend, unless you know how to put the products to use and share in the experience with your children.

The three sections of this book give you specific hints and ideas for how to get the most out of your hardware and software dollars while your kids get the most out of this fascinating new technology.

Section I: Nuts and Bolts

Whether you're shopping for a computer or whether you need to design a kid-friendly environment for your existing computer, you'll find the game plan here. This part of the book includes tips on what to shop for and where to find good deals on both hardware and software. Many tips come from the Ellison household, where we proudly declare we've never paid list price for anything. We'll tell you how to make the computer shopping tour a family experience and how to set up a rich computer environment for your home, while you "kid-proof" the computer to insure that the children do not inadvertently erase or tamper with adult programs. And we'll even give you some insights on what the latest generation of home computers—the so-called multimedia PCs—will look like, so you can start thinking about whether these little luxuries are right for you.

Section II: A Plan of Action for a Computer Literate Family

Once your computer is out of the box, set up, and ready to go, you'll be ready for what we give you in Section II, a step-by-step activity guide to computer literacy. Here are hundreds of activities you can perform using just eight different software programs. In this section, we want to give you lots of ideas on some of the not-so-obvious ways of getting the most out of the software you buy your kids. The software is too expensive to wind up on a shelf collecting dust. The tips in these chapters will show you how to lengthen the life of the software, while spicing up the computer experience for your child.

We provide you with a veritable cookbook of activities, all tested and approved at the Raskin family keyboard. And, you'll be happy to know that most of these programs are available for Apple Macintosh and Tandy computers, as well as IBM PC-compatibles—so you'll be able to use them no matter what kind of computer you have at home. This section provides a playful curriculum you can use at home to introduce your children to various types of software.

The eight programs we've selected to use as examples range from games and computer "paint" programs to a programming language, as well as an online service that you can dial up to access special features just for kids. Each chapter in the section is devoted to a specific software package. Each includes hands-on instruction and examples, tips and strategies for using the software, creative projects, and connections to make the software experience a part of your child's everyday world. There's even a chapter that points out all sorts of things you and your child can do with Microsoft Windows—a program that many grownups have purchased to use at home.

Section III: Software Classics for Kids

The tips we offer in Section II aren't just for the games we talk about there. They can be carried over to other computer games. We picked these as examples to show what you and a little imagination can reap from many other fine software programs on the market.

In Section III, we tell you what those many other fine programs are. You can use the tips to strengthen your child's experience with any of the excellent software titles we identify here. This isn't just a compendium of what's out there. In this section we talk about our favorite programs, the best and most recent we've seen at *PC Magazine.* And these programs, like those in Section II, are mostly available on IBM PC-compatibles, Tandy, and Apple Macintosh computers. Many are also available for the Apple II series. Here too, we'll give you tips on how to get the most out of these games. And, for those lucky enough to have a CD-ROM player at home, there's even a special section on new CD-ROM titles.

A Little Editorializing

We're sure that, like us, you believe computers are an important part of your child's future. If you didn't believe it, you wouldn't have bought this book. We've said it many times before—in person and in print. But there are those who believe that technology has little place in education. So we say it again, and loudly: *We can no longer divorce technology from learning!*

Our children will grow up in a world we can only begin to imagine. They will have jobs that have not even been invented yet. The child who is an "information navigator," who can wend his way around the computer, is the child who is best prepared to succeed in this exciting new world. Computer games, reading programs, electronic paint programs, and newsletter-makers may seem rather pedestrian when discussing such lofty notions as the future, but they are the building blocks that will teach children to be comfortable with the tools that will drive the computer age.

And the best news about the world to come is happening today. Computers have finally become mature enough to be kind to parents, so that you can work with your child on a computer. We couldn't have written this book a few years ago. Back then, you either had to be a computer guru or a fanatical parent to do all the work that was needed to make computers and kids true partners in learning.

A few years ago, parents had to forage through quarter-inch ads in mailorder catalogs to find decent children's software programs. And, unless you knew what you were looking for, good programs were hard to find. Setting up a PC so that you could install the software meant fiddling with I/O ports and copy-protected software and reading cryptic manuals. And, when you were done, the games often looked no better on screen than pictographs drawn by prehistoric cave dwellers. No wonder Nintendo got such a strong early lead on the home computer! What child wanted to use a home computer when Donkey Kong, with vivid colors and animated graphics, lured them to the TV set?

But all that has changed. Today programs are colorful and compelling with their animated graphics and sound. Computer characters like Carmen Sandiego are as appealing as Super Mario. The hardware is now rugged enough that you can let even your littlest ones play without fear of doing damage. And the prices are low enough that it's now possible to enter the computer age with limited impact on the family budget.

So why wait? As the kids say, "Go for it!"

SECTION I

NUTS AND BOLTS

In this section, we give you a game plan for shopping for a computer and for designing a kid-friendly environment for the computer once you get it home. If the mysteries of computer hardware have left you with a lot of questions and a fear of buying anything until you get some answers, read this chapter. It contains tips on what to shop for and where to find good deals on both hardware and software. You'll also get this advice from a couple of authors whose families have spent the last two decades shopping for computers, as frequently as some families shop for shoes. The Raskins and the Ellisons have populated their family rooms with computers and display these discount wares with pride.

In Chapter 1, we give you a primer to demystify computer jargon and help you understand the kinds of hardware that make up a basic computer system. We'll tell you what we think are the best buys in computers and report on the various options available for IBM PC-compatibles. Here, too, we'll fill you in on some new developments that are making home computers more exciting than they have ever been. These are the multimedia PCs, complete with built-in audio, and CD-ROM players. Chapter 2 briefs you on how to make decisions about what software to buy. Buying software can be tricky because it's hard to tell how good a program is by just looking at the box. So, in addition to telling you what we like, we'll give you tips on how to read the information on a software package and share our ideas about what makes good computer software for kids. In Chapter 3 we'll show you how to make shopping for a computer a family experience, and we'll show you how to set up a rich and kidproof computer environment at home.

CHAPTER
1

WHAT YOU'LL NEED:
HARDWARE

Kids today grow up with many things that we never had and that's an advantage. But the flip side is that they'll grow up depending on these things as they move through life. Our children will need to use word processing software the way we used pencil and paper. They will use spreadsheets as we used calculators. When there are lists to keep and records to file, they'll perform those tasks with a database manager. And, if electronic media haven't already become the focus of their home entertainment, they will very soon. In the time that has passed between the moment we sent this book to the publisher and the moment you have started to read it, computer vendors have produced and marketed all sorts of wondrous innovations. Some of the most exciting products that are now entering the market bring voice and music to the computer. Suddenly, the personal computer is more lively than television. Not only can children hear voices and watch animation on the screen, they can also interact with it. These electronic worlds bring their imaginations to life in ways no other home entertainment device ever has.

But before a child can experience the best that computers have to offer, she has to have a computer. Consider this chapter a primer. You'll find it useful if you don't already own a computer and are thinking of buying one, or if you do already own a computer and are thinking of adding devices to upgrade it. With IBM PCs especially, it's easy to refurbish an old computer to help it keep up with modern times. If you already own a computer and aren't thinking of upgrading it, you may want to jump to the next chapter, where we talk about how to evaluate good software.

So now, we begin at the beginning—with the computer you'll buy.

The Basic Box

The first question you have to ask yourself is: "What kind of computer should I buy?" And that question alone could keep you busy for a while. It's not as if you don't have a choice. There are literally thousands of companies selling computers these days. How do you assure yourself that you're getting what you want? Making a choice isn't as difficult as it might seem, once you've learned a bit about what makes up a computer. Basically, there are two families of computers with which you should be concerned—the IBM PC-compatibles (the PC stands for Personal Computer) and the Macintoshes, or "Macs," from Apple (others like the Commodore Amiga don't really have the market share, or the support of the software and hardware development community, even though they are interesting machines from a technical standpoint). PCs and Macs both are "personal computers," in that they're designed for use by one person at a time and they sit on top or under a desk; IBM coined the name. But the Macintosh and IBM PC-compatible computer designs are fundamentally different and, for the most part, software for one cannot run on the other. So opting for one or the other is a choice you'll want to make with some care. Once you've bought into one, switching to the other, will require buying some, if not all, new software as well as hardware.

Note

When we say "IBM PC-compatible," we're referring to computers that run the same kinds of software as several models of personal computers made by IBM, using the MS-DOS or PC-DOS operating system. Later in this chapter, we'll provide more specific information.

Debates rage over whether the Macintosh or the IBM PC-compatibles are the best. Up front, we admit that we have a bias on the subject. The Raskin and Ellison households are home to more IBM PC-compatibles than to television sets, toilets, or clock radios. For us, it makes sense to own PCs because those are the types of computers we use at work. (You, on the other hand, may use a Macintosh, or you may not use a computer at work.) And while they are not the kind that many children use at school, we believe parents rule the roost, and kids readily become "bilingual" when it comes to using computers. A home computer should complement the needs of everyone in the family, adults who will be bringing work home from their offices, as well as children who will be using it as a tool for fun and learning. So the two questions to ask yourself after you've decided to buy a computer are:

- What kind of computer activities are my kids performing at school? And what kind of computer do they use?

- What kinds of activities do I perform at the office? And what kind of computer do I use?

If you're buying the computer primarily for the kids, you should, at least briefly, consider purchasing the same kind of computer for home that they use at school. If you expect to use the home computer to work on projects that you bring back from the office, you should consider purchasing the same type of computer that you have at work. With luck, your kids' needs will match your own, and the choice will be easy. If the two don't match, (as is quite likely) you have a decision to make. But it isn't one that should worry you too much. Virtually all the software available for PCs, and that includes just about all of the programs we discuss in this book, are also available in Macintosh versions and vice versa. However, a lot of the software available on Apple's other computers, like the Apple II series, is not available in versions that can run on PCs or Macs. And many programs designed to run on Macintoshes and PCs cannot run on Apple IIs. Also remember that there's no such thing as a bargain, even if someone makes you an offer you can't refuse. Although Apple IIs still abound in schools, Apple computer has identified the Macintosh as its computer of the future. If you're buying an Apple computer today, don't buy an Apple II. A Macintosh will meet your present needs and will serve you and your children much longer. Software that runs on an Apple II cannot run on a Macintosh, without adding special hardware, and developers are producing more and more software titles for PCs and Macs and fewer and fewer for Apple IIs.

We've already confessed our bias, but we do have reasons for believing that, when all else is equal, the IBM PC-compatible is the better choice for many people. And here's why:

- They're less expensive. There's competition in the PC market, and that tends to keep prices on PC-compatibles lower to much lower than prices on Macintoshes. (Apple has a monopoly on Macs!) Careful shoppers can turn up real deals on PCs. The options aren't as plentiful when shopping for Macs. Likewise, the PC versions of software are often priced lower than Macintosh versions.

- They're more likely to serve the entire family's needs. The PC is the dominant computer in American business offices and that makes it the computer of choice for people who frequently bring work home from the office.

- They can be made to do almost everything that the Macs do. Even if your child uses Apple computers at school, you can usually find PC versions of the software to use at home.

- Your child is likely to need PC skills. Because the PC is currently dominant in the business world, it is the one that offers more career opportunities and the one your child will eventually want to train on as she seeks jobs.

But Macintosh aficionados can make a good case too:

- Macintoshes feature high-quality sound and built-in graphics. On an IBM PC-compatible these features cost extra and require adding equipment to the computer.

- There's much more uniformity among Macintosh software programs than among those you'll find for IBM PC-compatibles. Once you learn one program, it's very easy to learn others. Software for IBM PC-compatibles sometimes uses vastly different conventions.

- Macintosh computers can run software designed for IBM PC-compatibles.

- It's easy to set-up a Macintosh and install new software. The Mac clearly shows where you should plug in a keyboard, monitor, and mouse. And because features like sound are built into the Mac, you don't have to worry about adding components, as you do with an IBM PC-compatible.

- There are certain kids' programs that exist only on the Macintosh—those fascinating HyperCard products that we'll discuss later in this book. And some programs like Broderbund's Kid Pix actually have more features on the Mac version of their software than on the PC counterpart.

- The Macintosh is easier for a child or adult to learn and use because of the friendly, visual way it interacts with people.

But, for all the arguments you'll hear on either side of the debate, the most important thing is that you expose the kids to computers. A keyboard is a keyboard, and children are remarkably adaptable. They love computers, and they won't let differences in appearances or keyboard layouts or command sequences hold them back when there's electronic fun to be had. They're able to make the switch from PC to Mac with little or no coaching. (It's a little harder for them to go from Mac to PC without your help, but it's still not very difficult.) And, in the end, the exposure to different types of computers has to be valuable. So there is no reason to wring your hands over which one to buy or to suffer parental guilt at the notion that you may have opted for the wrong computer. Macintoshes and IBM PC-compatibles are excellent computers. Either one represents a good, safe investment. Both are likely to be with us for some time to come. And your kids will feel just as much at home on one as on the other.

Macintosh computers are easy to purchase and set up. Apple has produced a friendly, plug-and-play system that you can boot and run almost the minute you take it out of the box. About all you need to worry about once you look at the price tag is how fast a system you need and how big a hard disk and how much memory you should get. PCs are made up of components that are generally sold separately. You can buy them as a unit, but you usually need to specify what you want when you order one. So you'll need to know a bit about those components when you make a purchase.

Here's the minimum you'll need when buying an IBM PC-compatible for your home:

- The PC itself, its memory and hard disk (yes, we consider a hard disk a necessity, not a luxury)

- A keyboard

- A mouse

- A video system, which includes the monitor, a video card that fits inside the PC, and a cable to connect the two

- A printer

When buying a Macintosh, the smaller and older machines include the video system and mouse so you need only think about the keyboard, printer, memory, and hard disk. On more powerful Macs you can add larger, color monitors, more memory, and bigger hard disks.

There are all sorts of things you may—and probably will—want to add to this basic setup. You'll need a modem, for instance, to use online services, such as Prodigy, which we discuss later in this book. But the items listed above are what you'll need to get started, so we'll talk about these first. We'll recommend what we think is best. And then we'll tell you about the options you can add to enhance this basic system with quality sound and graphics.

The Home-School and IBM-Apple Connections

The fact is that most U.S. schools are too impoverished to afford the same kinds of computers—IBM PC-compatibles and Macintoshes—that are current in today's businesses. Many have already made a sizable investment in Apple IIs or Commodore computers, which they cannot afford to undo. So schools primarily have Apple II series or Commodore-64 computers, if they have computers at all.

Companies like Broderbund, The Learning Company, and Davidson and Associates, to name some leading examples, still sell titles for the Apple II series. But the numbers are dwindling, and these machines are no longer being improved.

So, you may not want to match your home computer with the one your child uses in school. Don't be too concerned. You most likely will be able to buy the same software that your child uses in school; at home it will simply be running more smoothly on a more modern computer.

(continued)

The Home-School and IBM-Apple Connections (continued)

Parents often worry, unnecessarily we think, over which type of computer to buy for their home. "Which one is best for my child?" they ask. The truth is: Any computer will be right for kids. Buy something that will serve the whole family. The hardware is only a mechanism. It's the software you install on it that your child will learn from. As long as there are plenty of software offerings for kids—and you'll find many for both Macintoshes and IBM PC-compatibles—you are making the right choice.

If you opt for a Macintosh, you'll need to know a bit about the models that Apple offers. Choosing an IBM PC-compatible computer requires a somewhat different sort of knowledge because of the many different vendors who give their models different names. But, whatever name a vendor puts on a computer, they all use the same classifications of microprocessor chips, the brains of the computer. So, when shopping for an IBM PC-compatible, you'll make comparisons according to the type of microprocessor that's inside. Below, we'll tell you about the various models of Macintoshes that are available. Then we'll give you a short lesson on microprocessors for IBM PC-compatibles.

Whether you buy a Macintosh or IBM PC-compatible, you'll still need to make decisions about the things you want to add to your system. So later in the chapter, we'll give you pointers about the kinds of equipment you might want to add to build a better computer for your kids. You can mix different computer components to come up with just about as many custom computer designs for your desk as there are customized automobiles on the road. Understanding all the options can be confusing for anyone who is just starting out with their first computer. So this chapter is designed to give you a quick debriefing on computer lingo. There are many fine books that offer much more detail on the options we discuss here. (At the back of this book, Appendix C lists some of the better books we've seen. If you're interested in learning more about how computers operate and what you should know when buying equipment to enhance your system, you'll want to refer to that list for further reading.)

Big Macs: A Hearty Selection

Macs come in four basic model groups: compact, low-cost modular, Nu-Bus modular, and PowerBooks. (The PowerBooks are laptop Macs. Since they are probably not the most appropriate machines for family use they are not discussed here.) Each group serves a different purpose and price bracket, but in terms of raw power, the high-end of one group usually overlaps the low end of the next more expensive group.

Like PC's, Macs also use different generations of the same microprocessor. In the Mac's case, they all use the Motorola 680xx family of processors with the 68000 being the oldest and least powerful and the 68040 the newest and most powerful. (See the general discussion of microprocessors in the next section.) Apple has configured the Macs so that the most basic machines use the least expensive processor, while the machines with high-powered options have the most expensive, fastest processor.

The original Mac used the same basic compact design that is sold today as the Classic and Classic II. The processor, disk drives, and monitor are all housed within the computer's case, and a basic keyboard and mouse are included with the unit. This makes the Classics transportable. You can't use them on an airplane like a true portable, but it's easy to pick them up and move them from one room to another or even occasionally from home to office.

The Classic is the least expensive Mac available. It has the same 68000 processor that the original Mac had, but other features make it faster than its progenitor. For word processing, basic calculations, and some games, it's powerful enough. Unfortunately, it is not capable of running the latest releases of the Mac's operating system, System 7, and comes with a built-in black and white monitor.

The system software is what you see first when you start a computer and what most differentiates Macs from PCs. This is often referred to as the user interface and it includes everything you see when you aren't using your store-bought applications software. It also in-cludes the underlying operations that all applications share. The desktop with program icons and data folders, the file system that keeps track of your data and disks, the menu bars from which you choose comands, and the input/output system that lets you read and write data or send files to a printer are all part of the operating system.

The 68000 processor is not capable of executing certain advanced features of System 7. (It's also not capable of supporting color moni-tors.) Therefore, the Classic must use a previous version of the sys-tem software, which, logically enough, is System 6.

System 7 requires more system resources in the form of additional memory and disk space than System 6, so there are important cost savings in System 6's favor. Also, there are very few applications that won't run under System 6. So if expense is your most important con-cern, you shouldn't feel handicapped with a Classic. On the other hand, if features like virtual memory, multitasking, or file sharing mean something to you, or you want to be able to upgrade easily to take advantage of whatever becomes the latest feature, don't buy a Classic.

For those who do buy one, the Classic has built-in ports for a printer, modem, and external hard disks, but there are relatively few options for expansion designed into the machine. However, several third-party manufacturers sell external monitors, internal hard disks, and accelerator boards than can boost the power of a Classic into the Mac II range. So if a Classic is all you can afford now, you're not re-ally stuck.

The Classic II is just like the Classic in appearance and options for expansion, but it comes with a 68030 processor that is considerably faster and is compatible with System 7. This should be considered the home starter system for anyone who can afford it.

The only model in the low-cost modular group is the LC-II. The original LC with a 68020 processor was recently replaced by the faster LC-II with a 68030 processor. (The 68020 was not System 7-compatible unless you bought an additional chip for it. Apple no longer manufactures 68020-based Macs.)

The LC-II is a clear winner. It has everything the Classic II has, but without the nine inch monitor, which turns out to be the LC's biggest advantage over the Classic II. A plethora of monitors can plug right into the LC's built-in video port. There is also a single expansion slot inside the box that allows you to add many features, including even bigger, more colorful displays, faster networking, or faster processors.

The LC is the only Mac that can support an Apple II coprocessor card. Plug it into the expansion slot and you can run any Apple II software on your Mac. If you're worried about compatability with a school computer, this will solve your problem without jeopardizing future compatability. With lots of options for expansion and no obsolete features in sight, the LC is a superior home computer.

Even better is the deluxe home Mac, the IIsi. While it is the bottom of the line for NuBus modular Macs, it has everything the LC has and more. The Mac II's are distinguished by the ease with which they can be customized. This is because the expansion slots within the Mac II's are self-configuring and can communicate with the central processing unit relatively quickly. In other words, like most Mac features, all you do is plug in the board and it works.

The si has a hybrid slot that can use either NuBus boards, of which there are many, or boards similar to LC-II boards. Not all NuBus boards of LC-II boards will fit, but there is still a bewildering array of powerful expansion options.

The built-in video in the si is more powerful than on the LC-II, so you can display more pixels and/or colors before you have to add an additional video display card. The si can also have more total memory than an LC, 65 megabytes versus 10 megabytes. (See the discussion later on memory and megabytes.)

None of these features is essential for home use, but if you're buying your computer for a family that performs some desktop publishing, graphics, database management, or numerical analysis, you won't regret paying for the extra power of an si.

If the emphasis of your purchase is for a home office, and educational use is a secondary issue, then you might consider the more powerful IIci or the most powerful Quadra 700 and 950, the first two Macs to have a 68040 processor.

In fall 1992 Apple announced a new series of Macintoshes. The Performa line includes four models specifically designed for home use. The 200 is a revamped Mac classic II with a 68030 CPU. The 400 is a revamped LC II with the newer 68030 chip. The 600 has three NuBus slots for expansion and the 600 CD has a built-in CD-ROM drive. These computers promise to set new records for aggressively priced Macs and they'll be sold in places like Sears Roebuck.

Finally, there are used Macs available from many sources. You can probably find an old Mac Plus or SE for under $500. (Don't buy a really old 512k or 128k machine unless you know how to upgrade it to current standards. Upgrading an old Mac is more difficult than upgrading an old PC.) At the high end, there are also many old Mac II's on the market and these make good home office machines and can be upgraded fairly easily.

You should remember that buying a used computer is more like buying a used television than a used car. You can't really look under the hood and see if everything is okay. But chances are, that if it works when you buy it, it will continue to work for some time. Still, electronic components do age and can fail without warning at any time, and you want to have the capabilities that come with newer electronic components.

Inside IBM PC-Compatibles: The Chip's the Thing

Like Macs, IBM PC-compatible PCs are often described by the type of microchip that makes them work. These microchips, called microprocessors or CPUs (Central Processing Units), more or less determine the power and speed of the PC. The microprocessor is, essentially, the ringmaster inside the PC. It's what receives the signals or information you type in at the keyboard and directs that information to where it needs to go. If you tell a program to print a document you have on screen, the CPU directs the job to the printer. If you tell the PC to save or store the document, the CPU directs it to the hard disk. If you enter a command to load a program you previously stored on the hard disk, the CPU retrieves the program and brings it up on screen.

Microprocessors have numeric names which indicate how powerful they are. For home use, the ones you'll most often find are the 8088, 80286, and 80386 PCs. Think of them roughly as being so-so, pretty good, and the best, respectively. You'll also find more powerful computers—80486s and the high-performance 80386 PCs called MCA and EISA—but home users really needn't worry about these pricey machines. They're designed for intensive corporate applications and possess far more computing power than you need for family use—unless, of course, you and your kids happen to be designing jet propulsion systems or calculating the distant reaches of the universe. As lower and somewhat less capable variant of the 80386 processor is the 80386SX. These processors are not quite as powerful as the 386, but they are less expensive. And they are probably the best bet you'll find when shopping for an IBM PC-compatible for the home.

The original PCs were powered by 8088 processors. Few manufacturers make these kinds of computers any more, but they abound at garage sales and in the Sunday classifieds. You'll often find these systems being sold for as little as a few hundred dollars. Good deals? Not really. PCs equipped with 8088 processors are antiquated and very slow by today's standards. They just don't deal with information very well. Technically speaking, computer information is made up of "bits," in the way words and sentences are made of letters. The 8088 chip is able to process only eight bits of information at a time. Then it processes eight more, then eight more. So the person at the keyboard must wait until the computer processes all the information, eight bits by eight bits. Think of reading a document eight letters at a time, then another eight letters, and so on. It'll take a while to get to the end. And you're likely to become impatient with the process before you do.

So it is with an 8088 computer. At the time it was developed, in 1981, it seemed fast enough. But it isn't anymore. The processor functions well enough to run many of the programs you'll read about later in this book. But the most exciting programs, those with lots of graphics and sound, contain a lot of electronic information that's likely to overload the processor. Many do not even run on an 8088. And, as your child becomes a sophisticated computer user, she'll grow bored waiting for the old processor to come up with new information or change the graphics on screen. And many 8088s don't have built-in hard disks, which we heartily recommend. No matter how good a deal you find on an 8088 computer, we recommend you don't buy it. It's a little like buying a 1968 Ford. Unless you're a collector, you'll regret the decision. The machine just isn't designed to meet the computing needs of the 1990s.

The 80286 chip, commonly known as the 286, is a little newer. It was first installed in systems called IBM PC-ATs. The 286 processes twice the information of the 8088: sixteen bits at a time instead of eight bits. But it too is old and underpowered for much of today's sophisticated software. You can run all of the software you'll read about here on a 286 PC and, unless you've experienced a faster PC, you may not notice the fact that it plods by comparison. If you're only buying a PC for your children to run their software and if you can find a tremendous deal on an AT or AT-compatible (a used system, including the monitor, may sell for as little as $500 or $600), you might want to consider it. If it's a hand-me-down from a friend or relative, why not give it a whirl? But be aware that this isn't a PC that you can grow with, and, if you and your kids become PC power users, you'll want to trade it in quickly. Trade-in prices on PCs of any kind aren't particularly good. You almost never get back what you invested, and often you lose quite a bit. So it's best to purchase a PC you know you can live with for quite some time.

And that brings us to the 80386, or 386, as it's more commonly known. It is capable of processing 32 bits of information at a time, and that's exactly what it does in the high-performance PCs we talked about earlier. However, you'll most often find it installed in such a way that it only processes sixteen-bits of information at once. Even so, it processes the information at much faster speeds than a 286 chip. Speed, in the personal computer world, is measured in clock frequencies called megahertz, which you'll usually see abbreviated as mhz. The 80386 chip runs at anywhere from sixteen to 40 megahertz, compared to the slower 286 chips, which run at eight to sixteen megahertz. So, just as the 80286 chip was a great advancement over the 8088, the 80386 is a great advancement over the 80286. Software programs that feature sounds and digitized voices are able to play on the 386 at speeds fast enough to replicate natural-sounding voices and sounds. You don't hear a phony computerized voice. And also, on a 386, lustrous screen graphics, filled with many colors and electronic details, are displayed much more quickly. That means any children's software that features animation—and a growing number do—presents images that move fairly naturally and almost as smoothly as the action on TV.

The 80386 chip is also capable of multiprocessing, which means that it can handle several processes at once. This means you can run several different computer programs or processes at the same time.

In an office environment, for instance, you could write a letter while your Spreadsheet formulas are recalculating. That may be more computing power than you need in a home computer. But the 386 chip has a little brother, known as the 80386SX, which runs at speeds on the low end of the 386 spectrum and is ideal for home use. A 386SX computer runs at sixteen, twenty, or sometimes 25 megahertz and provides sufficient computing power to generate sound and animation that's smooth and almost natural.

Disks: Electronic Filing Cabinets

Whether you buy an IBM PC-compatible or a Macintosh, you'll need to think about how to store the library of software your family will accumulate. Software programs come on floppy disks that fit neatly into a box on a computer store shelf. But at home, shuffling floppy disks in and out of the computer is inefficient and tedious. For fast access and convenient storage you'll want to store the programs right inside the computer, on what is known as the computer's hard disk.

If you think of a disk as a filing cabinet, a place where lots of information is stored, you'll get some idea of how useful a hard disk can be. The floppy disks that contain your software programs come in two physical sizes—5.25 inches square and 3.5 inches square—on an IBM PC-compatible. On a Mac, they come in one size, 3.5 inches square. To run the programs, you insert a disk into the floppy drive on your computer. Some PC-compatibles have one size or the other; others come with both. But these days, most have a single floppy drive and a hard drive. Unlike the floppy drive, which is a slot at the front of your computer, you cannot see the hard disk drive. It is encased inside the computer. Where floppy disks are called "floppy" because they are made of flexible media (even if enclosed in a hard case), a hard disk drive really is hard. To store programs on it, you copy them from the disks you place in the floppy drive. The floppy drive becomes a vehicle for passing information onto a more permanent media, the hard disk.

There are several reasons why you'll want a hard disk. You can run software programs from the floppy drive. But since most computer systems come with hard disks, you'll be wasting a valuable resource if you don't use it. Software programs also run faster from a hard disk.

Games are more fun to play when you don't have to switch disks, as you often do when operating a program only from a floppy drive. Hard disk sizes are measured in megabytes, more often known by their abbreviation, MB; at a minimum they hold approximately 20 times as much information as a 3.5" floppy.

Technically, a megabyte is a million computer instructions. That's a lot. And hard disks are typically sold in sizes that contain twenty, 40, 60, 80MB, or more of information. The software programs you purchase and install on a hard disk can take up any amount of space on a hard disk, but most of those we review in this book consume well under two megabytes. Nevertheless, it seems that no amount of hard disk space is ever enough. Sooner or later a hard disk fills up. And no matter how large a hard disk you possess, you'll eventually start to feel as if you're in need of more space. That's because, once you own a PC, you continue to purchase new software that consumes the hard disk space you have available.

Naturally, you'll want to choose a computer system that conforms to your budget. And, the size of the hard disk inside a PC does have an impact on the bottom line. But do think of the future as you make the choice. A 40MB hard drive may seem like a lot of extra storage space right now. But if you're going to be using adult programs such as word processors, spreadsheets, and databases, alongside your children's programs, and if you expect to live with the system over a number of years, you should opt for one of the larger hard disks—80 or 100MB—now. Naturally, you want to buy what fits your budget, but it's actually cheaper in the long run to purchase a larger hard disk up front than to install a bigger hard disk later. Disk prices have fallen dramatically over the last two years. Buying an extra twenty or 40 megabytes of disk space now will cost you less and cause less hassle than having to add a larger disk later on.

However, if you think you will want to add a hard disk or install a larger one later, be sure you purchase a system with an extra, unused drive bay. A drive bay is a space in which new drives can be installed. With an additional drive bay, you'll be able to easily add a new disk, if you need one at a later date. Without a spare bay, you'll have to scrap your old disk and replace it with a new, larger one. The extra drive bay helps you preserve your original hard disk investment and spares you the headache of having to copy all your programs from a cramped old hard disk onto the newer, roomier one.

All Macs are equipped to house at least two drives internally, usually a floppy drive and hard disk. (Quadras can house even more.) They also all have SCSI ports (Small Computer Systems Interface) that allow you to chain up to five external devices—hard disks, cartridge drives, CD-ROM drives, or scanners—to your Mac. Just give them a unique SCSI ID#, 0-6, and plug them in.

Tip

When space gets tight on your hard disk (and it always does) you can use file compression software to make some of your files take up less space. These programs condense the data in your files when you aren't using them and expand them when you need them. One such program for PC-compatibles is Stacker from Stac Electronics. For the Macintosh, DiskDoubler from Salient Software is very popular.

Memory: The Ultimate Desktop

In choosing options for your computer, you also need to give some thought to memory, the chips that receive program information that the processor moves off the disk and makes it available for you and your child to use. If you think of a hard disk as being a bit like a filing cabinet, and a microprocessor as the clerk who retrieves information from the cabinet and brings it to your desk, the memory is your desktop—the place where the information becomes readily available.

Memory is also known as RAM (short for Random Access Memory). It keeps track of the activity of your software program as well as the task or document you're working on. It puts it on the screen and handles any quick changes you may make. RAM is where the computer stores the interesting events that await you when you and your child play games or explore the wonders of a simple desktop publishing program. When you turn on the computer and boot a program, RAM is where the computer moves those portions of the program that it thinks you'll use first. The more RAM installed, the bigger desktop you have for available information. A larger desktop, in the form of more memory, can keep more of the program available for ready use. A smaller desktop with less RAM requires the processor to perform extra work, grabbing and retrieving data from the hard disk more often. So, with more RAM, your computer will work faster. The more information you have stored in memory, the less work the processor has to do to ferry the information back and forth from the hard disk. Just as a faster processor improves the quality of animation you see on screen and the sound coming through the PC speaker, so does more memory.

Computer RAM is measured in kilobytes and megabytes (one megabyte equals 1024 kilobytes). The 80386 PCs typically come with at least one megabyte of memory built-in. (Two megabytes has become the standard; four megabytes is a hedge against obsolescence.) For the Mac, System 7 users can squeak by with two megabytes, but four megabytes will give you much more flexibility. System 6 users need only one megabyte, but, again, two is better. Also, there is usually enough open area inside the computers to add megabytes of memory later on if you feel you need it. The average price for memory is about $40 per megabyte. We recommend that you have at least four megabytes of RAM installed in your system. You won't need that much to run many of the educational programs and games we discuss here. But you will need that to run Windows, the graphical interface software that is becoming so popular and that we talk about in Chapter 9. If you don't plan to install Windows, one or two megabytes will do, but if the family computer doubles as a work-at-home computer for the parents, it's a good idea to install more memory. It will make your adult applications run more smoothly and speed the amount of time it takes the computer to load programs and make calculations. And the more Windows applications you're running, the more memory you'll need. Heavy-duty Windows users, particularly those who plan to do a lot of graphics work and desktop publishing, should consider installing at least four megabytes or even as much as eight megabytes of memory.

It's also a good idea to find out how much additional memory the system can accommodate later, if you wish to add more. In computer jargon, computer systems are usually described as having expandable memory configurations. For instance, you'll see systems advertised as possessing two megabytes expandable to eight megabytes. This means the computer comes equipped with two megabytes of memory, but as much as six megabytes more can be added, to give you a total of eight megabytes. A computer that is expandable usually costs little to no more than one that isn't. So, if you want to be sure of getting a computer that will grow with your family, get an expandable one.

Video: Getting the Picture

The best children's games are filled with color and wondrous screen graphics that you'll want your children to see. For home use, you need a good video system on your computer. On most PCs and Macs, video systems are made up of two components—a monitor and a card called the display adapter. The two are joined by a cable. (On some Macintosh models, the CPU and monitor are on one unit. Some new PCs and Macs have video built into the mother board, which means you won't need to buy a plug-in card and can also mean faster performance since the information path is more direct.) When buying a video system for an IBM PC-compatible, you'll want to be sure that the monitor has the ability to display all the colors and the sharpest resolution that the display adapter card can deliver. On a Macintosh, black-and-white screen graphics are much better than on an IBM PC-compatible because there are more dots-per-inch on the screen, making it higher resolution. For this reason, color may not be so important on these computers. However, color is still an option you should seriously consider.

Not all video systems are alike. Even if all the computer monitors look more or less the same on the outside, you'll find as much or more variation among their screens as you'll find on television sets. There are black-and-white systems, just as there are black-and-white TVs. In the computer world, these are called monochrome monitors. And, like black-and-white television sets, these are unable to display colors. They're really not acceptable for home use of an IBM PC-compatible unless you're only buying a computer for yourself. And then, only if you plan to do no more than write letters and run calculations. On an IBM PC-compatible, the display adapters that run only black and white are called monochrome, usually MDA (for Monochrome Display Adapter) and Hercules. MDA can display only text. And although the Hercules cards can display graphics, they only do so in black, white, and shades of gray. You'll want a system that runs color for your IBM PC-compatible. And the quality of color systems varies according to the number of colors and the degree of resolution the screen can display.

Resolution is the sharpness or crispness of the images that you see on screen. It is measured in the number of pixels that the screen can display at one time. A pixel is a tiny dot of light on the computer screen. Images in games and other software programs are made up of different colored pixels. Have you ever looked at a newspaper photo or color postcard through a magnifying glass and noticed how the image is actually made up of tiny dots of ink? That method of displaying an image uses more or less the same principle as computer monitors use to display screen images. But instead of dots of ink on a page, you see dots of light on a screen. The tinier the dots, the closer they are together, and the more that appear on screen, the higher the resolution and the better the image.

Macintosh Video

As mentioned before, all current Mac models have either a built-in monitor or built-in video capability. They all display the same sharp text and graphics. There are no competing graphics standards like the CGA, EGA, or VGA standards in the PC world. Mac graphics are controlled by QuickDraw, a part of the Mac's operating system all the way back to the first Macs.

While you don't need to worry about the quality of the Mac's graphics, there are still many options when choosing a monitor.

- Size. The built-in displays on the Classics are small nine inch screens. Most software is designed to be usable in this area, but it is a tight restriction when you start running multiple programs simultaneously. For home use, a twelve or thirteen inch monitor is ideal—not so big that it takes up the whole table, but big enough to let you get a lot of work done. Both sizes can plug directly into an LC or IIsi. The thirteen inch model has better, sharper color, but the twelve inch model, which comes in monochrome or color, is less expensive and can display more colors on an LC.

  For writers or desktop publishers, the fifteen inch or portrait monitor is capable of displaying a full page of text without scrolling. There are also sixteen inch monitors which are becoming more popular in the busines market for spreadsheet users, and big nineteen and twenty-one inch monitors that can dsplay two pages side-by-side and are very popular for graphics applications.

The rule of thumb for monitor size is that you will pay twice for a bigger one. First when you buy it, and second after you plug it in. The Mac's processor has to work harder to display more information on the screen, and so big screen equals slower performance. Bigger monitors may also require an extra video card. And bigger monitors that aren't top quality often produce images that are distorted looking.

- Color depth. The Classic is a black-and-white machine. All other Macs are capable of displaying over sixteen million colors. Once again, you'll pay twice for this capability. For home use, 256 colors (or what is commonly called 8-bit color) is great. A thirteen inch, 8-bit color system works well for almost all Mac application and all Macs with built-in video can display 256 colors on a 13" monitor.

There are also gray-scale monitors that can display up to 256 (8-bit) shades of gray. These are most useful for desktop publishers who are not using color in their printing.

Most Macintosh users buy Apple monitors, but there are other choices. Some multisynch monitors (See PC the video systems description.) will plug directly into a Mac video port. They are often the lowest cost color monitors for Macs, but the multisynch feature is of no particular advantage on the Mac unless you plan to share it with a PC. Also, you should be aware that a fourteen inch multisynch monitor will not necessarily display more information than a standard thirteen inch Mac monitor.

- Density. The amount of information displayed on the screen is dependent on the dot density as well as the size of the screen. The number of dots (pixels) on thirteen and fourteen inch monitors is usually the same, 640 by 480. The difference is in the dot density, 72 dots per inch (dpi) for the thirteen incher versus 68 dpi for the fourteen incher. It doesn't sound very important, but the denser screen is likely to be the clearer one. Too much white space between the dots can make the image appear fuzzy.

Like buying a television, buying a monitor is subjective. It's nice to be able to see a monitor in action before you buy it. That way you'll know whether the image looks clear and the colors are true.

Video On IBM PC-Compatible Computers

Video systems for IBM PC-compatible computers are sold by standards that define their quality of resolution and the number of colors they are able to display. The standards most commonly used in computers that are sold for the home are CGA, EGA, MCGA, VGA, and Super VGA.

CGA, which stands for Color Graphics Adapter, is the lowest quality standard, and you really don't want to buy one. You'll find lots of CGA video systems sold on computers at garage sales and in the Sunday classifieds. You still even occasionally find them advertised by discount computer stores and in mailorder catalogs. If you buy one, you'll only be disappointed. CGA was the first color graphics system on the market, and it's the worst. It's capable of displaying no more than four colors on screen, at a coarse resolution of only 320 by 200 pixels. In fact, when it was introduced in 1984, it was so grainy and hard to read that most PC users just stuck with their black and white systems. CGA adapters support monitors called RGB (red, green, blue). Like the CGA adapters, RGB monitors are yesterday's technology. They're antiquated, out-of-date, and not what you need to get the most out of the software programs we describe later in this book. It's enough that you simply know to avoid them when you shop for a computer.

EGA (which stands for Enhanced Graphics Adapter) came after CGA and was the first acceptable color graphics standard. EGA systems are still available and still acceptable. But there are better systems than EGA. A lot of new software, particularly colorful software for children, is being produced to take advantage of display systems that deliver much more than the sixteen colors and 640 by 350 resolution that you get from EGA. With an EGA adapter, you'll need at least an RGB Enhanced Color Display monitor. Some real bargains can be found on these types of monitors because they're old technology that support only EGA graphics. But you should keep in mind that, if you want to upgrade later to a better video system, you'll have to scrap the monitor, because an RGB Enhanced Color Display cannot "see" beyond the EGA standard.

Tip

The wisest buy in PC monitors is a multiscanning or multisync monitor. These monitors are capable of displaying as many colors and as much resolution as the software and display adapter can deliver.

So, if you want to improve the graphics you see on screen, you can upgrade your video system at any time by simply replacing the adapter you have installed with one that supports more colors and higher resolution. A multisync monitor will grow with you. Unlike RGB monitors, which support only one display mode, it won't have to be replaced when you upgrade.

MCGA, or Multi Color Graphics Array, is a video standard that is not commonly used. You'll find it in some of IBM's PS/2 model computers. But it's not as widely supported as the other video standards discussed here. It's kind of a hybrid. It can produce an impressive number of colors on screen (256) but its resolution is a grainy 320 by 200, the same as CGA. We don't recommend it.

To use all the software we recommend in this book, and to be sure you get a video system that you and your family can enjoy well into the future, you should buy at least a VGA system. VGA stands for Video Graphics Array. It supports all the display standards discussed above. With sixteen colors on screen, it delivers a nice crisp resolution of 640 by 480, which is pleasant to look at and easy on the eyes. VGA systems will cost you a bit more than EGA, but they're worth it. This is the minimum we recommend for the home. Beyond VGA there is Super VGA. A lot of manufacturers produce video adapters capable of displaying as many as 256 colors (sometimes even more!) and resolutions as high as 1024 by 768.

Prices on video adapters have dropped dramatically, and there is no reason why you should opt for less than a VGA video system. It's tough to steer you to specific monitors and display adapters. There are many good ones on the market. Paradise, Orchid, and ATI make outstanding video adapters. There are also many good deals to be had from other makers. NEC's Multisync monitors are among the best.

Video adapter boards, like computers themselves, have RAM built in to help speed performance. The key thing to remember is that if you're buying a VGA monitor, you should buy a video adapter with 256K memory on the board. If you buy a Super VGA, you'll need at least 512K memory on the board, preferably one megabyte. Prices on IBM PC-compatible video adapters have fallen dramatically in recent years, and Super VGA cards with one megabyte of memory are affordable for many.

Within the last year, there has been a lot of competition among makers of video systems. Prices on adapter boards have plummeted, as have prices on monitors. In the Ellison household, we found a Super VGA card with one megabyte of memory for $96, from a "homebrew" computer manufacturer in New Hampshire. (Homebrewers are regional manufacturers who build computers from scratch, and they usually offer great deals, sometimes the best deals, on IBM PC-compatible computer systems. We'll tell you more about them in Chapter 3.) So, if you're buying a new system, there's no reason not to enjoy the best, the most colorful, and most vivid screen images your PC will deliver. Look for bargains on super VGA systems. There are many out there.

But be careful to buy a video adapter that will display the software you want to run. When making a purchase, be sure to ask whether the display system is backward compatible, meaning that it's as capable of running software written to support nothing better than CGA resolutions as it is of running software that delivers high-quality Super-VGA images. That way, you and your child will be able to use any of the games we look at here.

Also, remember that video adapters, like computers, come with their own memory and in eight and sixteen-bit designs. In the same way that the CPU moves information in blocks of eight and sixteen bits, and the computer holds information in memory for ready use at the keyboard, the video memory holds information so that it can quickly redraw images on the screen. Be sure to get a sixteen-bit board, one that has at least 256K of memory, to insure speedy graphics performance and guarantee that your child will see natural-looking animated movement on screen.

Tip

One of the more subtle differences in monitors has to do with the way they display information on the screen. The two methods used to do this are called interlaced and non-interlaced. Non-interlaced monitors present a full image, every line of pixels, on the screen at one time. Interlaced monitors, which are usually much cheaper, display every other line of pixels in such rapid succession that you really don't notice that you're not seeing a full image at one time. However, your eyes do notice. And, if you spend a lot of time in front of the computer, interlaced monitors are likely to contribute to eyestrain. Whatever you do, don't buy one. Remember, your child will be spending a lifetime in front of a computer screen. Why compromise on something that could affect her eyes? A non-interlaced monitor is well worth the additional investment.

Finally, many new monitors are advertised as having 70 Hertz or higher refresh rates (the number of times per second a picture gets painted on the screen). These high refresh rate monitors are superior because they draw the screen so many times per second that the image is "flicker-free." Other monitors are advertised as having low emission of radiation. While it hasn't been proved that monitor emission can be dangerous to your health, it hasn't been disproved, either. You can't go wrong buying a modern monitor with a high refresh rate and non-interlaced picture.

Plugging in Keyboards, Mice, and Modems

Keyboards and mice are the means by which you communicate with your computer. Modems are devices that allow computers to communicate directly with one another via a telephone line.

By typing in commands at a keyboard or using a mouse (so-called because the device is small, moves around on the table like a mouse, and has a long tail—the cord) to click on objects on a screen, you tell the software programs what to do. Macintosh computers are sold with a mouse. You'll often find IBM PC-compatible systems that are too. But, with IBM PC-compatible computers, many times you'll want to specify your own or replace the one the computer comes with.

Computer purists debate the merits of various types of keyboard layouts, but for home use, any good keyboard with a comfortable touch will do nicely. Don't underestimate the comfort factor, however. A new malady, called Carpal Tunnel Syndrome, is making itself known among computer users. Carpal Tunnel Syndrome is comparable to writer's cramp but can be much more serious. In the same way you get writer's cramp by doing a lot of writing, Carpal Tunnel Syndrome is caused by excessive typing on a keyboard. It causes pain through the fingers, wrist, and sometimes, arms. And, unlike writer's cramp, it can have longlasting and even permanent effects. So you'll want to be sure that the devices you and your child use to communicate with the computer are ones that won't cause discomfort or cramping.

Tip

When and How Should You Teach Touch-Typing?

One of the great ironies about the computer keyboard is that the design is a holdover from the days of mechanical typewriters. The QWERTY keyboard, the keyboard layout we are familiar with, placed keys in a strange, illogical order based on frequency of use. It was designed to slow the typist down, so that the keys would not jam in manual typewriters. That explains, in part, why touch-typing is such a frustrating skill to learn. Children are particularly discouraged by the seemingly random keyboard setup.

(continued)

Tip (continued)

A more modern design, the Dvorak keyboard, arranges keys in a logical order, so that the typist's fingers don't have so far to move. You can purchase Dvorak keyboards for computers. But, for the most part, the QWERTY keyboard dominates, just as it continues to dominate typewriters.

Touch-typing on either keyboard is a crucial skill to master. Children think faster than their hands can hunt and peck for keys. Once they master touch-typing, their ideas can flow, unencumbered by the mechanics.

We recommend using a hunt-and-peck approach for the first months of your child's computer experience. Once the child is comfortable with the positioning of the keys, she is ready to learn proper fingering. Even children as young as five years old can benefit by learning touch-typing.

Luckily, there are software packages designed to make learning touch-typing more enjoyable. The best we've seen is *Mavis Beacon Teaches Touch Typing* from Software Toolworks. Mavis Beacon is a fictional typing wiz. The Mavis Beacon software teaches touch-typing to kids of any age over five and at any one of three difficulty levels. Lessons take place inside a simulated classroom. Your child's keystrokes are shadowed by a graphical representation of hands on a keyboard. She simply watches the monitor to see a graphic representation of where to place her hands.

There's also a "workshop," where a metronome ticks the number of words she needs to type to attain her speed goal, while a meter records her speed and accuracy as she goes along. Graphs and charts display her progress, and the manual includes a history of typewriting and information about typing posture, finger position, keyboard basics, and business letter forms.

(continued)

Tip (continued)

There's even an arcade-like automobile race to help sharpen skills. The text of the typing exercises is taken from famous quotations, which are infinitely more enlightening than the "asdf;lkj" technique you probably learned in school.

Other good typing instruction programs include *Dvorak on Typing* from Interplay Productions and *Typing Tutor 5* and *Typing Tutor 5 for Windows* from Que Software.

Likewise, when choosing a mouse, you'll want to select one that accommodates the way your child moves her hand. Logitech makes something called KidzMouse, a designer mouse for tiny hands. It's easy on little fingers because it's smaller than an adult mouse. Its buttons are closer together so that children needn't reach to press them. And it's even cute! It actually looks like a mouse with a long blue tail (the cord) that trails from its back and with matching blue plastic "ears" as its buttons. The front is pointed like a mouse's nose. It comes with software that features an outstanding tutorial to teach kids how to use a mouse by pointing, clicking, and dragging objects across the computer screen. And it's bundled with an educational game for youngsters called the *Dinosaur Discovery Kit* from First Byte. The Discovery Kit includes an on-screen coloring book, a match game, and a very simple desktop publishing program that allows kids to create picture-book stories about dinosaurs.

Tip

If you opt for the KidzMouse, and adults in the family will be using the PC, you'll probably also want to purchase a second mouse for big hands. KidzMouse's buttons are closely spaced. They're perfect for the under-twelve set but can be painful for adult fingers.

Keyboards plug into a special computer port, or opening, designed just for them. Many computers come with a mouse port as well. Macintoshes use the same type of port for the keyboard and the mouse as well as the other input devices like track balls and graphics tablets. But on an IBM PC-compatible, you should specify that you want one. And, you'll need other ports to plug in peripherals—devices like printers, sound boxes, and modems. So, when selecting a computer, it's important to get all the ports you need to operate the devices you want. The minimum you need on a PC is one parallel port and two serial ports. And, for a home computer, you should seriously investigate computers that feature a game port. This is a port especially designed to accommodate a joystick or a yoke (a kind-of airplane pilot's steering wheel) and to make game-playing more fun and realistic. The joysticks you'll find on personal computers are more or less like those you see on Nintendo systems, and yokes spice up road race games as readily as they do flight simulators.

All Macs have two serial ports for modem and printer. Joysticks and other game-oriented controllers are connected to the same port as the keyboard and mouse.

You'll need a parallel port to attach a printer (some printers connect through serial ports, but the vast majority on today's market connect through a parallel port). Some mice and modems connect directly to the computer through serial ports on the back of the computer. These are called serial mice and external modems. Bus mice plug into a card that is inserted in the computer. And internal modems are installed inside the computer. Unlike external modems, which are box-like units that sit on the desk alongside the computer, internal modems are actually no more than a card equipped with electronics that is installed in the computer. Both connect to a telephone line and allow you to use your computer to dial other computers and online services like Prodigy. The advantage of using external modems and serial mice is that installation is easy. There are no cards to plug in or switches to set. The configuration is all done automatically through the serial port on the computer. These devices spare you from using slots inside the computer, which computer manufacturers reserve so that you can add devices later. We recommend serial mice and external modems for those reasons. However, there is a disadvantage with external modems. They take up room on a desk, diminish the work area, and add a cluttered appearance.

When buying a modem, you'll need to consider how quickly it moves information across a telephone wire. Working with information that you retrieve by way of modem is always a lot slower than working with it from the hard disk of your computer. The reason is that telephone lines move information one bit at a time. Manufacturers speed the process by designing modems that send the information at various speeds, measured in bits-per-second (bps, also called baud rate). The first modems sent information at 300 bits-per-second and were extremely slow. You rarely find these modems anymore. When you do, they're very cheap, but they're not worth buying. Modems that are faster but still not acceptable by today's standards, send information at 1,200 bits per second (1,200 baud). They too are quite cheap but not worth the investment. The 2,400-baud modems, which are rapidly diminishing in price (around $100), are ideal for home use. You'll find faster modems, but they're often quite expensive. When you choose an external modem for an IBM PC-compatible, be sure to get advice from the vendor on the correct cable to match both the port on your computer and the port on your modem. Whatever type of modem you buy, make sure it's Hayes-compatible; this is the industry standard and is supported by most of the software programs you will use with your modem.

Printers

You'll also need a printer to publish the newsletters, invitations, and storybooks we talk about later. A printer really is an essential item. By printing all the creations your child assembles on screen, the stories she does in a word processor, and the art she creates with paint programs, you give her something tangible to show off. Three types of printers are practical for home use: dot-matrix printers, inkjet printers, and laser printers.

Dot-matrix printers, so-called because they print by laying down dot patterns with print heads that feature either nine or 25 pins, are good, inexpensive printers for home computer systems. And they may be the best choice for children because a number of programs designed for kids support only dot-matrix printers. For this reason, we recommend dot-matrix over other types of printers, if you're buying a printer specifically to accommodate the kids. If color is a must (and those who spend lots of time drawing at the computer will think it is), a dot-matrix printer is a good choice because such printers offer color at a much lower cost than other types of printers.

We have no particular favorite in this category. There are a number of low-cost, dot-matrix color printers to choose from. For IBM PC-compatibles, you'll find the Star Micronix NX1020 Rainbow, which lists for $299 and the Tandy DMP 136, which is also priced at around $300 (both can be bought considerably cheaper than the list price when you shop by mail or from a discount warehouse). The popular ImageWriter II for Macintosh, available from Apple Computer, is a bit more expensive, at $595.

Color inkjet printers lay down dot patterns by spraying ink over the page. They offer dramatically better color than dot-matrix printers because they produce a more solid swatch of color, but not all children's software programs support them. Inkjets are good, affordable options if you plan to share the computer with your children. Business correspondence simply looks better when printed on an inkjet printer. Inkjet printers range in price from a couple hundred dollars for black and white to more than $1,000 if you select a color, plain-paper printer acceptable for home and office use, or a thermal inkjet printer used in sophisticated publishing operations. Among the best-known and least expensive inkjet printers for IBM PC-compatibles are Hewlett-Packard's black-and-white DeskJet 500 and color DeskJet 500C. The 500 lists for $599 and can be gotten for as little as $300, if purchased mailorder; the 500C, which lists for $1,095, can be purchased mailorder for as low as $690. For the Macintosh, there is the DeskWriter C, also from Hewlett-Packard, a color inkjet printer that runs more than $1,000. Apple Computer's black-and-white StyleWriter inkjet for the Macintosh sells for $599.

Laser printers cost even more than inkjets, and they offer the best-looking printed output. We don't recommend them for home use, however, unless you're also using your computer for a home office and need the printer to give business correspondence and projects a snappy professional look. As with inkjets, Hewlett-Packard offers one of the best buys in reliable but inexpensive laser printers for the home. The HP LaserJet IIIP for IBM PC-compatibles, which carries a list price of $1,595, can be purchased for about $800 from mail-order firms and computer discount stores. But the LaserJet IIIP only prints in black. On the Macintosh side, Apple computer offers a variety of laser printers. The two least expensive, the LaserWriter IILS (lists for $1,299) and the Personal LaserWriter SC (lists for $1,499), are excellent printers for a home office. The GCC PCPII is a reliable, no-frills laser printer for Macs that cost around $800. Color laser printers for either Macintosh or IBM PC-compatibles generally fall in a price range of $3,000 to $8,000.

Tip

If you need high-quality printing but don't want to spend a small fortune for a color inkjet or laser printer, you'll probably buy one that prints only in black and white. Keep a pack of crayons near the printer, so that your child can color inside her printed line drawings. If school projects and reports are your primary concern, then black-and-white printing is sufficient.

Sound, Action

Macintosh owners enjoy the luxury of high-quality sound built into their personal computers. Tandy also provides sound in many of its computers. But owners of IBM PC-compatibles have to give their computers a bit of help to achieve the same results. Most IBM PC-compatibles have some sort of speaker built in. But the sound you'll get from the IBM PC-compatible's speaker is tinny and unnatural. Many of the programs you'll read about later in this book make fine use of sound. They combine music and voice with animated screen graphics to bring the action in computer programs to life. Several manufacturers make sound devices that enhance the sound coming from the PC speaker. Some of these feature jacks into which you can plug speakers and make the music and voice sound even better. Others have earphone jacks, which spare parents from the repetitive sound of so many children's games. The kids have fun, and you won't have to listen to the game music over and over again. So a sound card is a nice option to consider when upgrading your PC.

Our favorite sound card for home computers is the Sound Blaster from Brown-Waugh Publishing. The Sound Blaster features a special chip that picks up speech in computer programs and broadcasts it so that it sounds like a real human voice. The Sound Blaster is an add-in card which must be installed inside your PC. Its list price is $240, but you can usually find it in discount stores and mailorder catalogs for $175 to $190. Another excellent sound device, which sells for only $49.95, is the Sound Source from Disney Software. The Sound Source is easy to install. It simply plugs into the parallel port on the back of your PC, and it comes with an adapter, so that you can use it and leave your printer plugged in at the same time. It is not as widely supported as the Sound Blaster, and the sound is a bit raspier, but it's quite a bargain. Disney sells its software with the Sound Source, offering special discount prices for the bundle.

Other excellent sound cards come from AdLib and Roland. In fact, Roland is a big name in electronic music circles, and its cards are especially good at squeezing orchestral quality out of just about any program that features music. But the Roland lacks the ability to deliver voice and is a bit more expensive than other sound cards on the market. It is really designed for the musically inclined. If your child develops a special interest in electronic music, you ought to investigate it, but if you want to get voice and sound out of your child's software programs, a Sound Blaster is your best bet.

CD-ROM and Multimedia PCs

A CD-ROM player is another nice option for either an IBM PC-compatible or a Macintosh. These readers are the computer equivalent of the CD player that you may already have in your home or car. They "play" programs instead of music, although quite a few of the programs feature music, and the players actually deliver both. CD-ROM disks can store much larger programs and data files than what you normally get on a standard floppy disk. The readers plug into a serial port on the back of a PC and the SCSI (Small Computer Systems Interface) port on a Mac. The disks that you play on them feature such things as electronic encyclopedias and children's stories, illustrated with intricate color graphics and enhanced with lively sounds. At this writing, the players remain rather expensive (at least $399), as are the disks that you use in them. However, one CD-ROM disk can contain ten, 40, or 75 different programs, compared to the one you'll get on a floppy disk. They're good values if you want the programs that come on them, but the purchase price for a CD-ROM disc is quite a bit higher than for a single program sold on floppy disks.

CD-ROM players and CD-ROM discs are too expensive for many homes. But they are rapidly diminishing in price (the least expensive but still high-quality CD-ROM players are made by NEC and Tandy, and you can find them for as little as $399). As prices continue to fall, you'll find it economical to have these devices at home. So you should know about them and keep an eye open for bargains.

There are also IBM PC-compatibles that come equipped with CD-ROM players; many of these also feature built-in sound cards and speakers. These are called multimedia PCs, and you'll soon be hearing more about them. In November of 1991, Microsoft and a group called the MPC (Multimedia Personal Computer) council introduced a new specification for designing multimedia computers. These are IBM PC-compatibles that have all the hardware needed for sound and high-quality animation built right into the computer. They have the built-in ability to play CD-ROM software that features the same quality of sound that you find on audio compact disks, along with high-quality animation. Because sound and graphics require so much disk space for storage, floppy disks are no longer an acceptable means of distribution for these types of packages. Ultimately, the multimedia PC will also feature full-motion video, so you will be able to watch movies on your computer screen.

Apple's new Performa 600 CD features typical high-quality Mac sound and video and includes a CD-ROM drive.

Multimedia PCs are the wave of the future. If you are buying an IBM PC-compatible today, you might want to consider buying a multimedia model from Tandy or CompuAdd. These two companies are pioneers in the movement and have MPC certified components guaranteed to be able to play these new software titles. These machines sell for about $3,000—expensive, but not altogether unaffordable for high-tech households that want the best in entertainment equipment. Other companies are beginning to offer multimedia upgrade kits—a way to transform your existing IBM PC-compatible into a multimedia PC. The kits, from companies such as

New Media Graphics and Creative Labs contain CD-ROM players, sound boards, and the required Windows software . These can cost anywhere from $500 to $800, and they typically include five or six multimedia CDs to get you started. In order to play multimedia CD-ROM software, you also need a system with at least a VGA display. The new software titles (See Chapter 17, CD-ROM Software —The Wave of the Future is Here Now) are extremely impressive. They include products like Microsoft's Multimedia Bookshelf, an animated, colorful set of reference works and exotic games that talk.

If you are buying a computer today and expect it to last well into the second part of the decade, then you should seriously investigate a multimedia PC. If you already own a PC and want to enter the next generation of computer software, think about buying an upgrade kit.

If you have or are considering a Macintosh and want to install a CD-ROM player, consult with your Apple dealer to ensure that you have the needed amount of memory (four megabytes is a safe minimum).

Putting It All Together

IBM PC-Compatible Systems

Quite a number of PC manufacturers spare you the pain of figuring out exactly what you want in an IBM PC-compatible by putting everything they think you need in a single package. Below you'll find two PCs that are sold with the devices you need in a good home computer. Best yet, these systems come preassembled, so that you don't have the hassle of setting them up yourself. The cards are installed and the devices are ready to plug in.

One of these is IBM's own PS/1. It comes with a 16mhz 80386SX processor, two megabytes of RAM, a 2,400 bps modem, and a mouse. There are two different models, and the difference is in the size of hard disk in the computer and the number of preinstalled software offerings. A $1,399 model, the 2121C42, features a 40MB hard disk; the $1,799 2121B82 features an 80MB hard disk. Both models include DOS 5.0 and Microsoft Works (a handy set of home office programs) installed as software. Both also come with the software needed to access the Prodigy Service, a great interactive service for the whole family, which we tell you how to use in Chapters 10 and 11. There's also software for accessing IBM's Promenade online service, exclusively for PS/1 owners. The more expensive model also features Microsoft Windows, which we discuss in Chapter 9. Both computers feature expansion slots, so that you can plug in additional cards, such as sound boards. A CD-ROM player can be added to the system.

Our favorite, however, is Magnavox's HeadStart SX-20 CD. It's a solid, speedy PC that's not tough to set up. It features a built-in CD-ROM reader, 80MB hard drive, and a floppy drive. And it comes with an impressive collection of software. It sells for a suggested price of $1,899 without a monitor. Magnavox sells a 14-inch color VGA monitor, which you can purchase for $399. For a total of about $2,300, plus the cost of a modem, if you want one. Its installed video controller supports standard VGA and Super VGA resolution, up to 800 by 600 with sixteen simultaneous colors. The system's two megabytes of RAM can be expanded to eight megabytes. There are two serial ports and one parallel port. The CD-ROM controller has RCA connectors that allow you to connect stereo speakers and enjoy high quality sound. With three slots and two open drive bays available, there's room to grow. It even comes with a mouse and headphones.

Best yet, the HeadStart SX-20 CD is stocked with an impressive number of software programs, including Microsoft's Bookshelf, which includes reference materials such as *The American Heritage Dictionary*, *The World Almanac*, the *U.S. Zip Code Directory*, *Bartlett's Familiar Quotations*, and *Roget's Thesaurus*. Other disks contain some of the programs reviewed in this book that are normally found on standard floppy disks: *PC-Globe* and *The New Grolier Electronic Encyclopedia*. The system does not come with a video system or a modem, but the HeadStart SX-20 CD is an excellent home computer that will serve you for some time to come.

If you buy a HeadStart SX-20 CD system and follow our recommendations, this is about what you're looking at in cost:

Component	Approximate Cost
HeadStart SX-20 CD	$1,900
Magnavox VGA monitor	400
2,400-baud modem	100
Color dot-matrix printer	300
Total	$2,700

Macintosh Systems

Earlier we recommended the Mac LCII for families who prefer that platform. You can purchase an LCII system that is comparable to the Headstart described above for about the same amount of money:

Component	Approximate Cost
Mac LC II 4/40:	$1,400
Sony 14" RGB monitor:	350
Apple StyleWriter Inkjet printer:	350
NEC CD-ROM drive with bundled software:	500
2400 baud modem:	100
Total:	$2,700

CHAPTER
2

WHAT YOU'LL NEED: SOFTWARE

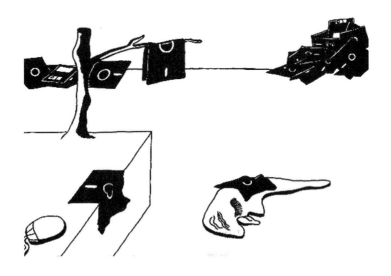

The computer itself is just a machine. Until you install the software that contains the games and learning programs you want to use with your child it is an idle appliance. So you'll immediately want to start building a software library. Building a software library is a balance between getting the most mileage out of your software dollars and varying your personal software collection to keep your child interested. In this chapter we'll give you some pointers on how to identify good computer games, both for their longevity and for their content.

Choosing Good Software

We're often asked: What is the educational value of a computer game? Should I be steering my child to other kinds of software? The happy truth is that many of the computer games available to children really are educational. Unlike TV video games, which present kids with sports, shootouts, and road races, many computer games challenge kids with logic puzzles. Just like a good movie or a good novel, a good computer game does more than entertain. It prompts a child to think. And like movies and novels, there are classics in the world of computer games. We identify many of these in Sections II and III of this book. These games present problems that children must figure out and mysteries that they must solve in order to win. When a game challenges children with worlds to explore, letters and numbers to learn, shapes to match, stories to write, and newspapers to produce, kids are drawn into using the computer. And through the activity, they begin to discover things they may not have realized about the world around them. The classic programs we discuss in the next two sections share certain characteristics that make them endure. Ask yourself these questions when you evaluate new software:

1. Is the program interactive?—Does the program put the child in charge of controlling the environment? Does it let them make their own connections to the world around them and gain their own insights into the logic of the activity? The more a game challenges a child to explore, the more it piques curiosity and builds problem-solving skills.

2. Is it open-ended?—When children assemble Legos, Lincoln Logs, or building blocks, they can walk away from their creations one afternoon, then pick them up the next day and transform them into something completely different. They use

the toys to proceed in different directions. The boat they built on Monday becomes a dinosaur on Tuesday, a tow truck on Wednesday, and a gas-n-go on Friday. Computer games should also present children with opportunities to expand their play. Open-ended play puts children in control. It lets them proceed in a nonlinear fashion. The fun simply continues as kids find new ways to use the tools the software gives them.

3. Does the program incorporate non-computer manipulatives: books, maps, stickers, crayons, posters, and even toys?—Children are multi-modal learners. That means that they will use whatever means are available to them to solve a puzzle or meet a challenge. Learning experiences are made up of many things besides computers, and the best computer games challenge children to link information in intuitive ways. The greater the assortment of learning tools that a program offers a child, the greater the experience. Programs that integrate computer and non-computer activities in the same package offer livelier, healthier, more challenging play.

4. Can the program be used in a group?—Contrary to popular belief, computers offer kids a lot more than a solitary pastime. The best games encourage group brainstorming and creative problem-solving ("group hubbub," we call it). In other words, games that offer kids a social experience, as well as a learning experience, are the best ones to buy. There's usually a lot of good group learning taking place when parents can hear chatter, as well as clatter, coming from the direction of the computer keyboard.

But these questions are more easily asked than answered. The question we face as parents when we enter a computer store is, how do we figure out what kind of opportunities a game offers a child just by reading the back of a box? It sounds difficult. But it really isn't. Software companies give you all sorts of clues in text they display on the box. When you go to make a purchase, you should carefully read the publisher's description of their program and note what they tell you comes in the box.

For instance, Broderbund's *Where in the USA is Carmen Sandiego?* features the usual glitzy packaging with a photo of a glamorous villainess on the front. But you'll also find a little tag that tells you that the program includes a reference book, *Fodor's USA*. And on the back, you'll find pictures of the program's screen graphics, the ones your child will see when he plays the game. In this case, the pictures of maps and historical monuments clue you in to the fact that your child stands to learn a bit about history and geography as he plays the game. Even the game's advertising slogans, such as, "Crime busters should have an inquisitive mind, an adventurous spirit and an uncanny knack for interpreting clues," suggest the kinds of challenges that await your child. You'll find similar packaging on all children's software. Learn to read between the lines, and you'll find all sorts of clues about what's inside.

Packaging on programs for preschoolers usually features a lot of information that parents will find useful. Disney Software's *Mickey's Memory Challenge*, for instance, offers an extensive description of the games inside. Descriptions like, "Different player number settings let your child play alone, with a friend, or against a Disney character," tell you that this is a program that can be played singly and in groups. And the packaging tells you that you can set the game's level of difficulty, so you know that it will grow with your child as he masters the tasks it presents to him.

Packaging also tells you what you'll need to know to be sure that the software will run on the hardware you own. All software packages feature small labels, usually found in the lower lefthand corner of the box, which tell you what kinds of computer systems the software will run on, how much memory you'll need, what kind of screen graphics the software it supports, and whether a mouse or a sound card is recommended.

So one key is to learn to read software packaging as carefully as you do food packaging in the grocery store. You'll soon learn to recognize good products on a software shelf as readily as you do healthy low-cholesterol products in a dairy case. We're not saying you should simply fall for fancy packages. Look for details that tell you what's inside.

Of course, the best way to know what the software is all about is to "test drive" it. This isn't always possible. But a lot of computer stores have demo systems on the floor, where the computers are equipped with popular kids' games. Drop by and let the kids try it out. It's a sure bet that they'll quickly assemble a wish list of favorite programs. Ask the kids to demonstrate the program to you. They'll have fun doing it, and you'll get a preview of the program before you buy it.

There are also numerous guides to children's software, including the one we give you in Section III. You can also turn to magazines for descriptions of the products. Lots of publications review new products as they come onto the market. Look in Appendix C for a list of publications that specialize in reviewing software for the home. In any product review that you read, however, note whether the reviewer appreciated the product for its educational value, its entertainment value, or both. The best products offer both.

Tip

Six Characteristics of a Good Software Package

1. It is interactive. The child is not a spectator but an explorer.

2. It is highly graphical: The days of Pac Man-like circles and stick-like mazes are gone. Brilliant images make software more compelling.

3. It combines content and amusement: Learning on a computer should be fun.

4. It allows exploration: It encourages children to make choices and arrive at decisions.

5. It has ties to the world outside computers. The game should relate to off-screen activities.

6. It stays with a child over time. There should be enough content and a variety of ability levels to amuse your child for quite some time. You don't want the game to gather dust on the shelf.

Sorting through the Kids' Software Maze

Children like variety even more than adults do. And while we certainly appreciate games with some educational or creative bent, it's been our experience that the best software libraries have representatives from several categories:

- Simulated environments
- Edutainment: Games that combine educational themes with arcade action
- Arcade games
- Role-playing and fantasy games
- Creativity tools
- Drill-and-practice games

Simulations

Games that plunge children into simulated worlds are the Legos and Lincoln Logs of computer software. They give children the tools to participate in a mythical world, using whatever resources the game puts at their disposal. There is no wrong or right way to play. The child explores for exploration's sake in a "world" created by the computer.

Broderbund's *Playroom* is good example of a simulation for very young children (although it also includes more traditional competitive games). In the *Playroom* game, we enter the world of a child's bedroom, where different games and activities can be found behind the various pieces of furniture. Good examples of simulations for older children include games like Maxis' *SimCity*, where players are asked to manage the budget and services of a simulated city. We'll tell you more about both of these programs later in this book.

Edutainment

Electronic games that combine elements of education and entertainment are sometimes referred to as *edutainment*. Misguided educators occasionally argue that edutainment software is more entertainment than education. Some say it trivializes education because it attempts to make learning as compelling for kids as Nintendo! These programs look like video arcade games but the content can be reading or math or geography. They're not as deep as a reference book or as intellectually challenging as a simulation, but they can be lots of fun for children. And learning *should* be fun.

Some of the best examples of these games come from The Learning Company. They present kids with math word problems, spelling, and reading comprehension exercises. But the child moves from one problem to another with fast, arcade-like action, often featuring sound and animation. In their reading comprehension game, Super Solvers' *Midnight Rescue!*, you try to stop a mischievous villain by hurling objects at his robot henchmen.

Arcade Games

Games like *Super Mario, Pac Man*, and *Space Invaders* are what we call "twitch reflex" games. They are computerized versions of the arcade games that have populated kids' lives for the last decade. These are marksmanship games that pit you against the clock and send you off into some hostile territory to earn a high score by shooting down, dodging around, or gobbling up your electronic opponents. They get your adrenalin pumping. And, for children, they can help foster a certain amount of eye-hand coordination. Most software libraries include one or two of these types of games.

But there are better games on the market. We call them simply "twitch games." They include programs like Spectrum Holobyte's *Tetris*, Microsoft's *Flight Simulator*, and *Links: The Challenge of Golf. Tetris* is an addictive game in which the sky rains puzzle pieces that must be oriented and placed correctly inside a contained area. *Flight Simulator* asks you to navigate your own plane, using some seriously realistic controls. *Links* puts you on the golf green and gives you a slew of clubs and swings to choose from, as you take on the challenge of the course. Because they do require sound strategies to succeed, all of these games are geared more to teens and adult children than they are to preschool and elementary school-age children. In addition to requiring the same eye-hand coordination as the simple arcade games, they also challenge big kids to think logically. These games require a strategy to win, and they give your brain, as well as your hands, a workout. None of them claim to have a strict educational mission, but they are fine for what they are—engrossing eye-hand-brain coordinators. Usually parents find them as entertaining, sometimes more entertaining, than the kids do.

How Should You Feel about Arcade Games?

Computers are no different than any other consumer item when it comes to advertising, brand-name recognition, and the power of word of mouth. Your children will find out all too quickly when a Dick Tracy computer game hits the stands or when the kid next door gets a new version of *Flight Simulator*. You may be well aware of the benefits of educational computing, but you'll have to work hard to lure the kids past the captivating displays of popular games. With a few exceptions, educational games, like most educational products, are marketed to parents and not children. Recreational games are marketed at children.

Yet, when it comes to computers, there's sometimes a fine line between recreation and education. Chuck Yeager's *Combat Trainer* develops eye-hand coordination and reflexes. *Tetris* is a compelling puzzle that keeps kids absorbed and dexterous for hours. Games like *Scrabble*, *Jeopardy*, and *Wheel of Fortune* are challenging computer counterparts to their real-life games and, yes, they foster knowledge and encourage children to spell. So what's a poor parent to do?

We tend to take a practical rather than a purist approach to the dilemma. A little computer gaming now and then never hurt anyone. And having computer games around the house shows your child that you view the computer as a true multipurpose tool, both for work and play.

Role-Playing and Fantasy Games

Role-playing games ask a child to assume a role and then follow certain clues to reach a reward. (*The Oregon Trail* from MECC lets you accompany a pioneer family across the nineteenth century wilderness.) These games are similar to the simulations we mentioned earlier. They also present children with new environments to explore but are a bit more challenging because they require the kids to participate in the environment, to take on the role of a character who lives there.

Role-playing games typically are designed for children who know how to read. Many of the descriptions of the world and its challenges are presented in text as well as graphics. Some are very elaborate. They include multidimensional scenes and require players to keep track of many things in order to earn a high score. Children often instruct the computer on what to do, using commands like *Slay Dragon* or *Get Medicine*—the language is a bit imperative. These games often require some suspension of belief; players must be willing to think the way the game thinks, in order to retrieve clues and navigate in a prescribed way. Role-playing and fantasy games are good for building problem-solving skills.

Creativity Tools

You wouldn't think that a computer would be very adept at music and art. But there are some wonderful things you can do with a computer in the world of the arts. A number of software packages on the market give children electronic versions of their favorite art materials. Some are electronic coloring books, some are painting and drawing tools, and some even allow you to produce computer animations.

Music, while it can sound a bit tinny if you don't have a Macintosh or a sound device on your PC-compatible, is also possible on a computer. With programs like *MetroGnomes* or *Treehouse*, children can learn the basics about musical notation or enter a electronic musical appreciation class. With a program like Microsoft's *Beethoven*, they can take a detailed look at a composer's life and music.

Drill and Practice

Drill-and-practice software falls into the it's-a-tough-job-but-some-body's-got-to-do-it category. Because computers are good at automating repetitive tasks, they're good at drilling kids on spelling lists, multiplication tables, foreign-language vocabulary, and SAT practice problems. At the same time, a computer can easily keep track of the progress being made along with the problems kids encounter. In fact, they're often far better than adults at doing this. Computers are patient. They wait for an answer and never rush off to answer the phone. They're nonjudgmental; they don't think any answers are silly. Computer drill is less painful than the drills kids are likely to encounter in school. All of these reasons help make the computer pretty adept at teaching basic facts. The problems presented by these programs are much like those you'll find in your children's school workbooks.

Computers are expensive devices if all you want to do is turn them into electronic workbooks. But a few drill-and-practice programs will round out a software library and reinforce skills your child is learning in school.

Adult Programs

Finally, a lot of programs that are not marked specifically for children can still be used by children. Kids don't shy away from the challenge of an adult word processor or drawing program. Robin's children use adult programs, such as Microsoft's *Word for Windows* word processor and *Microsoft Publisher* desktop publishing program, without any real difficulty. They certainly don't use all the features of these programs, but they master enough so that the programs can assist them with their stories and book reports. We've found that children who are between eight and twelve years old can typically use about half the features of an adult program. So don't shy away from teaching your children how your own programs work. You'll want to help them grow into the more advanced software that you use as an adult.

CHAPTER

3

FINDING THE BEST BUYS

Shopping for a good home computer system isn't terribly different from shopping for any other major purchase. First, you have to know what you want. Then you have to find the best buy. In Chapter 1, we gave you a primer on computers. This background information should help you determine what your family needs from a home computer. In Chapter 2, we gave you pointers on selecting good software to use with your computer. And in this chapter, we'll give you pointers on how to find both. We'll offer a few buying tips, such as how to deal with warranties and tell you how to evaluate policies on hardware returns and repairs.

We have to tell you right up front that buying a computer isn't the easiest purchase you'll make. This is a major investment—not as major as an automobile—but often as costly as a room full of new furniture. And it is as personal, perhaps more personal, than furniture. A computer is an item you and your child will be spending a lot of time with. You'll want to be sure to purchase one you all like, one that everyone in the family can be comfortable with. Its keyboard and mouse should be kind to your hands, your eyes, and your posture, as well as your child's. Determine what you need, how much money you have to spend, and the kinds of vendors that are likely to deliver what you want in your price range.

Buying a computer requires a much greater commitment in money and patience than buying other home entertainment systems like Nintendo or Sega. It also returns greater dividends. The options you get on a computer far exceed those that you can get on a home entertainment system. A computer offers much more than just entertainment. Every new software program presents you and your child with a whole new range of options for using the computer.

You can build a library of games and educational software for the kids while you add to your own storehouse of word processing and spreadsheet software. The kids can play and learn on it. And after they've shut off the computer and gone to bed, you can use it to balance your checking account, write letters, work on projects you've brought home from the office, or launch a small business of your own. Not only can a personal computer be a fun-filled home entertainment machine and productive office companion, you can put it in a separate room where children can attend to homework or play to their hearts' content, while you settle down with a good book or in front of the TV with *LA Law* or a championship basketball game.

So you owe it to yourself to comparison shop to be sure that you get what you want and that you get it at the best price. Take your children with you when you go shopping. This will, after all, be a device they'll be spending a lot of time with. Children are surprisingly sensitive to the quality of screen color, graphics, and sound. Ask them how they like the look and feel of different computers in the store. Older children will be able to tell you. Younger ones will show you by indicating their preferences.

Most stores will have models on display. Turn them on. Try them out. Be sure the keyboard feels comfortable to you and your child. (Do be considerate, though, of other shoppers and don't let the kids linger too long at the keyboard when others are waiting to try it.) If a store does not have demonstration models on display or has a policy against children using the display machines, don't protest. Just be sure the store has a good return policy. You'll be trying out the computer once you get it home. If it's not what you wanted, you can take it back.

Tip

It's sometimes possible to try out software too. Many software vendors have short demo disks that you can run from a computer's floppy drive. Some of these automatically scroll through several screens so that you can see what the program looks like. Others actually offer several minutes of play. When shopping for software, ask the salesmen if the store has demo disks of the programs you are looking for. If it does, ask if you and your child can run the program. It's a good way to preview the software, right there in the store, before you buy it.

Where to Buy

Personal computers are turning up everywhere, from the Sunday classifieds to garage sales on August afternoons, from stores like ComputerLand to mailorder vendors, like Gateway and Insight, which advertise in computer magazines. You'll even spot them on shelves where, five years ago, you'd never have seen a computer. We've seen them near the appliance section of Sears and alongside office supplies at Staples Discount Office Products, as well as two aisles over from canned goods and fabric softeners in the buyers' clubs. There are now also shop-on-the-run stores that specialize in computers, software, and computer-related books and magazines. Throughout the South, for instance, you'll find the SoftWarehouse, which markets personal computers and all that go with them in the same way Toys 'R' Us markets dolls, backyard swings, and train sets. And you'll also find places that sell custom-designed computers; the yellow pages in most cities' phone books boast a few so-called home-brewers, people who will actually build a computer to your specification—usually at outstanding prices.

Finding the Best Buy

No one store, distributor or manufacturer offers the best buy on personal computers. Prices are constantly changing. New models are being introduced and old ones are coming off the market. So the best advice we can give is to tell you how to shop well and evaluate the information you get.

Before perusing the ads, review the information in Chapter 1. You'll be better able to make good price comparisons. You'll need to be aware of this information, whether you are buying a new computer from a mailorder firm or a used one from the Sunday classifieds. By understanding what the specifications mean, you'll know what you are getting. At the end of this chapter, we give you a checklist to help you compare values on hardware. You can use this sheet to record such things as the price, disk size, and memory of the systems you're comparing. Make multiple copies and use them to record details on each computer system you're evaluating. You'll be able to quickly identify the best deals.

Before you head out to buy a new computer, find out if your place of employment offers purchase options. Corporate data processing departments and Management Information Systems (MIS) managers are big purchasers of computer equipment. They usually have standing accounts with vendors and, often, the volume of business they do qualifies them for significant discounts off purchase prices. Many companies pass these discounts along to employees by allowing them to order equipment through the company. Get a list of models and prices that you can take home and compare against ads in computer magazines and in your local newspapers. It might be wise to talk to your accountant too, since many PC purchases can be tax-deductible.

Shopping Tips

Be sure to ask the store or vendor about their policy on returns. Make *sure* you can send back a system that you're unhappy with. If you're a first time buyer, particularly, you'll want to have the option of taking back a system, even if it is not defective. There are times when you'll exercise this option, not because of any fault with the system, but because you realize that the system configuration you selected was not the one you really needed.

Suppose, for instance, that you order a PC with two megabytes of memory and then find that the system is slow when running Windows or graphical applications—too slow for your taste. You'll want to send it back. Often stores and mailorder houses charge restocking fees for handling returns on their end, and you'll want to know what those are before making the purchase. Ask, too, about who's responsible for freight and shipping. Most vendors will assume these costs if a system is defective but will charge them to you if you simply decide you don't like the system or ordered the wrong one for your needs. Paying a restocking fee can be worth it. A $40 or $50 restocking fee is a more comfortable price to pay than living with a system that cannot do what you need it to and taking a large loss on it when you trade it in to buy a more powerful one later.

Tip

Always pay for hardware purchases with a credit card. Hardware systems represent major purchases, and you do not want to leave yourself at risk for thousands of dollars. Credit card companies have policies to insure that you won't be billed for something you did not receive. If your orders are not delivered and the vendor bills your credit card account, you only need to notify the credit card company that this is a false charge. The credit card company will prevail upon the vendor to deliver your order or will cancel the charge from your account. Be aware, though, that credit card companies generally intervene only when you did not receive what you ordered or when you send it back before paying for it. If a dispute over the return policy arises later, they may insist that you work out your problems with the vendor.

Look for special deals on software and services as you shop. Just before Christmas last year, The Prodigy Service, which offers a lot for kids that we tell you about in Chapters 10 and 11, made phenomenal deals available at regional computer fairs. For simply signing up for the service and logging on before the first of the year, they gave you the software, a $39.95 value, along with miscellaneous premiums, including two free audio compact discs. This is just one example of the kinds of deals available to you if you keep your eyes open.

Sources for Products and Information

Perhaps the best place to begin making comparisons of computer systems and prices is advertising. Magazines offer information on various computer systems. Local newspapers reveal which stores in your area are having sales and special offers.

One tour through a computer magazine, from front to back, will turn up a wealth of information on various systems, components, and prices, in both the advertising and editorial copy. Vendors who don't detail all their offerings in their ads often provide 800 numbers that you can call for sales information. Interestingly, you'll find that different computer magazines carry different types of advertising, according to their format. Some ads are designed to promote your awareness of computer products. Others are presented catalog-style with shopping lists of all the products a distributor offers, so that you can call up and place your order directly. Among the Ziff-Davis magazines that we work for, *PC Magazine* and *PC/Computing* feature a great deal of product advertising, while *PC Sources* and *Computer Shopper* offer catalog listings of mailorder vendors. But even in these mailorder listings, companies typically advertise the hottest products they currently have on the market. You should phone to find out if these ads offer a complete run-down of all that is available. Sometimes, there are unadvertised specials. Remember, too, that prices often change (usually becoming less expensive) between the time a vendor places an ad and the time you see it in the magazine. So if you decide to shop directly from magazines and see a system you like, you should always phone for an updated price list and ask if other special prices are available.

If you're happy to buy mailorder, you can often do all your comparison shopping from within the pages of a magazine like *Computer Shopper* or *PC Sources*, which specializes in the mailorder computer business. These magazines also often offer insightful articles for consumers. *PC Sources*, for instance, frequently runs articles that give tips on how to read and interpret the information you see in computer ads. They can also point out information that is likely to be misleading. If you're new to computers, you'll find *PC Sources* and the consumer sections of *PC/Computing* and *Computer Shopper* to be quite helpful.

After you peruse the ads and direct mail literature and before you purchase, you'll want to make comparisons with the prices and systems that local distributors are offering. Good buys are everywhere, and a little comparative shopping is sometimes all it takes to turn up dynamite deals. See who's having the sales and what they're selling.

Many regional distributors, such as 47th St. Computer in Manhattan, offer excellent discount prices on computers and electronics. And they often accept telephone orders from customers outside their regions.

Mailorder Companies

Often the best buys available come from computer mailorder firms like Gateway, Swan, and Insight. (See Appendix A for the addresses and telephone numbers of popular computer vendors and mailorder firms.) Not only are they able to offer low prices by selling directly to customers, heavy competition among mailorder firms has driven prices down dramatically, while raising the quality of warranties and service you're likely to get from them.

> **Tip**
>
> When buying software, be aware that some mailorder firms offer cut-rate prices on old versions when new versions of the software are released. These are marvelous deals if you're not particularly picky about having the most up-to-date software on the market. Once you register the old version, you're usually eligible for attractive discount prices on the new release. Often it's cheaper to upgrade your software this way than to simply buy the latest version.

Even better are the deals you'll find on software from mailorder firms. And if you have any qualms about shopping mailorder, software is a good, safe buy. It is not terribly expensive and rarely needs to be returned. Certain specialty catalog distributors, such as DAK, buy large volumes of popular home-oriented software products and inexpensive systems, selling them through direct mail catalogs that look like electronics versions of the Lillian Vernon or Fuller Brush catalog. They pass along to their customers some of the savings they garner from volume purchases.

Tip

Find out a bit about the company you're dealing with. In these recessionary times, particularly when you're dealing with a mailorder firm in a distant city, you'll want to assure yourself that the vendor will be in business for a while and able to deal with returns and any necessary repairs. When you call for information on systems and prices, be sure to also ask how long the company has been doing business under its current name. Don't be alarmed if the company is new or hasn't been in business for more than a year or two. Computers are a young and fast-moving industry. Do ask a few more questions if the firm has changed names recently. This is sometimes an indication that a firm has entered bankruptcy and reopened under another name.

Discount Stores and Buyers Clubs

These days you'll find computers everywhere. And discount stores of all stripes—from the Wal-Mart discount department stores to Staples Discount Office Supplies—have begun to stock personal computers down the aisle from refrigerators and typewriters, paper clips, and tissue paper. This makes it easy to make shopping for a computer part of a family shopping trip. Once you've determined more or less what type of system you want and what kind of prices you can get if you order through your employer or through a mail-order firm, you're ready to see what's also available from local stores.

Discount stores, buyers' clubs (such as the Wholesale Club, Makro, and Sam's Club) and even retail stores (such as Sears), typically carry two or three different lines of personal computers. There are also "superstores" that specialize in selling computers, software, and other computer-related products like computer books and magazines. A computer superstore is a bit like an electronic Toys 'R' Us. They stock computers and computer components in cartons that you can take down from warehouse shelves, hoist into a shopping cart, and carry through a checkout line. Superstores carry many more different types of computers and brand names than what you'll typi-cally find at a discount store, buyers' club, or retail department store.

Where mail-order firms, such as Gateway or Swan, usually sell only computers that they manufacture, discount stores and buyers' clubs will stock two to three different manufacturers' computers. Certain computer vendors—including Magnavox, Packard-Bell, Epson, and Sun, Moon, Star—specialize in selling their products through discount and retail outlets. It's always wise, when buying through any of these outlets, to ask how the computers are war-ranted. Most discount and retail outlets have no facility through which to service computers and computer parts, and so service ar-rangements must be made directly with the manufacturer or through a third-party service organization, such as TRW. This can mean shipping the computer back to the manufacturer or to a regional re-pair center if something goes wrong. It is important, when buying through such a store, that you gather details on returns and warran-ties. If a computer must go back to the manufacturer, find out who pays shipping. Ask how long repairs typically take and whether the vendor is likely to simply replace the computer, instead of repairing it, so that you'll be without the computer for only a short time.

Tip

Beware of bundles. Many times computer manufacturers will "bundle" software with their hardware systems. A bundle is a collection of software that is included in the basic price of the system. It may include games and per-haps a word processor or spreadsheet. Sometimes these represent a great value, but at other times you'll pay some-what more for a software bundle with your system with-out getting software you would really use. Always ask the names of the programs that are bundled.

Superstores, such as the SoftWarehouse across the South and the HardWarehouse in the Middle West, offer a wider variety of selec-tions and better terms on service than you'll find from other types of stores. This is simply because they specialize. In addition to comput-ers such as those mentioned above, you'll usually also find Macintosh and IBM products, as well as computer systems from companies like AST and NEC. Here too, you'll usually find a wide selection of modems, printers, sound cards, joysticks, and mice. These stores maintain their own service departments to configure the systems and help you troubleshoot problems if they turn up later. And, because they specialize, their sales and service people tend to be much better informed than the people in stores that sell computers as a sideline. After all, at stores like the SoftWarehouse, a sales person only needs to be knowledgeable about computers. No one will ask them about other household products. Typically, too, a superstore offers an extra layer of protection on service and warranties. Many offer their own terms, in addition to what you'll get from the manufacturer. The SoftWarehouse, for instance, maintains its own service department that will set up, service, and warrant the computer.

At a SoftWarehouse in Dallas, the Ellisons called ahead to get directions and asked a few questions about the specials of the week. Friendly salespeople told us how to get there, what was on special, and advised us by phone which systems were most likely to match our needs. That's what impressed us most. It's tough for a furniture or appliance salesman to quickly learn enough about computers to be able to give customers enlightened advice about what they need and which systems will best serve them. However at a specialty computer store, the salespeople specialize as well. And, typically, the advice you get from them is as good or better than the advice you'll get anywhere. This makes superstores ideal places for novices to shop. All you have to do is be willing to ask for advice.

Tip

Ask about the company's policy regarding returns. Will you get 100 percent of your money back if you are not satisfied? Is there a restocking fee? Some vendors, particularly mailorder firms, charge a restocking fee to cover their costs in handling your order and putting the system back in their warehouse if you return it. If you are buying mailorder, also ask who pays shipping charges if you return the computer. Typically, you do.

Be careful not to confuse superstores with specialty retail stores, like ComputerLand, which specialize in selling computers. These stores also staff knowledgeable salespeople, frequently maintain their own service departments, and often even train people in how to use computers and various types of software. But stores like Computer-Land (and Nynex on the East Coast), primarily cater to the needs of business customers. In general, they are set up to negotiate volume sale prices and large-scale service warranties. They are great places for the business customer. But individual consumers who are simply buying for their homes can usually find better prices and warranties elsewhere.

Homebrewers

Homebrewers are people who will actually build a computer for you according to your specifications—if you know what type of computer you want, how large a hard disk, how much memory, and what kind of video system. And if you're not too picky about the brand names that are on the components that make up the system, you can often get incredibly good deals from a homebrewer. The Ellisons purchased their first homebrew system in 1986 from a Jersey City homebrewer who also operated a wholesale Chinese food distribution warehouse and would literally build the computer while you waited among sacks of rice and dried fungi.

A homebrewer might maintain a storefront in your city. Or, he might simply do business out of his home, basement, or garage. Homebrewers tend to be unusually savvy about computers and electronics. They order computer parts from catalogs and magazines according to who is offering the best price on components in any given week. And then they build computers from those components. Because they are small and can move quickly to take advantage of special pricing, they can usually offer excellent deals on systems. The difficulty in buying from a homebrewer is that, often, you have to be as savvy about computers as the homebrewer is in order to specify what you want and be sure you are getting a good system. A good way to find knowledgeable homebrewers, who will stand behind their systems, is to get in touch with a local user group. Most cities have computer user groups, clubs of computer enthusiasts and computer professionals, who are happy to welcome newcomers and proffer advice. In Appendix D, we give you a list of regional user groups that can steer you in the direction of reputable homebrewers. Often too, their members will advise you on how to make a good purchase.

Computer Fairs

Frequently, local and regional computer fairs are held in arenas and hotels. These are often great places to find good deals on computer equipment and software. And even if you don't find what you want, you'll have a great time looking. For admission fees of a couple of dollars, you'll be able to browse the offerings of local and regional computer distributors and programmers who set up tables at the fair. Sometimes the distributors are actually homebrewers who have built their trades into thriving businesses.

You'll usually also find many computer aficionados who can answer your questions and offer advice, and you'll generally find really great deals on new software. Many of the software products sold at these fairs are old versions or versions that the manufacturers soon will upgrade, and the shrink-wrapped boxes you see on sale are being sold at closeout prices of half or less of what stores charge.

Garage Sales and the Classifieds

There are many risks in buying used electronic equipment of any sort, and that is especially true when it comes to buying personal computers. Typically, the PCs you find on sale in the classifieds or at garage sales are old models that we don't recommend buying.

And don't think that because the equipment is old, you'll be getting a good deal. We've found that most computer owners seek to get back the costs, usually high, that they have invested in their equipment. Computer prices, even on Macintoshes, have fallen dramatically in recent years, and they continue to fall. A person who tries to sell a two-year-old PC for about ten to fifteen percent less than what they paid for it will still be charging you more than, or about as much as, what you would pay for a new system of the same type. And remember, a used system isn't warranted. Unless you know the computer is in excellent shape, you may be inheriting the former owner's problems and a lot of repair bills.

If you do find a good deal on a used system, you'll need to exercise some caution to insure that what you're getting is in good condition.

The classifieds are good places to find used computer systems. But you should exercise the same amount of caution that you'd use in buying a used car. Always ask why the person is getting rid of the system. Very often, it's because they want a new, bigger, and better model. But you'll want to specifically ask if the user has experienced problems with the system. What are the problems? Try to get the owner to warrant the system. Ask them to give you a signed letter insuring that the system is in good working order and itemizing any difficulties they've had with it.

The truly good buys we've found on used computer goods are on software. These games, of course, aren't the hot new ones, but you'll often find popular old games and classics that have endured the test of time. Just as young children grow out of the shoes and clothing that you find being sold for pennies at garage sales, they also grow out of toys, games, and software.

Our friends the Haverburgs make shopping for used toys and software a Saturday outing. On any sunny, summer Saturday morning, you'll find father Bruce with his two sons, Brandon (five), and Kyle (three), cruising garage sales near their home. They find some excellent deals. Programs that typically sell in retail stores for $19.99 and higher will be on sale for a dollar or two. It's not unusual for the Haverburgs to return with fistfuls of floppy disks. For just a few dollars, the family purchases software and shares in a fun outing.

Mac Simplicity

Shopping for a Mac is a somewhat different experience than shopping for a PC. There are no clones, homebrews, or worries about poor quality knockoffs, because all Macs are manufactured by Apple. There are no questions of quality, and all Macs have the same one year warranty. Furthermore, Apple now has a 900 number so you can get technical support direct from the source.

While you don't have to worry about brands, you still have to decide what model you want and the final configuration. Then you can shop for the best price. Mailorder may be the best bet for the lowest prices, and since Macs are so easy to set up, you probably won't need help from a dealer. If you think you're going to need local help and you know a good dealer, that might sway your decision. In either case, you won't find yourself stranded. All Mac dealers are required to do warranty work and general service, so getting your sales and support from a single source is not necessary.

Tip

Buying a used computer requires asking a few more questions than you might ask when you buy a new one. When following up on an ad in the classifieds, ask what peripherals are included in the price. On new systems, things like modems and printers, and sometimes even monitors, are priced separately, but owners of used systems usually price them together. You may find a system with many extra options that were not listed in an ad for just a slightly higher price. Find out what, if any, software you'll be getting on the hard disk. If the software is included, ask the owner for the manuals, so that you'll have reference materials to teach you how to use the programs. Be aware, too, that if the owner has no manuals and original disks, there's some likelihood that the software you're getting was pirated. It's highly unlikely that a software company's technical support departments will help you through a problem if you are unable to provide them with a registration number when you call for assistance. Furthermore, pirating software is illegal and ultimately results in higher prices.

Whether you shop retail or discount stores, computer fairs, or garage sales, you can use the following checklist to keep notes on the computer systems you see. If you're evaluating several systems, you'll want to make copies of this sheet and fill out separate sheets for each system. After noting all the pertinent statistics on the systems you are considering, you can compare these sheets and make a decision on what seems to be the best buy.

Do a little research and consider what you need. Take your time looking. There are hundreds of computers to choose from. Get what you want and enjoy the hunt.

To Help You Shop

Macintosh computers include such things as sound, a mouse, and a high-density floppy disk drive built-in. These things are often optional on a PC-compatible. Use this checklist to compare PC-compatible components and prices.

Computer

    Processor type (circle one): 80286   80386 SX   80386 DX   80486

        Processor speed: _____ mhz

    Memory: Total RAM _____ K or _____ MB   Hard Disk _____ MB

    No. serial ports _____   No. paralell ports _____

    No. 3 1/2-inch floppy drivess _____   No. 5 1/4-inch floppy drives _____

    DOS included?   Yes   No   Windows included?   Yes   No

                                        System Price $ _____

Video System

    Graphics adapter, manufacturer _____

        Brand name _____

        Amount of video memory _____ MB   **Price $ _____**

    Monitor Type: (circle one) EGA   VGA   MCGA   Super VGA

        Maximum resolution: _____

        Maximum # colors: _____

        Brand name and model _____   **Price $ _____**

Peripherals and Accessories

    Mouse Included? (Circle one)   Yes   No   **or Price $ _____**

    Printer Type: (Circle one) Dot Matrix/9-pin

        Dot Matrix 25-pin,   Inkjet   Laser

        Brandname _____   **Price $ _____**

    Modem Manufacturer and model: _____

        Speed: (Circle one):   1200 bps   2400 bps   9600 bps   **Price $ _____**

    Sound Card Manufacturer and model name _____

        Reproduces sound, music and voice   Yes   No   **Price $ _____**

    Bundled Software: What's Included? _____

_____

                                  GRAND TOTAL $ _____

Policy on Returns

    Moneyback guarantee? 30 days   60 days   Other   None

    Restocking Fee? $ _____

    Freight? $ _____

BRINGING HOME BABY—
THE PERFECT SETUP
FOR YOUR NEW PC

Bringing home the computer is a great deal like bringing home the baby. You've done your reading and your shopping. You've even managed the computer version of a mother's labor—buying the perfect machine. You've collected a nice library of software; your credit line is kaput. Despite all your new knowledge, once you unswaddle the computer, you find yourself quite alone and a little unprepared for the next step. At least with a baby, you can count on your mom or someone else to get you through. But your infant computer just sits there, and you've got to start bonding. Now what do you do?

Childproofing Your Computer

The very first thing you should do is establish yourself as master of your machine and let the family decide how to mediate and monitor the activities on it. This means establishing a few household rules to insure that this new electronic member of the family will live in harmony with the other children.

You can love your computer, and you can love your child, but it's hard to love the two of them together unless you're prepared for the chemistry between them. Things you never expected to go wrong can go wrong when your child's pint-sized sweetness and exuberance meet the keyboard. As with most parenting tasks, the key to a successful union comes in setting a good example and using some common sense. If you don't eat, drink, or make too much merry around your computer, neither will your children. So we're going to give you a few rules to lay down. You may have heard them before. They may seem like everyday common sense. But they bear repeating:

1. Keep Cords and Plugs out of Sight. If a cable or cord is in harm's way, a child is apt to find it. A power strip, a sort of multi-socket extension cord, is a great $20 investment for tidying up loose ends. (Even better is a $50 surge protector that acts as a power strip and keeps outages and brown-outs from damaging your equipment.) You can plug your computer, printer, and other devices into it and use heavy duty duck tape to secure cords that may wander.

2. No Food, No Drink, No Dirty Hands. Cleanliness, they say, is next to godliness. It's also the preferred way to compute. It takes only a few computing sessions with unscrubbed kids

before your keyboard is ready to audition for a Mr. Clean commercial. Washed and dried hands should be part of the children's pre-computing ritual. Insist on a "no food and no drink" policy around the computer. A little bit of liquid spilled over a keyboard will, at a minimum, gum it up. Worse, it can cause shorts (and we don't mean the pants variety).

3. Stow away Pencils, Crayons, and Implements of Destruction. Robin once caught her son using a crayon to draw a map on the monitor to find his way through the fairyland in *Mixed-Up Mother Goose.* Crayons can come off monitors, but it takes only one crayon or scissors blade shoved into a disk drive or paper clip wedged into a keyboard to create technical dilemmas that make you lose faith in the next generation. Why risk the heartbreak (not to mention cost)? Keep office tools away from the computer.

4. Don't Touch the Screen. Manufacturers of glass-cleaning products profit most from the kiddie computing crowd. Small children instinctively want to touch the screen. Break the habit gently by reinforcing keyboard and mouse skills when your children want to show and tell what they just did on the computer. Show them how to point with the keyboard arrow keys or by moving the mouse pointer.

5. Make the Right Space. Adult-sized desks and chairs can be dangerous places for kids. Tiny arms and necks have a much farther distance to reach than adults' to touch the keyboard and see the screen. Most of us don't have the wherewithal in space or money to outfit our kids with their own private setup, but there are ways to accommodate a kid's-eye view. Some families use adjustable height desks and chairs; others simply stock up on telephone books. For the very young, a parent's lap is the ultimate child's seat. A child's chair should be a comfortable height, and the child should remain firmly planted. Accidents happen when kids balance on their knees or come tottering off an office swivel chair.

6. The Après-Computing Ritual. When the computing session is over, don't let the kids scamper away and make you the computer's Cinderella. Make sure they help put away the software and documentation. The children should be involved in

the post-computing cleanup process. Let them watch at first, then have them help you return disks to their proper places. Older children should help you label disks and make backups according to the manufacturer's instructions.

7. Teach Kindness to Floppies. If you ever want to write a book on a thousand and one uses for a floppy disk, observe your child in action. Floppies can be thrown Frisbee-style across the room or dissected with scissors or pen points for close inspection. Or hand one floppy disk to two children and watch the tug o'war that ensues over who gets to insert the disk. This is not what you want to happen, but don't expect your child to automatically understand the delicacies of a floppy disk. It's up to you to explain the proper care and handling of magnetic media. Tell them:

  • No fingers in the disk's inner circle. Oil from fingerprints can corrode the media. Floppies should be handled at the outer edges only.

  • Use the disk jackets. These are the paper envelopes that the floppy disks come in. Whenever the floppy is not in use, it should be in the paper disk jacket. 3.5-inch floppies are made of plastic and are much sturdier; these rarely come in disk jackets, but children should avoid handling the metal edge.

  • Insert the disk properly into the floppy drive. Children should hold a 5.25-inch disk at its top edge with the notch to the left, keep it horizontal, and insert the disk. They should hold a 3.5-inch disk at its top with the metal piece away from them and keep it flat as they insert it into the drive.

8. Camouflage Floppy Disk Drives. Who can resist taking a peek at what's behind a door, especially when that door has that nice flipflop lever and flashing lights? Leaving a disk drive in sight of a very young child is pure temptation. You can either stand guard over the drive or remove the temptation. Once the disk is inserted, a good tactic is to camouflage the disk drives by taping a large piece of cardboard across their doors. Keep the cardboard in place while your child is computing. Draw a picture on the cardboard if you're artistically inclined. Out of sight, out of mind is the rule for disk drives.

9. Teach Keyboard Etiquette. Ever see a kid use a keyboard? Children's computing styles fall into different categories. Consider The Hulk—this kid has a force so powerful that a key he depresses may never bounce back. There's also the Dead Weight—this is the kid who leaves a finger on the key, sending a line full of "a's" with each single press of the A key. Then there's the Speed Typist—the kid who thinks you've got to hit the keys as fast as you can to look like a grownup.

The best way to break these patterns is direct intervention. In the beginning, the parent should be there, hand atop the child's hand, to offer tactile feedback about the correct pressure to exert. Children as young as two years old can be shown the proper way to press a key. Older children should be introduced to touch-typing as soon as possible (see the tip on typing in Chapter 2).

10. Discourage Keypushing for Keypushing's Sake. Kids of all ages have a "because it is there" mentality about pushing buttons. All of us have the tendency to press a key before we think. While you don't want to squelch a child's enthusiasm for the keyboard, you do want to discourage wanton key pressing. If saying "no" doesn't work, gently restrain your child from pressing a key until he's looked at what's on screen. Encourage him to talk about what he sees. This helps your child understand that there's more to computing than touch-typing.

Most important, let the children know that you never walk up to a computer and start pressing buttons for no reason (especially when there's something on the screen).

11. Store Important Documents Safely. Whoever said computers would mean the end of paper was a little daft. Most computer programs, especially those for kids, have all sorts of paper accoutrements: quick tips, speedy manuals, and even sheets of paper that serve as copy protection devices. You don't want to see these lost or destroyed. One handy idea is to buy a tacky-back folder from an office supply store and affix it to a wall near the computer work area. Store all paperwork in the folder, so you and your child can quickly retrieve it and easily put it away.

Encouraging Independence

Unless you're willing to run to the keyboard and change programs for your child every time he finishes with one program and wants to start another, you should set up a system that makes it easy for your child to use the computer when adults are not around. This is not something you want to do until your child is well-schooled in the rules of etiquette we outline above. You will want to be on hand when very young children use the computer, but as they become aware of how to deal gently with the system and you become more confident that accidents won't happen, you'll want to encourage self-sufficiency. This can be tough if the kids are young and cannot yet read software labels or identify their favorite programs. But it is not impossible.

Very young children can identify their software by color or pictures. You may want to limit small children to running their programs only from a floppy disk. Very often, you can teach your child to recognize a favorite program by the color and typefaces on the program labels. Broderbund's *Kid Pix*, for instance, uses a funny typeface in which the dot over the *i* looks like a target and the center of the *p* looks like an eye. Children are quick to identify traits of their favorite playthings, so you usually only need to point out the distinctions once. If the floppy disks have no distinguishing characteristics, you can color-code them using markers or purchase stick-on stars and funny faces to help your child differentiate one program from another. You might also think about purchasing a storage box for your child's diskettes, to separate them from your own. These boxes can be purchased at any computer store or electronics store that carries personal computers. You could, for instance, put your child's software in a red box, while you keep your own in a black or grey one.

It's helpful, too, to give your non-reading preschooler clues to the appropriate keys on the keyboard. *The Playroom* comes with its own set of stickers—a smiling mouse face for the spacebar and a dragon's head for the Enter key—to guide your child to the keys he will need to operate the program. But if your software includes no such aids, you can create your own by using stickers or color-coding the keys by making tiny dots on them with different colored markers.

If you have older children in the house, they can help you with the process. Big kids usually enjoy manipulating disks for the young ones and showing them how to get started. But don't ask your six-year old to help your three-year old until you've had a chance to observe the dynamics. Children have a tendency to forget the rules, and they can be very territorial when a computer is in the room. Be on hand to mediate disputes and discourage hand-to-hand combat over who controls the keyboard. Once children become comfortable working together, the kid-helping-kid sessions can be rewarding for all involved.

Choosing from a Menu

Software programs are getting more and more complex. Often they are too complex to fit on a single floppy disk. When programs come on more than one disk, children have an easier time operating them if they are installed on the system's hard disk. Macintosh programs are easy to find once they're installed on a hard disk because they appear as icons or little pictures that your child can launch by double-clicking on the icon with a mouse. But finding a software program on an IBM PC-compatible's hard disk is a little more difficult.

Unlike the Macintosh, which operates graphically, the IBM is "character-based," which means that it cannot deal with graphics without a little bit of help. You can make an IBM graphical in nature by installing Microsoft's Windows software. Windows puts a Macintosh-like look on a PC-compatible's screen. (We'll tell you more about Windows in Chapter 9.)

If you own an IBM PC-compatible, you'll probably want to create a menu for your child. A menu is simply a list of programs that can be launched by pressing a single letter or number. It can come up on screen as soon as the computer is turned on. Or you can assign a menu a name, so that, when the computer comes on and you see the C:> prompt in the upper lefthand corner, you can type your name to bring up a menu of your programs. Computer menus are similar to menus you might find in a restaurant. They list the offerings; all you need to do is press a key to indicate the one you want, and it will be delivered.

A menu allows your child to automatically load his favorite program simply by selecting it. Having different menus come up with different people's names is a good idea if you want to keep the kid away from your own software. You can simply have him type his name to bring up his own menu.

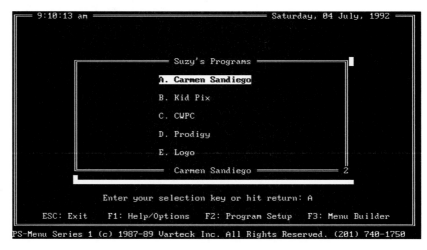

Figure 4.1 A menu can be set up to appear on the screen of your IBM PC-compatible as soon as your child turns on the system.

You can create menus like the one above by using software for IBM PC-compatibles that builds menus automatically. Programs like PC Dynamics' *Menu Works Personal* or OSCS's *QuickMenu III* walk you through necessary steps to setting up a menu. Some multi-purposes computer utility programs, including the popular *XTree Gold*, will also help you build menus. The ultimate menu system for kids is KidShell from EdMark. This clever program looks like a child's desk, including accessories. When you click on a drawer you gain access to software programs. And adventuresome computer users can build their own by typing the appropriate commands directly into the computer, creating DOS batch files.

We don't recommend the roll-your-own approach for novices, but IBM PC-compatible owners who have grown comfortable with their systems will find it isn't too difficult. Here's how:

Rolling Your Own PC Menu

Below, we'll give you a simple menu that will make it easy for children to load their favorite programs after turning on a PC. We recommend this only to parents who understand the disk operating

system (DOS) on an IBM PC-compatible and have had some experience writing batch files to control it.

Use a word processor or a program like *XTree Gold* to add a line to
the end of your AUTOEXEC.BAT that says:

```
type menu.txt
```

Be sure you save the AUTOEXEC.BAT as an ASCII text file.

Then use the same word processor to create MENU.TXT file as
an ASCII text file (a file with no formatting from your word processor) that lists your child's favorite programs. Give it the filename
MENU.TXT and store it in your root directory. At the top of the
file write Main Menu, then list your child's favorite programs giving
each an alphabetical designation. At the bottom, write Type a letter
and press enter. Depending upon the programs in your child's software library, the file might look something like this:

```
MAIN MENU
A - CARMEN SANDIEGO
B - PLAYROOM
C - TREEHOUSE
D - MICKEY'S JIGSAW PUZZLE
F - READER RABBIT
TYPE A LETTER AND PRESS ENTER
```

Now name the file MENU.TXT and save it. That was not too
tough, was it? But the work doesn't stop here. For each program that
you listed in the menu, you'll have to write a batch file that will launch
that program when your child types the appropriate letter. For instance, on the menu above, you'll need to create a batch file with the
name, A.BAT, to call up *Carmen Sandiego*. You'll need one named
B.BAT to call up *Playroom*, and so forth. For the menu to work, all of
them must be saved in flat ASCII format and must be stored in the
main root directory. The file A.BAT might look like this:

```
CD\CARMEN
CARMEN
CD\
CLS
TYPE MENU.TEXT
```

The strange-looking words in the file above are DOS commands.
CD\ is shorthand that tells the system to Change the Directory. CLS

tells it to CLear the Screen. The file above tells the PC to automatically change to the directory (in the current drive) where Carmen Sandiego is stored (CD\CARMEN) and load the program (CARMEN). When your child quits the program, the rest of the file will go into effect, changing back to the main root directory (CD\), clearing the screen (CLS), and returning the menu to the screen (TYPE MENU.TXT). Remember, you'll need to create separate batch files for every software program you add to the menu.

The procedure we outlined above will bring the menu to the screen whenever your child turns on the computer.

The Pictorial Approach

If you're running the kids' programs from a Macintosh or an IBM PC-compatible with Windows installed, you can simply teach your child which little picture or icon to click on in order to launch a favorite program. Both the Mac and Windows are designed for a mouse. There are a number of preschool games on the market to teach young children how to use a mouse, including First Byte's *Dinosaur Discovery Kit.*

Macintosh users and PC-compatible owners who use Windows can customize what is known as a *desktop*, the first screen. It is called a desktop because here you'll find what you need to operate the computer. To launch a program you just click with the mouse pointer on the right icon for the program. Special software is available that can be used to make Macintosh icons talk, so that when young children click on the icon they hear the name of the program it represents.

Windows

In Chapter 9, we explain how you and your older child can explore the programs that come with Windows. These programs provide valuable training for your child in using adult applications, and some are quite useful for creating school reports, schedules, and more. Windows can also provide a friendly, easy-to-use environment for your younger child, although not all kids' programs are compatible with Windows. Chapter 9 also provides a useful introduction to Windows features and terms, so if any of the descriptions here are confusing to you, we suggest that you read the first section of Chapter 9 right now, before you customize Windows.

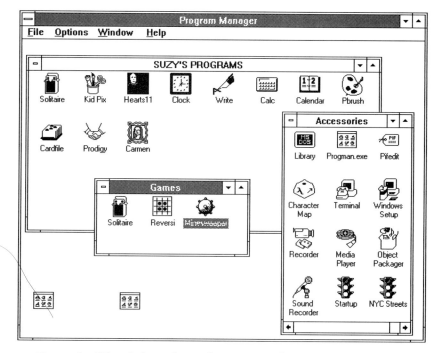

Figure 4.2 The *desktop*, shown here in Windows, organizes software programs according to little pictures called *icons*.

Readying Windows for the Older Child

If your child is at least ten years old, he can start using Windows for a variety of tasks. However, before you turn him loose on Windows (which we tell you how to do in Chapter 9), you should take a few precautions. Children can't "break" Windows, but they can accidentally change the way you have it set up. If a child does alter your setup, you may have to spend a lot of time correcting the problems. Here are a few tips for childproofing Windows:

- Windows allows you to run several programs at a time—in fact, this is one of its most useful features. In Chapter 9, we suggest several ways your child can take advantage of these *multitasking* abilities. However, not all computer systems are powerful enough for Windows multitasking. Before attempting to run several programs at a time, read Chapter 14, *Optimizing Windows* in the *Microsoft Windows User's Guide*. It's worthwhile to optimize Windows for your system, so that

Windows can make the best use of your hardware. Then, try the exercises in Chapter 9 on your own. If your system is not powerful enough for multitasking, attempting to use several programs at once can cause system crashes and loss of data.

• You and your child should always remember to save your work frequently when using Windows. Work with your child to make sure he follows this important rule.

• Put all of the programs your child will use in one Windows *program group,* so that he doesn't get into your own work while he works within the Windows environment. Make sure the child knows that he should only use the programs in his group —not any of the others in your system. (Below are instructions for creating a program group just for your child.)

Tip

You may have trouble understanding Chapter 14 of the Windows manual, because the writers assume that you know a great deal more about hardware and software than most people do. If you do have trouble, have your serial number ready and call Microsoft Technical Support, available Monday through Friday, between 6 a.m. and 6 p.m. Pacific time, at 206-637-7098. We don't recommend you use the Interactive Voice Support Service, whose number is also included in the manual. Whoever you call at Microsoft, it's at your own expense—and it can be costly.

A program group is a collection of Windows programs. An application can exist in more than one program group at a time without taking up more space on your hard disk. Here are the steps for creating a program group for your child:

1. After installing Windows, start it by typing WIN and pressing Enter. The *Program Manager* window opens. All program groups should be closed, appearing as rectangular icons. If any are open, close them by double clicking on the control menu boxes at the upper left corners of the windows.

2. Click on the File menu of *Program Manager*. Then click on the New command. The New Program Object dialog box opens.

3. Click on the Program Group button and then on *OK*. The Program Group Properties dialog box opens, with the typing cursor in the text box labeled *Description*.

4. Type in a name for your child's program group. If your child is named Suzy, for example, you might type in: Suzy's Programs. We'll use this name for our example. You can leave the other text box blank. Just press Enter or click on *OK*. Windows creates a new program group for you and opens it. The name you entered is shown on the *title bar* at the top of the program group window.

5. When you first start Windows, the Windows programs your child needs are in the Accessories program group. Find this group now. (If necessary, you can move Suzy's Programs by positioning the mouse pointer on the title bar, holding down the left mouse button, and rolling the mouse.) When you can see the Accessories program group, double click on it.

6. In the Accessories window, click on the icon labeled *Calculator*. Do you use this application in your own work? If you do, click on *Program Manager*'s File menu and then on the Copy command. If you don't use this program, choose the Move command from the File menu.

7. Whichever command you choose, a dialog box appears; it includes a list box labeled *To Group*. Click on the arrow key next to the list box to open a pull-down menu. To see more of the list, click on the arrow key at the bottom of the list box. Highlight the name *Suzy's Programs* and click on *OK*.

8. Now the *Calculator* icon is moved or copied to Suzy's Programs. Your child can start *Calculator* by opening this program group and double clicking on this icon.

9. Repeat steps 6 through 8 to move or copy the following accessory programs: *Solitaire, Minesweeper, Cardfile, Notepad, Write, Clock*, and *Paintbrush*. If you don't find *Solitaire* and *Minesweeper* in Accessories, check *Program Manager* for a program group called *Games*; they should be located there.

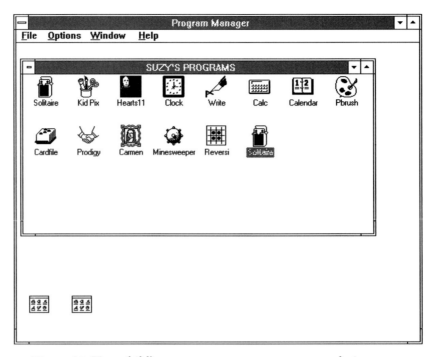

Figure 4.3 Your child's program group presents many choices.

This section has given you minimal instructions for childproofing Windows. The following section offers suggestions if you want to add more applications to your child's program group or further childproof Windows.

Readying Windows for the Younger Child

Windows can be used to create a visual environment where your younger child can easily find his applications. However, at this writing, many of the programs featured in this book are not compatible with Windows. Some are, however (The *Prodigy* service can be installed to run under Windows), and some, like *Kid Pix*, are even available in Windows versions. In the future, more and more programs will be able to work under Windows. Because of Windows' friendly face, it is worthwhile trying to install your child's favorite applications to run under it.

We have not tested all the programs in this book for Windows use, so you'll have to try out your own. Installing applications under Windows is not always straightforward, so we advise you to check the program's manual and the Windows manual for assistance. We aren't going to give detailed instructions here, but we do offer some general help.

1. To set up an application under Windows, open the Main program group by double clicking on it. Then double click on the icon labeled *Windows Setup*.

2. From the Options menu, choose *Set Up Applications*. When the Setup Applications dialog box appears, click on the button labeled *Ask you to specify an application*. Next, Windows presents a dialog box where you enter the full path and name of the file that starts the application.

3. To find the filename, click on *Browse*. In the Directories list of the next Setup Applications dialog box, double click first on the icon for your root directory (probably labeled *c:*) and then double click on the icon for the directory where the application is located. (If necessary, click on the scroll bars next to the list box to display the name you're looking for.) When you have selected the application's directory, Windows Setup displays the names of all files with the extensions .BAT, .EXE, and .COM.

4. Highlight the name of the file that starts the application. If there is a .BAT file where the letters preceding *.BAT* are the letters you type to start the application, choose it. Otherwise, the filename will end in .EXE (most likely) or .COM. When you have highlighted the correct name, click on *OK.*

Windows sets up the application or informs you that it cannot do so. It places the application in a program group, usually the Applications group. Before you go further, test the application and make sure that it actually runs. The program may crash or halt your system if it does not in fact work properly with Windows. An expert might be able to correct the problem, but the solutions are complex, and you probably should not waste your time in the attempt. Instead, this particular application should be started by your child using the DOS batch file that we described earlier in this chapter.

If you can run the program from Windows, your child will be able to find and use it easily. Follow the directions outlined earlier for creating a program group for your child and placing his applications there.

Next, you may wish to further childproof Windows, so that your younger child cannot accidentally ruin the effort you've put into customizing and/or installing Windows for your own use. It's fairly easy to protect your Windows environment using *File Manager,* an adult program located in the Main program group. We're not going to give you a lot of information about using *File Manager,* although its operation is fairly simple. Our suggestions assume that *File Manager* is still set up as it is when you first install Windows. (And if it isn't, you probably have already been working with it! For more instructions, consult *Van Wolverton's Guide to Windows 3.1* by Michael Boom and Van Wolverton, published by Random House, or your Windows manual. *File Manager* is a very useful program, and you will want to learn more about it.) Follow the steps below to prevent your child from altering program groups, your Windows color schemes, and other even more important settings:

1. Open the Main program group and double click on the *File Manager* icon.

2. In the lefthand portion of the *File Manager* window, click on the directory where Windows is located (it may already be selected), probably called *windows.* A list of the Windows files appears in the right half of the screen.

3. Click on the View menu and choose *Sort by Type.* The Name option should also be checked. In the righthand file list, the Windows files are sorted in alphabetic order by extension. (If you don't see a file list, click on *Tree and Directory* in the View menu.)

4. Use the scroll bars to display the files with the extension .INI.

5. Now, hold down the Control key. While holding it down, click on the following filenames: *control.ini, dosapp.ini* (if present), *progman.ini, system.ini,* and *win.ini.* If you highlight another filename by accident, just click on it again to remove the highlight from the name.

6. When these five filenames are highlighted, click on the File menu and choose the Properties command. Click the checkbox labeled *Read Only*, so that an *x* appears in the box. You can now exit *File Manager*.

Now your child will not be able to make changes to your Windows setup—unless he figures this all out and removes the read-only status from these files. If your child does make changes, Windows will appear to carry them out. But after he is finished and leaves Windows, the changes won't be recorded. That's because these files have been protected and cannot be altered. The next time someone starts Windows, a message will appear, saying that the changes have not been made.

You also won't be able to create new program groups, add applications, change color schemes, or perform other customization activities. However, it's easy to remedy this situation. Just follow the steps above. At step 6, click the Read Only checkbox and remove the *x* from it.

This method of childproofing is not foolproof against the savvy older child, but it is likely to protect you in most cases. Now you are ready to start teaching your child about Windows.

SECTION II

A PLAN OF ACTION

Playing is learning; don't let anyone tell you differently. Simple math takes place whenever a child plays pickup sticks, sells lemonade from a sidewalk stand, or builds a Lego castle. Just as those activities introduce children to numbers, computer games introduce children to all sorts of abstract and concrete concepts.

Playing computer games means cultivating new and special skills that don't come as naturally as playing Keep Away or Make Believe. Games offer joyous entrees to the world of computing, as well as challenging recreation for your child. But games should be a beginning, not an end, to learning. So in this section, we start with games and then introduce you to other types of software you'll want to use with your children. We'll show you, as parents, how to stretch the fun and usefulness of these games as far as your imagination can carry you.

Good programs give children new worlds and environments to explore. But every good explorer knows that you need to be equipped for a journey. Unless kids are given the right tools for learning, the benefit of software—and particularly computer games—can be superficial. Like a miner without a pick, your child won't get past the surface. Kids will explore on their own if left to their own devices. But if the child lacks the tools and guidance to delve deeper, the software can wind up gathering dust on a shelf after just a few plays.

Parents can enrich the computing experience in two ways:

- By giving children the tools they need to move deeper into the game

- By integrating the computer experience with real life.

In this section we show you ways to do both of those things using computer games and other types of computer programs. We show you how to help your child with electronic painting, electronic publishing, online services, computer programming, and Microsoft Windows.

Each chapter in this section focuses on a particular software program while introducing the important fundamentals for a particular genre of software. In this way, we'll give you all sorts of interesting activities to stretch your software dollars. The suggestions can be used well with other similar programs in your software library too. But even if you buy all of the programs mentioned in these chapters, you'll spend no more than $250 (and probably less, if you shop from reputable mail order catalogs).

We chose to give these programs special attention because they are very popular, are readily available in stores, and have staying power. These are not the kinds of software programs kids play with once and then toss aside. And with the additional activities we give you in these chapters, you'll greatly increase the active shelf-life of the packages, because your kids will have so many things to do with them.

A Word about Copy Protection

We'd be shirking our responsibility if we didn't say something about the copy protection you'll find on many children's games. Copy-protection schemes keep people from randomly copying software and passing it out, free, to friends. Generosity is nice, but it's also illegal. It's the equivalent of stealing the software from the company that produces it. For every free copy that's distributed, the company may well lose a sale. And that, in turn, hurts all of us by making software more expensive.

It should be enough to say, "Don't be a villain and steal this software. You'll quickly find that crime doesn't pay." But to keep pirates at bay, companies often embed code words at key places in their documentation or have a special floppy disk, called a key disk, that you must use to operate the program. Sometimes they bury a key phrase behind colored type so that it can only be read through a cellophane viewer that comes with a legal copy. This sort of copy protection can ruin your enjoyment of a game— if you lose the means of learning the code word, you won't be able to play.

(continued)

A Word About Copy Protection (continued)

Some companies replace lost manuals and copy-protection guards. Of course, you can always buy another copy of the program. It's thriftier and more convenient to keep your manuals on the bookshelf next to the dictionary and encyclopedia your kids use for homework.

It's vital that parents set a good example as honest software users. Good software takes enormous amounts of research and development to assure high quality. When parents respect software (and your children will know if you beg, borrow, or steal, instead of buying) children will grow up to do likewise.

CHAPTER
5

PLAN I: PLAYING GAMES FOR ALL THEIR WORTH— THE PLAYROOM

The software you'll need: *The Playroom*

What it costs: $49.95

Why it's special: Exposes children to a magical world through a tour of child's bedroom. Games and surprises wait behind the furniture; pets and toys are displayed on screen.

Ages it appeals to: 3 to 7

Activities: Learn to tell time; recognize the alphabet; pre-reading skills; number skills; mouse navigation; build a clock; create mixed up photos; fantasy play.

Introducing .... *The Playroom*

Did you ever watch a small child get acquainted with a roomful of toys. They run first to one, then to another, experimenting just long enough with each to discover what it's about. Then they revisit their cherished places again and again, finding new ways to play. Broderbund's *The Playroom* captures that busy intensity and sense of discovery.

The Playroom places your child in an on-screen bedroom and lets her manipulate and explore that environment. She uses a mouse to click on electronic representations of toys and gadgets in a child's bedroom. And something happens with every one she clicks on. Some objects make sounds. Others perform animated activities. The goldfish, for instance, jumps when you click on its bowl. Click on the computer in the bedroom, and a game designed to teach keyboard skills pops up. Six full-fledged computer games lurk behind playthings and are designed to introduce preschoolers to the alphabet, words, numbers, and deductive reasoning. So, in a sense, *The Playroom* offers seven games, the bedroom itself and the six games in it. With the Mac version you can record your own sounds and replace the ones that come with *The Playroom*.

The program works best when used with a mouse. Your child can point to objects and click on them to make selections. You can also use a keyboard, but your child will have to hit the arrow keys several times to make the arrow pointer jump in different directions.

Broderbund has actually done a good bit of our work for us. *The Playroom* documentation includes a lovely collection of activities you can do with your child. It gives you ideas and tips on making finger puppets, coloring books, name trains, and other wacky creations. Broderbund even supplies some cut-out items in the manual to help you start. And, once you get going, you can create others on your own. We'll take up where they leave off, but we applaud them for their creative activity guide.

Quick Start

The first screen you see in *The Playroom* is an illustration of a child's room. Toys and furnishings appear to the center and right; Pepper Mouse, the cartoon character hero, peers through a window at the back of the room. (A little stuffed Pepper Mouse toy actually comes with the software. You can keep him near your computer for your child to play with during breaks from the computer game.)

Even while you are idle, the playroom is busy. Every minute or so some object in the room comes to life and gurgles, yawns, tweets, or does something funny to get your attention.

Figure 5.1 The Playroom creates a world where computer games lie behind ordinary bedroom objects.

Explain to your child that she can choose various objects by using the computer's mouse, joystick, or arrow keys to move the arrow-like pointer on the screen. With the pointer on an object, the child clicks the mouse or presses Enter to select it. If your child has never played a computer game, demonstrate this by doing it yourself.

Tip
Explore before your child does. This advice goes for any new game. You should be very comfortable with the game before the children come anywhere near the scene of the action. Young children, especially, have no patience for a parent-in-training.

Very young children may appreciate a verbal tour of the room. Point out each object on the screen and name it. That way you develop a shared vocabulary. First, introduce the simple objects, the ones that offer music and animated rewards; these are immediately gratifying. Then move them on to games. Teach them the names of *The Playroom* characters. This helps build an affinity that lasts well beyond the world of the computer. The mouse is called *Pepper Mouse.* The Dragon is simply called *Dragon.* The one-eyed creature is called *Look-A-Lot.* You should also ask the child to name items in the computer playroom and then to name items in her own bedroom. This helps her understand the metaphor.

Tip

To teach good "sharing" behavior, when we play games with young children in a group setting, we keep some index cards with happy and sad faces on them nearby. When a child generously relinquishes control of the mouse (and their turn) to the next child, we reward her with a happy face. A child who tries to control the mouse gets a sad face. And the child with the most happy faces gets a snack or goody.

Step-by-Step Tour

In this whirlwind tour of *The Playroom,* we'll tell you about the activities and exploratory games in the playroom and talk about ways you can use them to encourage further play and discussion. First we'll discuss the activities associated with the objects. Then we'll show you how to use the full-fledged games.

The Activities

A Bed

Click on it with the mouse, and it plays a lullaby. It also snores and yawns. (There's something under the bed in the Mac version.) Sing along as the computer plays the tune. Ask your child what other lullabies she knows. And if your child wishes to sing them, sing those too. Discuss the difference between a lullaby and a wake-up song and the kinds of activities that start the day or night.

The Radio

Click on it, and the computer plays "Twinkle, Twinkle Little Star." (It plays *The Playroom* theme in the Mac version.) Once again, sing along with the tune. You might use the song as an opportunity to talk about stars and the night sky. Does your child know what stars are and how they differ from planets?

The Night Stand

The drawer opens when you click on it, and a balloon floats into the room. Click on the drawer again and it closes. Move the mouse pointer to the floating balloon and it pops, which is great practice for young mouse-hands in training. Close the drawer and open it again to release another balloon. (It closes by itself in the Mac version.)

The Window

Click on Dragon's face in the window. What does the dragon change into? What happens if you click again? Click on Mouse, and he falls down. Click on Dragon, and he breathes fire. In the Mac version Pepper Mouse is in the window. When you click on him he falls with a crash. Click on the curtains and Pepper Mouse is replaced by a dragon that breathes fire when you click on him. Name the characters as they disappear and reappear.

The Word Picture

Click on the word in the picture frame, and a voice speaks the word that is printed and illustrated in the frame. The words are also animated in the Mac version. Seven basic words and phrases are illustrated: *Yes, No, Exit, Poison, Walk, Don't Walk,* and *Danger.* These are important words in a child's life. Talk to your child about what each one means. Review the letters. Speak each one aloud, then ask your child to spell the word. Use the game to help your child recognize how important these words are to them. For instance, talk about the *Walk* and *Don't Walk* lights at crosswalks; when you're out for a walk, point out the lights and say "Remember the signs in *The Playroom.*" You can even practice these words with flashcards or have the children write the words on paper. Can you make up a story with these words? Make up a story that calls for the child to supply one of these words. For example, "I got to the red light and Mom said, "Don't walk." In this way, the game will reinforce important concepts children should know about the real world.

Other Objects in the Room

The bird tweets when you click on it. Click repeatedly to make it warble. In the Mac version, the bird wakes up and opens its eye when you click on it. While it's awake, it warbles when you move the mouse across the room. The rhino wags its tail when you first click on it. Click a second time and it bellows. In the Mac version, the rhino opens its mouth and yawns. The goldfish does a somersault when you click on it. And click on the green one-eyed monster, and it winks and makes a noise. The one-eyed monster is pink-eyed. It wakes up and the eye follows the mouse arrow as it moves around the room. He is called Look-A-Lot.

Connection

Draw a bird and a nest on a piece of paper. Cut out both shapes to create a game in which you give the child verbal directions on what to do with the bird and the nest, such as "Put the bird *in* the nest. Put the bird *near* the nest. Put the bird *under* the nest. This is a good way to teach vocabulary words that involve spatial relationships.

The Exploratory Games

Six of the objects—the clock, the toy on the carpet, the Spinner, the A-B-C book, the mouse hole, and the computer—lead to mini-games when you click on them. Each has different lessons to teach.

These hidden games take longer to understand and master than the objects you'll see on screen. Each has various levels of difficulty, so you can customize the play, making it easier for younger children, and able to grow as they grow.

When you first introduce your child to an activity, set the game to the easiest level. When the child figures out that there are more advanced levels or demonstrates that she's ready ("Hey Dad, why can't I count up to twelve in the spinner game instead of just five?"), it's time to advance. Here's how you can use each of the exploratory games to make connections to other games and activities you can construct at home:

The Clock

Behind the clock is a "learn to tell time" game. As you click on various numbers, the hands move around a large cuckoo clock on one side of the screen to show time passing. On the other side of the screen, you'll find a digital clock with a readout that coincides with the hands on the cuckoo clock. Pepper Mouse sits above the digital clock and, as you change the hour, he performs an activity appropriate to the time—sleeping, eating breakfast, getting a midnight snack. Click on the hands, and an hour is chosen at random. Click on the cuckoo or the digital clock, and the bird chimes the hour and a voice announces the time.

Connections

Use one of your own "play clocks" and have the child match the time on the physical clock to the time on the computer clocks. If you don't have a toy clock, you can build one from a paper plate, using paper-fasteners and cardboard for the hands. Set the clock for different times of the day and let your child physically act out what should be done at a certain time of day, like having a glass of milk in the morning or sleeping at night.

This is a good time to explain to your child about the difference between AM and PM. Point out how Pepper Mouse does something different at 10 AM than he does at 10 PM.

(continued)

Connections (continued)

Have the children cut out pictures of activities from magazines and associate them with certain times of the day. Make a collage, or poster with pictures of things that you do during different times of the day.

Figure 5.2 The Clock introduces children to analog and digital time. Pepper Mouse demonstrates time-appropriate behavior.

The Toy on the Carpet

If it's hard to tell what this little stuffed animal is—with portions of different animals on its head, body, and legs—it's because the creature is really a mixed-up toy game. It's called the Mixed-Up Toy. Your child can create silly combo creatures by clicking on the top, bottom, or middle of the toy to make it change to a different animal. The character may end up with a carrot top over an elephant's body and a dragon's feet and tail. Some children yearn for symmetry in this game and will try to match the same head, torso, and feet to the same animal. Others will giggle over the silly creatures they create.

Encourage your child to do both. Click on the toy surrounded by question marks in the corner of the screen to let The Playroom create its own new creatures automatically.

Connections

Broderbund suggests that you cut photos in magazines into pieces— top, middle, and bottom—to create three-part combo creatures of your own. We've also done this using old family and vacation photos that are too numerous or out of focus to put in the photo album. Kids love to create silly creatures from familiar people and things. They'll laugh when you mix their faces with the family pets' bodies.

Another game that's terrific fun is to take a sheet of paper and fold it in thirds, so that only one third is visible at a time. Have the first player draw a face in her third of the paper, turn the paper so the second third is visible, and pass it on to the next player. Have the next player draw the midsection of a body (human or animal), and have the final player do the same for the lower part of the body. Unravel your paper and view your "silly creation." We play this game at restaurants using napkins or placemats. It's a great way to wile away the time before your food comes. Try naming your silly creatures, a "carrot-opus," perhaps?

The Spinner Toy

A click on this grey-and-white toy (it's yellow on the Mac) on the bookshelf reveals two roulette wheels, one with pictures and one with numbers. If you select *10* on the roulette's spinner, ten objects appear in a display window. Pepper Mouse stands at the side of the window. If your child clicks on Pepper to wake him up, in the display window he'll present objects that your child can match to the number on the spinner. When your child answers correctly, an animated sequence plays out in the window. You can set the difficulty level on a color-coded disk displayed on the right side of the window; depending on which level you select, all or only a few of the numbers from one to 12 will be available on the spinner.

Connections

Counting things is an intriguing activity—*Sesame Street's* "count" has proved it so. It's easy to create your own variations on counting games. For example, you can get a shoebox and then draw 20 colored circles on separate pieces of paper. Place the circles on the floor. Ask your child to place a certain number of circles, ten, for example, in the shoebox.

Sometimes, to add an element of "gaming" to these counting events, we use drinking straws. The child must pick up the colored circle by sucking the paper up with the straw and then carrying the straw, with paper attached, to the shoebox drop-off place.

The Computer

The game behind the computer teaches spelling and keyboarding skills. The game places an image of a computer with a QWERTY keyboard on the screen. Pepper Mouse is resting to one side. When you click on a letter on the screen, the key on-screen is depressed, the letter apppears, and a voice pronounces the name of the letter. When you click on Pepper Mouse, he wakes up and the computer screen fills with gift wrapped boxes, each with a word under it. Click on a gift box and Pepper Mouse will help you spell the word beneath it. There is also a mystery box where a word is automatically chosen for you. You can set the level of difficulty by adjusting the slider to the right of the screen. Your child can match each letter that Pepper Mouse holds up, clicking on the appropriate key on the display screen's picture of a keyboard or typing it at the computer's real keyboard. Or you can spell out your own messages. You can set skill levels to control how many letters are used at one time—choosing to create words from a single row of keys on the keyboard or using the entire alphabet.

Connections

Children can take turns matching letters, words, or messages, scoring points for those they match correctly. This is a great way to play against a friend. It's a cross between a spelling bee and a typing contest.

You can also come up with a secret word for each day taken from *The Playroom's* on-screen list. Write your word on a card and go over the spelling with your child. If your child correctly spells the word the following day, put it in a box. In this way you can build your child's vocabulary by collecting word cards. At the end of the week, use these cards as flashcards. See which ones your child can read and remember. You may wish to work on a group of words that can be assembled into simple sentences or stories.

Robin uses this game to mimic the work her children do in school. For example, Reed, her five-year-old, learns phonetic spellings using it. He simultaneously works on words like *cat, hat, bat,* and *sat.* Then he practices typing these words. We believe that by typing them, he gains one more insight into the repetition of letter patterns. Sometimes Robin lines up his toy cars—five or so of his favorites—next to the computer. Each time he spells a word correctly, she takes away a car. Tactics like these help children see the finite quality of a given task.

Round Robin typing is also fun. When there are two or more children, you can have them take turns typing in a letter of the word to be spelled. There's a great deal of interaction among the players, and we stress that this is cooperative play—the idea is to spell a word correctly, not outspell each other.

Another variation is typing versus writing. For example, have one child write the word *good* on paper, while the other types the same word on the screen. At the Raskin house, they time these events for fun and see if the typing time decreases with repetition.

The Mousehole

By clicking on the mousehole, you enter a maze of mouse tunnels. Each of the three tunnels contains a computerized version of a board game with a different level of difficulty. This game teaches simple addition and subtraction. Each player clicks on the on-screen dice cup which rolls three dice, and then moves their character that number of spaces on the board. If you land on a square with a white circled number, you move ahead that number of spaces. Land on a square with a black circled number, and you move back that number of spaces. The first person to reach the end of the maze wins the game.

Figure 5.3 The Mousehole Game is an electronic board game that teaches simple addition and subtraction.

Connections

Point to the spots on the dice and count the numbers with your child. Count out the number of spaces aloud as her player moves forward and back. Explain the concepts behind subtraction (minus, to take away from) and addition (plus, to add to) whenever she lands on a black or white circled square. You can play a similar game on your kitchen table, using pasta shells or pennies. Roll the dice, then take that number of shells, or rehearse addition and subtraction by hiding pasta shells. Hide some under a dish and ask your child how many are left and how many are hidden.

(continued)

Connections (continued)

Robin's kids make their own game boards from cardboard. The themes vary, but there are always some squares with instructions like *Move forward 5 squares* or *Go back to start*. Again, if you bring a die in your pocket to a restaurant, you can whip up a quick "board" game on a napkin and play until the food appears.

The ABC Book

Hidden behind the ABC book is one of the most delightful and creative games in *The Playroom*. It's sort of a cross between color forms and alphabet pictures. Click on the book, and you're taken to a new screen displaying a fantasyland of castles, wizards, and dragons. A second game has a neighborhood theme. An alphabet appears at the top of the screen. If your child clicks on a letter an image appears. There is an image for each letter of the alphabet. A voice pronounces the letter and names the image. You can drag the picture anywhere you like on screen and then click again to place the image.

Click on the letter *A* and an *archer* appears. Click on the archer and you can drag it into the picture and place it in the scene. Click on *B* and a *bat* appears. (Put it in the castle belfry). Click on *C* and you have a *crystal ball* to give to the wizard, who appears when you click W.

Click in the upper right corner of the screen to change scenes. (The lower-right corner is always the route back to the playroom. Lower-left corner changes the scene) Now you're in a suburban neighborhood. Clicking on the letter *A* here produces an *ambulance* that you can place in the road. *B* brings up a *bike* that you can place on a sidewalk. Click on as many letters as you like to place more objects in the scene. The Mac has a third scene of a farmyard with barn and pond. There are some very unusual animals for the scene like an umbrella bird and an x-ray fish. With any of the scenes, you can switch the alphabet between uppercase and lowercase—important for beginning readers. If you don't want to use an image you can put it in the trash can. And you can click on the garbage truck to clean up and start over.

Connections

Playroom's special places afford wondrous opportunities to let the imagination run wild. Help your child devise stories to go with the scenes. You might begin by asking her to identify the objects in each scene and talk about why certain objects belong in a neighborhood, while others belong in a fantasy land. Ask her, for example, "Where does the ice cream truck belong? Where does the princess belong?"

Explain unfamiliar objects to your child; tell her what they do and how they are used in each world. When you play the game, encourage your child to place objects in different places and spin a new story to reflect the new scene ("And what is the wizard doing today?").

Some children live in settings that are not well represented in these scenes. Have them draw a picture of a land that represents common objects they find in their daily lives—one for each letter of the alphabet. Now have them create a fantasyland using completely unique items for each letter of the alphabet.

Another nice touch is to create a story about the scene you devise. You can take dictation and write down the story your child makes up. (If you have a dot-matrix printer hooked up to the computer, you can get a printout of the scene by holding down the Shift key while pressing the Print Screen key on your keyboard.) On the Mac, choose print from the File menu to print to any printer. Mount the picture and story on posterboard to build a library of your child's stories.

One of Robin's kids' favorite games is what we call the Take Away game. Place five items such as the king, ogre, unicorn, yeti, and magic wand in the fantasy scene. Have your child study the scene. Now take away one item by dragging it to the garbage truck with your mouse. Can they tell you which one is missing? Can they do the same thing in the hope of tricking you?

You can also play with the ABC game for "loot," such as pennies, toothpicks, or coupons. Pick any scene to work with. Say a letter, such as *C*. If the child, for example, selects the crystal ball for the fantasy scene and can place that item in the picture, she gets the prize. At the end of the game, the player with the most "booty" is the winner.

(continued)

Connections (continued)

You can also have a Playroom Day at your house. In addition to play-ing the computer game and doing the other activities suggested in this chapter, you can invite children to bring their favorite toy from their personal playrooms over to your house. Line the toys up and ask each child to make up a story that uses all the toys. A child can even act out their story or tell where her favorite toy came from and how long she's had it.

Let the children sing songs about toys and make up playroom songs based on common traditional songs. Try a song like,

"There was a Pepper Mouse and he had a playroom, Ei-I-Ei-I- O ...."

"And in his playroom he had a ...."

and so on.

Give each child a square of paper to draw a picture of her favorite toy and then glue all the pictures together to create a quilt.

You may even want to talk about toys from other lands and explain how a playroom in another country or from another culture might look very different.

And if your children really enjoy *The Playroom*, but you find they've outgrown it, don't be dismayed, there's more fun ahead. *The Playroom* was so popular that Broderbund decided to create a sequel for slightly older children. It's called *The Treehouse*, and this time special things happen as you explore the abode of some playful pos-sums. (We'll tell you more about it in Section III.)

6

PLAN II: WHERE IN THE WORLD IS CARMEN SANDIEGO?—TAKING CARMEN BEYOND THE DISPLAY SCREEN

The software you'll need: *Where in the World Is Carmen Sandiego?*

What it costs: $49.95

Why it's special: An entertaining blend of travel and mystery introduces kids to the wonders of geography and history, as it keeps their fingers walking through reference books.

Ages it appeals to: 8 to 80

Activities: Carmen Sandiego costume party; villains' international snack food buffet; trivial pursuit games; reference races; build a geographical database; create flashcards.

Introducing *Where in the World Is Carmen Sandiego?*

Now there's a question that can bring hours of pleasure at the computer keyboard. "Where is Carmen Sandiego?" is the question at the heart of one of the most enduring educational series of computer games available for children. Carmen is a nefarious protagonist. She is the attractive, fashionable leader of a band of electronic henchmen known as the Villains' International League of Evil, VILE for short. Carmen and her VILE companions appear in five different PC games produced by Broderbund Software. In each game, a VILE villain absconds with a cultural treasure and takes off to a hideout somewhere on an unknown place on the globe or in time. It is your child's mission, should he choose to accept it—and the kids always do—to track down the henchman and return the treasure to its rightful owner.

Though she only rarely appears in these games (leaving the villainy to the henchmen), Carmen Sandiego has become a legend in her own time. She may be the closest thing to a cult figure ever to come to the personal computer. Try as they might, computer game developers have a tough time instilling any sort of personality into their digitized creations. But they succeeded so well with this one that Carmen has reappeared in more computer game sequels than Sylvester Stallone has in Rocky movies. The six games in the software series have sold more than 2 million copies. And no wonder! They pack enough fun into geography and history that teachers across the country have used Carmen, her henchmen, and their globe-trotting shenanigans as a rubric for lesson plans. And Carmen endures both on and off the computer screen. Carmen is also the heroine of a series of children's books. She even earned a time slot on public television last year with her own TV game show.

All this makes Carmen a key link in that chain that is so important to a child's education—the home/school connection. Learning that takes place in school and is reinforced in the home, that a child can experience in a classroom and encounter again in a recreational setting, is learning that sticks. Children remember things they can assimilate. This knowledge helps them solve problems and succeed again and again. By welcoming Carmen into your home and installing her games on your PC, you'll take your child on adventures that relate to what he learns in geography and history class. Vacation travel, reading, and educational television programs only help enhance the experience. At home, Carmen takes the kids on a keyboard travel adventure—an adventure your whole family can share without ever leaving the house. In this chapter, we'll show you how to travel well and wisely with Carmen Sandiego.

The premise in every Carmen game is the same. And, to a large extent, so is what you see on screen. If your child has played one game, the others will seem as familiar as an amusement park the second time you visit. The games are available for both Macintosh and IBM PC-compatibles. The newer games make greater use of sound and screen graphics than some of the earlier ones, which rely more heavily on written text that appears on screen. But Broderbund has begun to revamp all the games to feature more sound and panoramic screen shots. PC owners will enjoy the games more if their system is equipped with a sound card and sophisticated video system to let them hear and see these extra features. But, with the exception of one deluxe edition, all will run on systems as simple as an 8088 equipped with a monochrome or CGA monitor. You just have to settle for tinny sound from the PC system and less-than-lovely screen graphics. The Carmen games are compatible with all Macs from the Plus up.

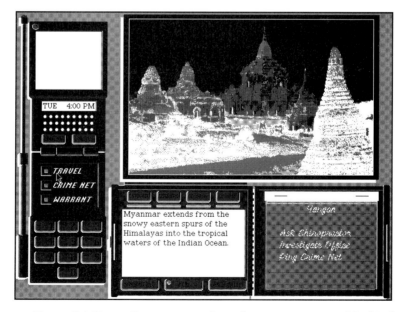

Figure 6.1 Every Carmen game introduces some geographical information as you query suspects in a crime.

A simple, ingenious plot sets the stage for every game. A member of Carmen's band steals a treasure—such as the keys to the Tower of London or Pizarro's sword—and flees the scene of the crime. Your child, as a member of the Acme Detective Agency, follows in hot pursuit, collecting clues about what the villain looked like and where he headed. But to get to the next spot and head the henchman off at the pass, so to speak, players must turn to a reference book—an almanac, atlas, or travel book—to make sense of the clues they've been given and to figure out where the bandit will go next.

The magic of Carmen is that she offers a playful introduction to the world of reference books and information-gathering. And books like those that come with the Carmen games are great introductions to the reference shelf. Children absorb geography and history, as they use almanacs to identify the villain's trail. And in doing so, they gain an appreciation of the wealth of information that can be found in an almanac. We've seen many a child take a break from the game to browse through the books on his own.

Tip

If your child is playing in a group, have one person man the almanac and one the keyboard. This encourages teamwork. The child at the keyboard can read the clues aloud, while the other looks them up. Together, they can brainstorm about where to look within the Almanac. For example, a witness might offer a clue such as; *She went to a place where the currency was rubles.* Since the mystery must be solved within a set time period, it's important for the almanac-reader to be able to "cut to the punch" and get right to the place in the almanac that lists a country's currency.

Depending upon the game you select, the theme may be historical or geographical, global in scope or limited to the United States or Europe. Below are brief descriptions of each of the six Carmen games. In the exercises that follow, we'll focus on the first game in the series, *Where in the World Is Carmen Sandiego?* But the tips and activities we offer here can easily be adapted to any of the games. So don't sweat it if your child prefers the historical games to the geographical ones. Whatever his preference, you'll find something here that fits the bill.

Where in the World Is Carmen Sandiego?

This is the original Carmen game. In it, Carmen's henchmen turn up in one of 30 cities around the world. The world almanac packaged with the disks helps kids decipher clues offered by the game's witnesses. The facts to be learned from this game tend to be somewhat random, making it a bit more like Trivial Pursuits than a true geography lesson. But after playing a few rounds, the kids will be spewing facts over the dinner table. They'll tell you where Port Moresby is and what the currency is in New Guinea.

Where in the World Is Carmen Sandiego? Deluxe Edition

This game plays much the same as the standard edition we discussed above, but the geographical information is a little more relevant to what kids need to know. And the game goes further than the standard edition, with colorful illustrations and detailed photographs from museum archives and the pages of *The National Geographic*. The world map in this game features 45 international cities, instead of the 30 you get in the standard edition. There are also more villains and more gadgets for sleuthing, as well as better sound effects and music. There is, for instance, a Videophone that appears in the corner of the screen to let players see who's calling with special alerts and updates from Acme headquarters. It displays the caller's picture as it gives the update. There's also a Dataminder, which contains facts that spare the kids from always having to look things up in the almanac. But, as parents, we still encourage the almanac practice and like to challenge the kids to look things up the old-fashioned way, even if the Dataminder is a bit more convenient.

The deluxe edition, with its beautiful screen graphics, is a remarkable improvement over the standard edition. But PC owners will need a VGA screen display to see what makes this deluxe edition really deluxe. There is no Mac deluxe version, yet.

Where in Europe Is Carmen Sandiego?

Unlike the deluxe edition, this game doesn't require special video for PCs. *Where in Europe?* comes with *The Rand-McNally Concise History of Europe.* The crimes and travels in this game take place in 33 nations in Europe.

Where in the USA Is Carmen Sandiego?

This one's a chase through the United States. And to solve the mystery, the game comes packaged with *Fodor's USA Travel Guide.* The familiar landmarks you see in this game make it fun. If your family has ever visited New York City, your kids will probably recognize the picture of the Empire State Building. And, if you've vacationed in different locations or stayed with friends and family in various cities and states, your kids will have a good time recognizing the sights from "the city where Uncle Rob lives" or "that place Aunt Eva took us to."

Where in Time Is Carmen Sandiego?

In this game, Carmen and her crew attempt to elude the kids by moving back and forth through time from 400 A.D. to the 1950s. Time travel to 48 different locations is made possible by a device called the ChronoSkimmer, which is a lot like a time machine.

The action in this game is more animated than in the other Carmen games. In earlier versions of the games, kids saw no more than a line move across a map to chart their movement from one locale to another. But in this one, the screen shakes when the Chrono-Skimmer takes off. Kids think it's cool because effects like these seem to put them right in the game, instead of making them watch from the sidelines like spectators. The ChronoSkimmer isn't the only animated movement that engages the kids. Henchmen appear at intervals to enact bizarre routines in which they throw knives or Molotov cocktails. All this is entertaining; it's also helpful when playing the game because when the animated henchmen appear, the kids know they're on the right track.

The New American Encyclopedia, packaged with the game, helps players research historical events—from the invention of fireworks to the invention of the telescope—and figure out which way to head in time. The kids will need this kind of help. *Where in Time?* is a bit tougher than the other games, because kids must keep track of two things, historical time frames and geographic locations. The game features a timeline to help with the chore, and Broderbund restricts slots on the timeline to certain possibilities. The history the kids see isn't one long inexorable march of random events but a discrete collection of events that they can more easily make sense of. On one screen, for example, they can only choose to go to Spain in the 1500s or Russia in the 1800s. This selective history keeps the game manageable, and, if the kids want to learn more about a particular period, they can always look it up in *The New American Encyclopedia.*

Where in America's Past Is Carmen Sandiego?

This is Robin's personal favorite. The focus is American history from the 1600s to 1975. Again, this one is tricky. To discover the VILE hideout, players need to make sure they're in the right geographic location within the US, and they have to be in the correct place on a timeline. Unlike *Where in Time?*, which gives players the dates that correspond to the locations, *Where in America's Past?* throws players to their own devices. Children need to determine where to travel in the United States. And they need to figure out when—that is, in what time period—to travel there. Because children must attend to both time and place, the game requires a sophisticated leap of learning. To help out the players, *Where in America's Past?* includes a fact-filled book called *What Happened When?*, an encyclopedia of American history and culture that parents might find fun to read, even when they're not helping the kids.

Quick Tour

If your child has been on this planet for any length of time, you probably won't have to do much coaxing to get him to play *Where in the World Is Carmen Sandiego?* But you can still generate interest in the game before you even open the shrink-wrap. The packaging is very attractive, and the detective manuals inside the box help draw children into Carmen's world. Review the materials and read them with your child.

Since there are so many Carmen games to choose from, we recommend beginning at the beginning. Start your child out on *Where in the World Is Carmen Sandiego?* It's a less abstract game than the others, since it brings the kids face-to-face with the villainess herself. Believe it or not, it's the only game in the series in which Carmen actually commits the crimes and runs for the bushes. The kids actually have the opportunity to capture Carmen. She rarely shows up in the other games; in those, she's gone into management and lets her henchmen do the dirty work.

From a more practical point of view, *Where in the World?* is a good game to start with because it will run on any PC as well as on Macintosh and Apple computers. That's probably the reason it still outsells the other versions, despite its lack of knock-your-socks-off sound and graphics. You and your child will enjoy this game even if you don't have a sound card and VGA monitor. The classic Carmen sets a marvelous stage for what's to come, although you may want to spring for the deluxe version if you have the requisite hardware.

Tip

Make sure the kids get a laugh. The Carmen games have their own subtle humor that you can point out to your children as they play. Some of the best examples of this are the henchman's names: Earl E. Bird, Ernest Endeavor, Gene Yuss, Minnie Series, Molly Coddle, etc. Be sure your kids begin to get the joke by pointing out the names and speaking them aloud.

Connection

Carmen can be a jumping-off point for artistic endeavors. Ask the kids to think up some funny henchman names of their own and then imagine what the person must look like and what kind of hobbies they have. Then have them make "Wanted for Arrest" posters for their characters. Ask the kids to draw each villain and list their characteristics on the poster. You can send the results to Broderbund (you'll find the address in Appendix B at the back of this book) and maybe they'll include them in an upcoming game.

The game begins when the players, who are employed by the Acme Crime Agency, enter their names as rookies in the crime computer and receive their assignments. Usually they're sent scurrying off to find the thief and the stolen treasure. The thefts are always imaginative: *Sybil's Secret stolen from Athens* in the *Where in the World Is Carmen Sandiego?* game or *Monsieur Cadillac's fur coat taken from Michigan in 1701* in *Where in America's Past Is Carmen Sandiego?*. The elements of play fit together beautifully and grow increasingly complex as your child solves enough mysteries to be promoted from gumshoe detective to supersleuth.

Tip

It's not enough to gather the clues. Clues are only good if they are entered into the Crime Computer. Don't forget: in order to obtain a warrant you must enter the clues and process them so that the computer can figure out who you're hunting for and issue a correct warrant.

Players learn about the missing treasures by interrogating witnesses and suspects. Clicking on a graphic of a character makes him speak. Witnesses and suspects say the darndest things. They may remark on what the suspect looked like, what their hobbies or habits were, or what type of transportation they used. All of the games, including *Where in the World?*, display the witnesses' remarks as text on screen. Future CD-ROM versions will have digitized speech.

Clues are logged into a Crime Computer, which is displayed on the screen and which the kids can call up at any time to review the evidence they've gathered. When enough clues are logged, a warrant for arrest is issued.

Once your child collects clues at one location to figure out a henchman's whereabouts, it's time for action. Kids should hit the reference book to figure out where to go next. This could send you scurrying back to the almanac to figure out how to get to a place where you can take a riverboat ride from Dubuque to Baton Rouge or to a place where you can borrow oodles of kroner. Once your child figures out the significance of the clue, it's back to the computer keyboard to select the location where he believes the thief is headed.

Tip

Work efficiently. After all, you didn't expect that you'd have forever to solve a case, did you? There's only a limited amount to time to each play (the limit depends on how high in the ACME Detective pecking order you've risen). To make matters tougher still, it's not enough to gather the clues. Clues are only good if they are processed and filed with headquarters. You save time by processing multiple clues in one fell swoop. On the other hand, you'll want to obtain a warrant as soon as possible, since without one you could bump right into Carmen or her henchfolks and be absolutely powerless to do anything.

Tip

Have your child put bookmarks in the world almanac, so he can quickly turn to the most commonly used pages: The world flags, currencies, and capital cities. Children should learn how to use the almanac, so don't insert the bookmarks for them. But they sometimes also grow impatient with having to flip back to the same pages again and again. Having them use bookmarks helps hold their interest in the game and shows them how bookmarks are used.

A timekeeping device in a corner of the screen clicks away the hours, as the kids travel to the suspect's location in an airplane. At each locale, the kids gather more clues about the suspect's hair color, hobbies, and other characteristics. They can record these in an Evidence File. When the file fills with clues (usually about three clues will do it), they can ask the game's Crime Computer to decipher the clues and determine which henchmen stole the loot. Once they do, the computer issues an arrest warrant. Without a warrant, kids can track the villains down, but they can't capture them. And, when they do make an arrest, the warrant must be for the right suspect, or they'll lose the game. This keeps the kids from just guessing by entering random clues.

Tip

Always question witnesses whenever and wherever they are available. The witnesses not only offer clues to the henchman's whereabouts, they also provide tips about the suspect's appearance and habits and give players what they need to piece together a description and secure a warrant. We've seen some enterprising kids sell little "cheat sheets" on the villains and villainesses in order to aid and abet their fellow detectives. We've even seen Carmen game book guides that publish profiles of each villain. We tend to stay away from these. To us they are sort of like Carmen *Cliff Notes*—an unnecessary item that can take some of the pleasure out of doing it yourself.

Time figures heavily into the play of the game, so kids have to keep an eye on the clock shown on screen. They have only so long to solve the crime, and each time they travel to a new destination or log a bunch of clues with headquarters, they lose valuable hours. On the computer game's clock, they're given days and hours, but in reality it's ten to twenty minutes, depending on how fast young players can look up the clues. Novices get more time than master detectives. Time does not progress while you search through the almanac. Only when you engage the computer directly. The more time children spend investigating a crime, the more clues they gather, and the more sure they are that they're on the right track. But travel and investigation consumes time on the game's clock, so children have to strike a balance between lingering at a location to gather clues and getting quickly to the henchman's hideout.

> **Tip**
> Don't waste your time when there's nothing happening.
> Start backtracking when you come up dry on clues. If you
> reach a place where there are no clues, you'll know it im-
> mediately. The first witness you question will say, "I
> haven't seen a thing" or, "I haven't got a clue." That's the
> signal to high-tail out of there and retrace your steps to the
> place you flew in from. If you don't, you'll just go on a
> wild goose chase. Kids will also quickly learn to avoid
> making a random guess about where to go next. There's
> nothing that chews up time faster than wrong guesses.

Step-by-Step Tour

When the game begins, your child is presented with a brief on-screen
description of the crime that took place. He learns a bit about the
treasure that the thief snatched and the place it was snatched from.
For instance, he may be told to report to Bangkok, where the thief
has stolen the queen's Siamese cat. This assignment heightens your
child's awareness of countries and cultures, even as it sets the stage for
the game. After this short briefing, your child is whisked to the scene
of the crime, where he learns even more about the locale: *Bangkok,
capital of Thailand, is a bustling city, laced with canals and dotted with
temples called Wats.* A picture that characterizes the scenery or landmarks of the location appears on screen. In this case, the picture is of
a brightly lit temple at the edge of a canal. Once at the location, your
child can explore one of three sites in the area and interview the witnesses he finds there. Usually the locations are places like museums,
airports, palaces, or sports clubs—some real, some fictitious. With
luck, the witnesses will tell him something that reveals essential information about the thief. This might include: physical characteristics (eye color, hair color), mode of travel, and hobbies.

The picture of the Crime Computer at the bottom of the screen
shows your child where to record his findings. After he's collected
enough evidence (three clues are sufficient), he can click on the
Send/Receive or Compute button (depending on which version you
are playing) to get the computer to issue the arrest warrant.

Figure 6.2 Witnesses tell what they know about a suspect.

Figure 6.3 The Crime Computer collects your findings.

Connection

Each scene in the game opens with a scenic description of the region of the world where your child detective is. For example, there are passages like these: *The Peoples Republic of China, with more than one billion people, is the most populous country on Earth,* or *Oslo is the capital of Norway, a country known for its beautiful fjords and rugged mountains.*

Kids quickly learn that reading the narrative descriptions about the countries doesn't reveal any extra clues. They'll often skip them. Encourage your child to read these paragraphs. Try sauntering past the computer a few times during the play session and popping the kids a question about the country they are in. Suddenly, their curiosity will be piqued. Children are proud to show off their knowledge when an appreciative adult is standing by. Don't be shy about showing them that you too are curious about what they're learning.

We sometimes use information from these passages to play Carmen trivia. You can easily make up a flash card to accompany each text passage. You could, for instance, write, Which country has fjords? on one side of the card and Norway on the other. Then use the flash cards for an impromptu game of geographical trivia.

Remember, without an arrest warrant, your child will be helpless to apprehend the criminal. The temporal element adds another dimension to the play. Kids must work quickly. Beginners have only "six days" (about 40 minutes or so on a computer) to solve a case. Each time a player travels to a new location he uses up valuable time. So it's important that your child conducts his worldwide hunt efficiently.

Tip

To save time, never enter one clue at a time into the Crime Computer's Evidence Folder. Each time you enter a clue, the clock ticks away valuable hours, so putting them in one by one just chews up case-solving time.

(continued)

Tip (continued)

It's better to collect the clues and wait to enter them as evidence when you have at least two and preferably three. Keep a piece of paper handy and jot down the clues. Then make one, efficient trip to the Crime Computer to record your evidence.

Remember to read a clue very carefully. In some games, a piece of evidence, such as the sex of the villain, is given away in a sentence such as, *She had a tattoo.* Occasionally, the suspect's sex is divulged when you receive your assignment.

Activities to Stretch the Fun

One of the best ways to extend Carmen's charm is to stretch the metaphor into the real world of everyday play. You can do this by organizing activities around the theme of the game. All you need is a little imagination, a supply cabinet of toys and household items you can use to embellish the activities, and a push in the right direction. That push is what we give you below, with activities for you and your child. Once you've explored these playful paths, we're sure you will find others all your own.

Carmen Cops and Robbers

Let the kids do a little role-playing by taking on the identities of characters in the game. You can help with the fun. Buy a detective kit, one that includes a magnifying glass, perhaps, and a fingerprinting kit. Encourage the kids to act out the little dramas they see in the Carmen games.

You can even turn this into Carmen Sandiego's answer to the classic children's game, Hide and Go Seek. Let one child be the detective; others can take the roles of witnesses and henchmen. Kids who elect to be the henchmen can choose identities from the Carmen Sandiego game manual. The Carmen games make role-playing easy by including little profiles of each henchman in the documentation; kids can even dress up like the henchman.

The kids who take the roles of detectives pretend they're on Carmen's trail. They can question one another using the techniques they learn in the game and use a fingerprinting kit, magnifying glass, and other playthings to assist in the chase.

Where In the World Is My Family?

Question your children about your family ancestry. Do they know how your family ended up living where you live? Have them use the almanac to read up on the geography and culture of their origins. You can create a natural connection between Carmen's emphasis on geographical locations and your own family tree. Is the country that your family comes from one listed in the Carmen games?

As the questions and answers continue, you can use pencil and paper to actually sketch out your family tree, including names, birth dates, and places, along with a sentence or two on what happened in each ancestor's life. (If you don't know much about the ancestor's life, perhaps you can research the important events that occurred at the time and in the place where the person lived.)

There's also a software program to do the job for you, if you'd rather let the computer do the work. Banner Blue's *Family Tree Maker* not only helps you create a family tree by prompting you to input the names of your relatives and their relationship to you, but it offers a multitude of ways to present the information. For example, you can print a family tree based on one family member's point of view. *Family Tree Maker* lets you delve quite deeply into anecdotal information, medical information, and other in-depth family information. The Raskin family tree was created using this program. They sent postcards to relatives asking them to list their relations. Then, at one family gathering, they printed a personalized chart for each member of the family based on their point of view. It was a wonderful event.

Inspired Carmen devotees might even enjoy using this software to create a genealogy for each of the Carmen villains. Ask the kids to make up a life story and family history for their favorite villainess. Where is Carmen from? Who is she related to? and so on. When they're finished, save the notes. In Chapter 8, we'll show you how to turn this into an illustrated story using yet another piece of software, the Learning Company's *Children's Writing and Publishing Center*.

The International Carmen Sandiego Party

Broderbund actually offers a "Carmen Sandiego Day" kit that includes activities, certificates, and goodies like Carmen stickers. It costs only $10. Although it's more often sold to schools, which use the game in geography classes, the company makes the kit available to parents who request it. Any parent who wants to host a Carmen party at home should call Broderbund's customer service number (800) 521-6263. But even without a kit, you can exercise a little home-grown ingenuity and throw your own Carmen Sandiego party. Just use your imagination and the resources that come with the game.

Assign identities to the partygoers when you mail the invitations. Include photos and descriptions of their VILE personalities in each of the invitations. Each henchman in Carmen gang has a distinct personality that's described in the manual.

Turn it into a costume party. Ask the children to come dressed as their assigned henchmen. As soon as the children arrive, have them take turns modeling their costumes and see if they can guess each other's henchman identity. If they can't, ask the henchman to act out the particular traits of the character. For instance, each of the henchmen has a favorite hobby (spelunking, skydiving, climbing). You can have a child act out his henchman's hobby and see if the others can guess which one it is. The other kids should be free to ask questions about the character.

Give the party an international flavor. Prepare food from some of the countries visited in the game. This will be fun for the cooks out there; you can even involve your own children in the preparation and teach them a bit about how cultures prepare their food, what spices they use, and so on. If you're not inclined to spend much time in the kitchen, collect a sampling of international foods from the local grocery, deli, or take-out counter: crusty Italian bread, crispy Chinese noodles with sweet and sour duck sauce, some small French pastries, Swedish meatballs, and the like.

Let the Music Play

Each of Carmen's henchmen has a favorite type of music (classical, rock, country, opera). As you play *Where in the World Is Carmen Sandiego?* and discover which type of music your henchmen like, play a sample tune. When you play the record or compact disc, take the opportunity to chat with your child about what gives that particular type of music its special sound. Note the folksy themes about family and love in country ballads, or how no one sings in classical orchestral music, or the the different voices you hear in opera. Ask your child if he agrees with the henchman's taste in music. Why or why not? (You probably already know the answers to these questions, but it never hurts to ask; your child may surprise you with an interest you never knew he had, one that you can encourage later.) And chances are, rock 'n' roll will garner more fans than string quartets. But at least your child will be introduced to different types of music that he might not ordinarily listen to.

Pad the Play

Here's a little trick Robin uses at home. When the kids are just about to put Carmen away, she grabs the almanac, looks up a fact, and puts it before the kids in the form of a question: "Who was the 22nd President of the US?" Then she returns the almanac and lets the kids look up the answer. It's a fun way to end a game session and it demonstrates to the kids that you're as interested in the game as they are. What's more, it gives them a chance to show off their knowledge and skill at using the almanac.

You can turn this little game into a competition by timing how fast it takes different children to look up different answers. Give them each a minute or a minute and a half. Don't allow too much time; children have short attention spans. This is a good game to play at bedtime, particularly if the kids are accustomed to getting a nightly snack. Reward the winner with an extra snack or treat, but be sure to give everyone in the group with a little something for the effort.

And don't ever forget that the world almanac included in *Where in the World Is Carmen Sandiego?*, as well as the reference materials in the other Carmen games, can be used as homework helpers. We can't tell you how many times we've turned to the almanac to provide that tidbit of information we're missing when completing a school report.

Trivially Pursuing Carmen

Use the reference materials that come with the Carmen Sandiego games to develop your own Trivial Pursuit game. If you have more than one Carmen game, you can even let the kids select the types of questions they should answer. Depending on which games you have in your Carmen library, this might be world geography, American history, places in the United States, or world history.

Let the kids divide into two teams. Team One keeps the almanac long enough to look up the answers to five facts, then writes down questions concerning each. Then they give the almanac to Team Two and time how long it takes them to look up the answers. Then it's Team Two's turn to use the almanac to come up with five questions for Team One and time how long it takes Team One to look them up.

This is a fun game and it's one you can use at a Carmen Sandiego party. Grab an assortment of prizes (perhaps cookies or small toys) to pass out to the winning team.

Digging for Definitions

An almanac isn't a dictionary, but it does include definitions children should know. Kids should understand the difference between a country and a continent, a sea and an ocean.

Challenge them to look up geographical terms such as *bay, channel, fjord, gulf, peninsula, strait, reef, atoll*, and *island*. Prompt them to accurately describe the term and distinguish it from similar ones. A reef, for instance, is a submerged bed of coral, but an atoll is a mass of coral that has collected into a small land mass. Atolls can grow into islands as the mass gets larger.

Use the maps supplied in the *Where in the World Is Carmen Sandiego?* manual to have the children point out examples of islands, peninsulas, bays, and oceans.

Record the World

Create a database of country information using Windows *Cardfile* or a more powerful (but still simple) database program such as *PC File.* (We'll tell you how in Chapter 9.) A database is a kind of electronic filing cabinet. Learning to use one teaches children skills in organization and logical thinking, because they must group pieces of information together in related ways. Using *Cardfile* as a means to do it will introduce your child to the rich, graphical environment of Windows even though it is really just intended for names, addresses, and phone numbers.

You could use any of a number of other database programs but *PC File* allows you to link information about countries in such a way that it's easy to look up. Building a database is an exercise in how to use the computer to record information in a logical fashion so that it can be easily retrieved.

To get the kids started, have them create a database in which they can enter information. The form should include blanks for *Country Name*, *Currency*, *Title of Head of State*, and *Capital*. Ask them to add their own ideas for any other subjects to be included in a country database (maybe the name of a national anthem or the major industry). After they've built the database form, have them use the almanac to look up the information to enter in the blanks. This gives the kids experience in using the almanac and in recording what they find.

After they have entered all the information for the database, show them how they can search on any field name to find lists of all the capital cities or names of countries. (You can't do this with *Cardfile*, but you can with *PC File*.)

Games and More Games

Milk the almanac for all it's worth to develop all sorts of game themes. An almanac is an almost inexhaustible source of information and entertainment. Pick a topic, any topic, and develop a game around it from the facts you find in the reference book. There are games to be created whenever you find a list of people, places, or things in the almanac, particularly when that list is accompanied by a series of drawings that capture your child's attention.

Create a Flag

Have your kids find the page in the almanac that shows the flags of the world and have them draw the flags on stiff pieces of construction paper. This can be a fun activity in itself, but you can extend it even farther by using the flag pictures as flash cards. On the back of each picture of a flag, ask the kids to write down the name of that flag's country. Then collect the flash cards, shuffle them, and hold them up one at a time so that the kids can guess which flag goes with which country.

This is even more effective if you use a paint program to draw the flags, print them on a dot-matrix printer, and then pass out crayons for the kids to color them in. (See Chapters 7 and 16 for more on paint programs.)

The National Anthem Game

Go to a library with a good record collection and see how many of the national anthems of various countries you can find. Discuss how the music differs from country to country. See if you can find translations of the words to these anthems. Point out the emphasis on fight songs. For example, our own anthem, "The Star Spangled Banner," was written as a glorification of a battle in the war of 1812. The French "Marseillaise" has recently come under attack by the French people for being a warlike song. And in South Africa, the new non-apartheid emphasis is making "Oh, Africa," a more well-known anthem than the old Afrikaaner anthem.

Changing Places, Changing Faces

The Carmen games are current but not current enough to keep up with the amazing speed of global change. Look at the portrayal of Russia and Germany in the Carmen games and use them as a jumping-off point to discuss recent global developments. If you already own Carmen games and possess an older almanac, you may find it beneficial to buy a new world almanac, simply to compare how the face of the map changes from year to year.

Stamps and Coins

Certainly, the geography of the Carmen games is a great stepping stone into stamp and coin collecting. Children have always been fascinated by the look of colorful stamps and the faces and emblems on international currencies. Consider taking your child along to a bank that trades in international currencies. Exchange a few American dollars for currency from your child's favorite country from the Carmen Sandiego mysteries. Ask friends to begin collecting stamps. If you have any friends traveling out of the country, see if they will send postcards to your child from wherever they're traveling. When the postcards arrive, look at the pictures on the stamp and see whether you can connect them with the information given about the country in the almanac.

Carmen On Trial

Once Carmen is arrested, you might want to ask the kids to stage a mock trial. Assign each child a role: judge, witnesses, felon, jury, and attorneys. Create a list of questions the lawyers might ask, based on the evidence. "Did you know the Sandiego gang member, Minnie Series? Where were you on the night of April 6th? Do you drive a sports car?" After hearing all the evidence, ask members of the jury "What's your verdict?" Can Carmen and her henchmen beat the rap?

Spy-Wear

Carmen is an attractive villainess, of that there's no doubt. The fashion-conscious child might like to create a paper doll of Carmen and give her a villainess's wardrobe. (Her trenchcoat is certainly getting a bit worn.) Ask the kids to trace Carmen off the packaging and try their hands at creating Spy-wear by drawing new clothing styles around her. They might even use their drawings to make Carmen dress-up puppets. Paper dolls are more durable when traced onto cardboard and cut out. Fashions can be designed on paper and fastened to the doll with traditional fold-down tabs drawn at the edges of the clothing or by using paper fasteners.

Once they've taken care of the wardrobe, it's time to start thinking about the accoutrements of the spy profession. If some kids aren't particularly interested in designing new clothes, they'll probably want to invent new gadgets. See if they can draw a new spy device more imaginative than Acme's ChronoSkimmer or Radio Controller.

Places of Interest

Many locales featured in the Carmen games make exciting future studies for group play, the Leaning Tower of Pisa or the Great Sphinx, for example. Give each child a place to look up and ask them report back to the group on what they've uncovered. Create a Place of Interest Inventory Sheet (or database if you're using database software). For each place, note its location, date of creation, and the reason for its historical influence. You can print this information, draw a picture of the location, and have a nifty travel guide when you're done. If your family travels often, you might even start checking off the places you've seen.

Ties to TV

You can capitalize on Carmen's popularity by encouraging your child to look for Carmen in all the places she appears. The public broadcasting stations, WGBH of Boston and WQED of Pittsburgh, began airing a series of Carmen Sandiego game shows to test kids' knowledge of world geography in a kind of trivia quiz. The shows were picked up by public broadcasting stations in many other cities. And, in many areas, they're still being repeated. If the shows are available in your area, encourage your child to watch. They can be fine reinforcements for the game.

The show mixes a trivia game, where kids are pitted against each other, with a fast-moving plot that includes zany antics, an a capella rock group, and lots of newsreel-type footage. It's fast-paced, fun-filled, and totally captivating—it beats Jeopardy by miles. As the kids play, the clues are unfolded in little vignettes, cleverly acted by a talented cast of actors.

Rumor has it that Carmen may in fact become a star of the big screen. Can you imagine a feature film about a computer character?

Carmen Online

Each week, the Prodigy online service sponsors a Carmen Sandiego episode (see more on the Prodigy service in Chapters 10 and 11).

Prodigy's version of Carmen Sandiego is a sort of online Carmen miniseries that changes from time to time, taking the villainess and your child to new and different locations. If you subscribe to Prodigy, you should encourage your child to try out this version. The game plays a bit differently than the one designed for PCs, in that it requires a bit more reading and a bit less action.

Carmen, Carmen Everywhere

Western Publishing has produced a series of novels about Carmen Sandiego, which you can use as a way of tying the game theme to reading exercises. With the game to pique his interest, your child may not even think of reading as an exercise. His interest in the game will give him reason to read the books. And from there you can introduce him to other adventure stories.

The books, by the way, are a sort of hypertext. The plot can go in a variety of directions, depending on how you choose to move through the text.

From time to time, teachers use the Carmen Sandiego party kits that Broderbund makes available to sponsor Carmen Sandiego Days. If your child is lucky enough to be enrolled in a school that sponsors one of these, he'll enjoy a full day of role-playing villains and detectives and a fun foray into geographical immersion.

And, here's a real flip-flop: there's a Nintendo game based on *Where in Time Is Carmen Sandiego?*, which you can use to introduce your child to the PC, instead of worrying that Nintendo will lure him away from the computer. If you've been looking for a way to wean the kids away from Nintendo and over to the computer, this may be your chance. Use your child's interest in the TV game to engage him in the more complex game available on the computer.

CHAPTER

7

PLAN III: THE ULTIMATE ELECTRONIC CANVAS— KID PIX

•

The software you'll need: *Kid Pix*

What it costs: $59.95

Why it's special: An electronic paint program just for kids, *Kid Pix* is imaginative, whimsical, and you can really paint with it.

Ages it appeals to: 3 and up

Activities: Create cards and party invitations, school worksheets, board games, connect-the-dot drawings, picture dictionaries, and maze games.

Introducing *Kid Pix*

Kid Pix was designed by programmer Craig Hickman for his three-year-old son, and it reflects the energy, curiosity, and unfettered imagination of a very young child. The many opportunities for exploration mean that your kids will never be bored with *Kid Pix.*

Kid Pix is as much for parents as for their children. It's like finger paints without the mess. *Kid Pix* has a mesmerizing power over anyone who uses it. It's irresistible, and because children can't stop playing with it—exploring all the tools and options—they can learn basic computer skills like mousing without realizing that they've been taught something. All of this makes *Kid Pix* a great first program.

Technically, electronic paint programs like *Kid Pix* work at the dot-level, changing the individual pixels that make up your screen. Everything you paint is a collection of dots. It's not important that you know this, but it makes painting programs inherently easier to use than drawing programs, which keep track of objects as vectors and arcs.

While *Kid Pix* shares this technology with every paint program, it is like no other. Paint programs simulate real painting and painting tools. They all have a palette of tools to select from and the tools behave pretty much as one might expect. The paint brush paints in broad strokes, the pencil draws lines, and the eraser rubs it all out in sections. That's only the beginning with *Kid Pix.* (For a discussion of a standard-style paint program, read about PC Paintbrush in Chapter 9.)

Kid Pix's tools are "wacky." Sure, you can draw a line, but you can also draw zigzags, pies, bubbles, echoes, pine needles, drips, and swirls. You don't just erase, you slip away, fade away, drop out, or explode. And *Kid Pix*'s tools don't just paint. They smile, gurgle, and go "kaboom!"

The sound effects and animation in *Kid Pix* are enchanting. With the Mac version, you can even attach your own recorded sounds to a drawing. Mac LC's, SI's, and Quadras have recording capability built-in. Other Macs will require a recording device like the Mac-Recorder from Macromedia.

Quick Tour

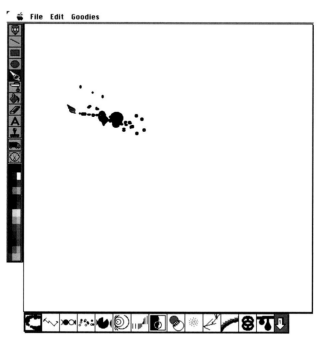

Figure 7.1 The *Kid Pix* drawing window in the Macintosh version: everything a budding artist needs to have fun.

There's no right way to use *Kid Pix*. Just grab your mouse and start painting. There are a few commands available from the menu bar across the top (We'll get to those later.) and a selection of tools from the tool palette down the left side of the drawing window.

At the bottom of the window there are tool options. Every painting tool has many options—so many options that you may feel overwhelmed at first. But don't worry, that's a purely adult reaction. For children, the seemingly endless options are their playground for exploration. They'll play contentedly with one thing for a long time before they even realize that there are more options. (And if your family manages to explore all of *Kid Pix's* possibilities, Broderbund sells the *Kid Pix* Companion, which has even more options.)

Nearly everything you do in *Kid Pix* will be with the mouse. Not only do you paint with it, but you select commands, tools, and options with it, too.

Tip

The mouse is a more natural pointing tool than painting tool, and learning to paint with it can be difficult for anyone. If your child becomes frustrated the first time she tries it, tell her not to despair. Take the mouse yourself and try painting some simple object like a house. The results are bound to be so hilariously pitiful that you will both get a good laugh out of it. In the future, digitizing pads that can record penstrokes will likely come down in price.

If you're afraid your preschooler will destroy your files by inadvertently choosing the wrong command, or if you want to keep her from straying into other programs and becoming frustrated, *Kid Pix* offers a thoughtful option that you won't find in other painting programs. Choose Small Kids Mode from the Goodies menu. This mode hides potentially dangerous commands and makes it impossible to stray out of *Kid Pix*.

Tip

For the youngest initiates to the computer, using the mouse will take some getting used to. You can help by guiding your child's mousing hand gently with your own. Children also like to point at the screen when they're asking questions or explaining their drawings. Encourage them to point with the mouse pointer. This will help keep your screen clean.

The first time you start *Kid Pix*, it's worth taking a few minutes to look around the screen. Find all the tools and identify them:

- Use the un-silly tools first. Try out the Line, Rectangle, and Oval tools. Select a color from the color palette, then choose the Paint Can and fill some of your shapes with color.

- Select the Wacky Pencil and draw some free-form shapes. Use the tool options to change the line thickness and pattern, then draw some more. Not so wacky? Try the last two patterns from the option bar. What's going on here?

- Your painting is probably getting pretty messy, so choose the Eraser and start rubbing out your drawing. That's a good way to erase little mistakes, but to start from a clean slate, choose the dynamite from the options bar and blow up your mess. If only cleaning your children's rooms were this easy.

- For those who find the blank screen intimidating, try the question mark option for the eraser tool. It's like a magic slate. When you rub in the drawing area, it reveals a hidden picture. *Kid Pix* has many hidden pictures that change at random.

- Still intimidated, don't know what to draw? Start decorating the background with the Rubber Stamp tool. There are more than 100 pictures in the Rubber Stamp option bar. Click on the numbered, down arrow on the right side of the bar to access them. (*Kid Pix* Companion has additional rubber stamps.)

- Go ahead and get really silly. Doodle away with the wacky brush. Move things around with the Moving Van. Mix things up thoroughly with the Electric Mixer.

Once you and your child have explored the tools and have a fair idea how they work, ask your child to draw a self portrait, or any portrait, for that matter. Faces are fascinating, and the results can be quite revealing.

Robin's kids start with the obvious, using the Oval tool to draw the head and eyes, and the Wacky Pencil to draw the nose and mouth. Then they start in on special effects:

- The Fuzzer option for the Wacky brush makes the mouth seem to ooze into the turtleneck.

- The Drip option is used to create an unusual hairstyle.

- The Bubbly option makes bangle earings.

- The background is a combination of many Wacky Brush options. From left to right the effects are: fractal trees (some inverse), concentric circles (some magnified), looping lines, the deck of cards brush, and the splatter paint.

- The entire image was shrunken with the Picture In A Picture option of the Electric Mixer tool, and then copied to make a wallpaper-like effect. (You can use this last technique to make and print a small piece of giftwrap.)

- The Text tool was used to label the painting.

Figure 7.2 Robin's daughter, Kari's, self portrait

Step-by-Step Tour

Now that you have mastered portraiture, it's time to explore *Kid Pix*'s options in more detail by studying city planning. Follow the steps outlined here to make a wacky city.

Wacky City

Use the Wacky Pencil tool to draw the outline of a cloud. Start by selecting the tool, choose a color from the color palette, and finally select a thin line from the options bar across the bottom of your window. Draw another cloud using a different color and line thickness.

Figure 7.3 Wacky Pencil

Tip

Be sure that you draw completely closed shapes. If there are any gaps in the outline, color will leak through when you color them in with the Paint bucket later.

Figure 7.4 Options Arrow

Click on the arrow at the end of the option bar and select one of the round end lines. (Some tools have multiple option sets and they are accessed through this arrow.) Choose another color and draw another cloud. With the rounded ends the cloud looks puffier, more cloud-like.

Figure 7.5 Paint Can

Choose the Paint Can from the tool palette, select another color, and fill in your clouds. Simply click with the Paint Can pointer inside your cloud.

Tip

It's sometimes difficult to fit the whole paint can inside the shape you are filling. Only the very tip of the spilling needs to be inside the lines. If you make a mistake, select undo from the Edit menu.

You can experiment with the tools as you use them. For instance, try using the Wacky Pencil and moving the mouse at different speeds. (With a Mac, you can set the responsiveness of your mouse with the Mouse Control Panel in your System folder.) If you still have the round end line option selected, you'll notice that moving the mouse quickly makes a series of dots, while moving it more slowly makes a line.

Try the other options. Select a pattern. What's the question mark for? Use different colors and try the tint option.

Notice how colors blend when they overlap.

Figure 7.6 Tint Option

Figure 7.7 Rectangle Tool

Put some buildings in your painting using the Rectangle tool. Put windows and doors on the facades of your buildings with smaller rectangles. You can draw a filled shape by selecting one of the patterns from the option bar at the bottom of the window. Have you figured out what the question mark does yet? What happens when shapes overlap?

Figure 7.8 Line Tool

Draw some pitched roofs with the Line tool. Hold down the shift key while using the tool to draw perfect horizontal, vertical, or 45° angle lines.

Figure 7.9 Oval Tool

Draw the sun using the Oval tool. To draw a perfect circle (or square), hold down the shift key while you draw with the Oval (Rectangle) tool.

Now is a good time to save your artwork. Choose the File menu and select Save or Save As. Give your painting a name like Wacky City and click OK. It can't be said too many times: save your work frequently and back up often.

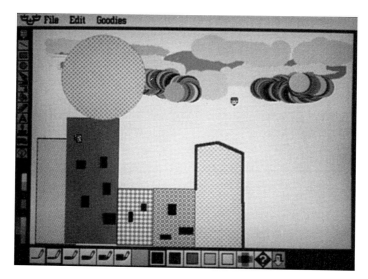

Figure 7.10 Starting A Wacky City

Figure 7.11 Wacky Pen

It's time to have some fun. Choose the Wacky Pen. Use the first option, which is the leaky pen, and draw a tree. Now choose the Pine Needle option and draw another tree. Choose the Zig-Zag option and try to draw a rooftop antenna. Try some of the other options and fill your background with bubbles, pies, echoes, splatters, stars, and loops. Make sure you try some of the options in the second option set. Remember, click on the arrow at the end of the option bar to change sets.

Tip

Many of the options in *Kid Pix* have additional hidden tricks. To use them, hold down the option key (or the PC's shift key) before you paint. For instance, several of the Wacky Brush options become giant sized when you hold down the option key. Try the Geometry and Tree options.

More Wacky Brushes

Among *Kid Pix's* many brushes is a Connect-The-Dots option. This is a great way for pairs or groups of children to play at the computer together. One child can create the dots and another can join them. Here's how it works: With the Connect-The-Dots option selected, any line you draw turns into a series of numbered dots. The next person can connect the dots by using the line tool.

Tip

If you draw very slowly, the dots will be too close together. If you want dots farther apart, you can click where you want them rather than drawing a line.

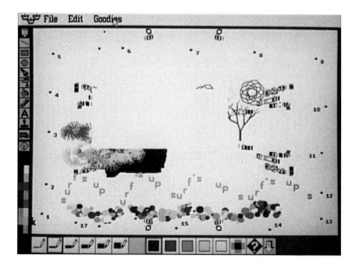

Figure 7.12 Connect the Dots and Alphabet Lines

Figure 7.13 Alphabet Line Option

The Alphabet Line option puts down a line of letters, a to z. If you hold down the option key, the font changes. You can also enter your own text instead of using the alphabet. Choose the Goodies menu at the top of the window and select alphabet text. (On the Mac you can also hold down the command key while pressing a, or you can click twice on the Alphabet Line icon in the option bar.) Type in the text you want and *Kid Pix* will paint with that.

Tip

When you drag from right to left with the Alphabet Line option, it draws letters in mirror writing. You can try sending secret messages by writing them backwards. Keep a mirror handy for decoding.

Wackier than Wacky Brushes

Figure 7.14 Mixer Tool

The Mixer Tool does not draw, it mixes things up. It can change black to white, throw paint blobs on your artwork, turn it into wallpaper, or shatter it like broken glass. It works on the whole drawing area rather than in any one place. Choose your option, click on your drawing, and instant mix up. If you hold down the mouse button or multi-click instead of clicking, things get more and more crazy.

Tip

We haven't talked about him yet, but you should know about the Undo Guy when using the Mixer Tool. If you don't like the effect you get on your first mix up, click on the Undo Guy to erase the last thing you did. Be careful, though. The Undo Guy can only back up one step.

We like to use the Mixer Tool to create backgrounds. You can get some very nice background effects, including some interesting 3D ones, and then paint your figures on top of these.

Filling, Erasing, and Stamping out Fun

Figure 7.15 Paint Can

The fastest way to fill a shape is to pour color into it with the Paint Can. As we mentioned before, you have to make sure that the shape you're filling doesn't have any leaks. If it does, remember the Undo

Guy. With the Paint Can options, you can fill with a pattern, or choose the question mark to fill with a selection from the rainbow. *Kid Pix* divides the drawing window into color panels and fills your shape according to its vertical position on the screen.

Figure 7.16 Eraser

Of all *Kid Pix*'s tools the eraser might just be the most fun of all. The eraser options are hilarious. So much so, that children seem to enjoy erasing their work as much as they do creating it. And blowing up a bad painting is a great way to relieve your frustrations.

Figure 7.17 Rubber Stamp

Can't draw a dog or a dinasaur to save your life? Just stamp a few into your painting with the Rubber Stamp tool. Hold down the option key to make big stamps. Use the option and shift keys together to make huge ones.

There are stamps for every occasion and more if you buy the *Kid Pix* Companion. You can even edit the stamps to change their colors, flip them so they face the other way, or turn them upside down; or, you can change them completely. You get to the Stamp Editor by choosing the Goodies menu and selecting Edit Stamp, by using the command-e key combination on the Mac, or by clicking twice on the stamp you wish to edit.

The Stamp Editor is like a small version of a painting program, but the only drawing tool is the pencil. You can select colors and turn the bits on one by one. Notice how on the left of the Editor the image is enlarged so that the individual bits show up as small squares, and on the right the image is shown at its actual size.

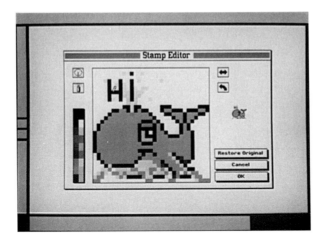

Figure 7.18 The Stamp Editor

Figure 7.19 Text

You may want to add text to your painting for labels, titles, or to attach a story to your artwork. While the Alphabet Line is fun, the Text Tool is more utilitarian. In its most basic mode, you can select individual letters and numbers from the Option Bar and stamp them on your painting like rubber stamps. However, if you hold down the option key when you first select the Text Tool, you can click on your painting and enter text from the keyboard. In this free typing mode, the Option Bar lets you select from eight typestyles for your text.

Last, but not least, Move and Undo

Figure 7.20 Moving Van

The Moving Van lets you pick up pieces of your painting and move them around. You can move specially shaped areas by choosing from thirteen shapes in the Options Bar. Select the shape, move it over the section you want to move, click and drag the mouse to the place you want to put it. The Moving Van leaves a white hole behind, or, if you press the option key when moving, it makes a copy of the section being moved.

There is one more option. By choosing the Magnet option, you can select any portion of the painting by dragging over it. You can move or copy the selection, and you can also use the commands from the Edit menu on your selection. On the Mac, this means that you can copy and paste to other *Kid Pix* documents or other applications.

Figure 7.21 Undo Guy

Finally, the Undo Guy, whom we've already introduced. He's a good guy to know, because he can save your painting from inadvertent mix ups, electronic spills, or just plain goofs. If you make a mistake, just click on the Undo Guy and it's gone. Remember, if you make two mistakes, the Undo Guy can only go back once.

Menus and Commands

Kid Pix has only three menus and just a few standard commands. Open, Close, Save, and Print commands in the File menu; Cut, Copy, and Paste, in the Edit menu; and *Kid Pix*-specific commands in the Goodies menu, most of which we've already discussed.

All of the commands have little icons so that non-readers can use them. You don't have to tell your three-year-old that the Open command is the second one down from the top, you can tell her to use the command with the open door.

The icons also come in handy if you choose the Switch To Spanish command from the Goodies menu. This displays all of the commands in Spanish and is a nice way to introduce your children to that language. Also nice if Spanish happens to be your native tongue. Hats off to *Kid Pix* programmer, Craig Hickman, for introducing our children to a little bilingual education.

We've talked about most of the Goodies, but only mentioned the sound capabilities. You can record and play back sound using commands in the Goodies menu.

A Gaggle of *Kid Pix* Activities

Floor Plan

Most children have tried drawing the facade of a house, but how many know what a floor plan looks like? Take your own house and draw all the rooms with the line tool. (Scale is not important here.) Wood, tile, and carpeted floors all have different textures. Show texture by selecting a fill option for the Paint Can. Use the Rubber Stamp tool to put some furniture in the rooms. You can use the Stamp Editor to add furniture that isn't in the stamp sets. Draw in the furniture that you only need once, like a piano or refrigerator. Label the rooms with the text tool. Label the drawing, too.

If you enjoy floor plans, try a site plan. Map out the whole neighborhood with several houses, streets, sidewalks, and even the neighbor's dog. What's a good fill pattern to use to show the texture of grass or the gravel in a driveway?

Figure 7.22 Have your kids start with a plan of their room

A Matching Game for PreSchoolers

This activity is particularly good if your pre-schooler has a literate older sibling. Have the older child make a column of pictures using the Rubber Stamp tool. Then make a column of letters using the Text Tool. Have the pre-schooler draw lines connecting the pictures to the first letters of their names.

Figure 7.23 Use stamps to create a matching game

Tip

Make sure you save the file before your pre-schooler starts drawing the connecting lines. That way, if she makes a mistake, it's easy to begin again.

Rorschach for Juniors

Use some of the Wacky Brushes that fill up the page quickly like Splatter Paint, Kaleidoscope, or Caterpillars to create a bizarre painting. Then let the other children try to interpret what it looks like. You can also make multiple copies of your bizarre painting and pass them around so that everyone can make up a story to go along with it.

Connect-The-Dots

We've already talked about the Connect-The-Dots brush, but we didn't tell you how to make a template to trace over. *Kid Pix* can import graphics like clip art saved in PCX format on a PC or PICT format on a Mac. Files in these formats are automatically listed in the

File Open dialog box, so that you can open a graphic as a new document. Trace over the image with the Connect-The-Dots brush, and then carefully erase the original image. Now you have a very realistic Connect-The-Dots drawing. Make sure you save your creation before connecting the dots.

Rubber Stamp

Rebuses

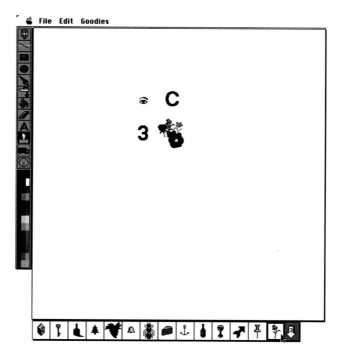

Figure 7.24 **Rebus**

A rebus is simply a puzzle where pictures or symbols are substituted for words in a sentence. You would read this rebus as, "I see three flowers." You can write whole stories in *Kid Pix* using the Text tool, changing to the Rubber Stamp tool to add pictures at appropriate places. If there isn't a stamp for the picture you need, create one using the Rubber Stamp editor. It's as much fun to decode a rebus as it is to create one.

Picture Dictionaries

Ask your preschooler to find a rubber stamp that corresponds to each letter in the alphabet. If you can't find one that matches, can she draw a picture of something that begins with that letter? You can help her by using the text tool to label each picture. If your child is particularly proud of her work, you can print her picture dictionary and bind it for future reference.

Matched Sets

Find like groups of rubber stamps. Stamp all the animals in one place, plants in another. What other sets are there?

Illustration

One of the best ways to stimulate the drawing imagination is to start out with a story. What could be more familiar to a young child than picture books? Well, here's a chance to create her own. If the prospect of writing and illustrating a whole story overwhelms your child, break up the game into smaller pieces.

Finish the Story

You can use the Text tool to start a story. Try typing, "Implacable November weather...," and ask your child to continue the story with an illustration.

Illustrate a Poem

Poetry is full of imagery that children can turn into pictures. You can type a line like, "Hey diddle diddle,/ The cat and the fiddle,/ The cow jumped over the moon," and have your child draw something to go along with it. Or you can have your child complete the poem with an illustration. Remember, older children probably aren't interested in illustrating nursery rhymes. Try something age-appropriate like, "'Twas brillig and the slithy toves/ Did gyre and gimble in the wabe..."

Familiar Stories

Use a story that you read to your children often. Fairytales are particularly good for this. Have your child draw a series of illustrations for Rapunzel or Rumplestiltskin. This is a good opportunity to practice the Copy and Paste commands since many of the drawing elements will be repeated. And if you have access to clip art, you can try opening some of those documents and using them for backgrounds.

Flip Books

Flip books, the predecessors of animated cartoons, are great fun. Draw a picture of a person or animal and save it. Change the arms and legs slightly to suggest movement and then use the Save As command to save the changed drawing as a second frame. Keep making changes to show a succession of movement and save each frame. Print all your frames and then staple them together at the top. Now flip through the book by fanning the pages with your thumb. Your image will jump, run, skip, throw, or perform whatever action you've drawn.

Group Activities

Here are some *Kid Pix* art projects that children can do together:

- Paint a wacky totem pole with each child contributing a section.
- Draw a comic strip with each child contributing a frame.
- Draw paper dolls and the clothing that goes with them.

With each of these projects, you can print out several copies and let each child color one in.

Further Explorations

If your children enjoy painting with *Kid Pix*, or any other paint program, it may be a good opportunity to introduce them to art. The key here is to find connections. For instance, look at paintings by twentieth-century artists. (You don't need to go to a museum to do this, any library has a section of art books.)

Take a close look at the Pointilist paintings of Georges Seurat. See how his entire composition is made up of colored dots. Have your child try to draw a landscape made up entirely of dots. Use some of the Wacky Brush options that make dots: the Leaky Pen, Dots, Bubbly, and Spray Paint options.

Move on to the Cubist paintings of Picasso and Braque. Notice how the forms are reduced to simple geometrical shapes. Try using *Kid Pix*'s Rectangle and Oval tools to draw a face.

Talk about some of the Abstract Expressionists. Ask your children if they like the paintings of Jackson Pollock. There are plenty of tools in *Kid Pix* to imitate the splatters and drips of Pollock. Talk about the simple forms and juxtapositions of color in Mark Rothko. These are also easy to copy in *Kid Pix*.

At all times, defer to the tastes of your child. Try to find an artist to talk about that your child likes. Why does she like his work? What does she like about it? Which artists and paintings do you like? Remember, technique is only part of the painting. Form and color are important, too.

CHAPTER 8

PLAN IV: ROLL THE PRESSES—CHILDREN'S WRITING AND PUBLISHING CENTER

The Software you'll need: *The Children's Writing and Publishing Center* program is for PC-compatibles only. A Macintosh version, simply called *The Writing Center*, is available for schools, and a home Macintosh version will soon be on the market.

What it costs: $69.95 ($89.95 Mac)

Why it's special: A unique desktop publishing package for young writers. *The Writing Center* for the Macintosh is even better, with a full-fledged word processor, better page layout, and more things to do with the artwork.

Ages it appeals to: 7 to 14

Activities: newsletters, invitations, sale signs, awards and certificates, reports, and diaries

Introducing *The Children's Writing and Publishing Center/ The Writing Center*

Here is a wonderful introduction to the world of computerized desktop publishing. With its kid-sized word processor, library of illustrations, and tools for electronic page design, children can create their own illustrated newsletters in no time, see their stories in print, and publish the reports they once composed in longhand. All this presents wonderful opportunities for learning and creativity.

As adults, we tend to think and act in a compartmentalized way. An idea is one thing. An expression is another. The acts of thinking, writing, and publishing what we've written are different disciplines, requiring different sets of skills and tools. Writing requires word processing and publishing requires desktop publishing. You get the text down on paper and then you format it with typefaces, borders, and images.

But children are much more holistic in their approach. Compartmentalized thinking isn't on their agenda. They don't see dividing lines between tasks, and they'll often think about illustrating a story as they write one.

Programs like The Learning Company's *The Children's Writing and Publishing Center* and *The Writing Center* recognize that our children will learn to write, compose, and edit as a single process. As an entry-level desktop publishing program, it encourages them to write, edit, design, illustrate, and publish, all in the same activity.

Desktop publishing helps bring a child's inner vision to the printed page. Good children's desktop publishing programs help kids design the pages of a book by giving them a means to integrate graphics and text in a single document. There are a selection of page layouts (templates) into which kids can place their written stories alongside artwork. Children can not only edit the text, but also revise the appearance of their text as easily as they can rewrite and revise what they've said.

Every child has a gazillion books inside him—little stories he makes up about his pets, family, friends, and neighbors. You've probably listened to many over dinner and bedtime snacks. Instead of just letting your child whisper his fantasies into your ear, you can encourage him to give the stories permanent life.

Of all the publishing kits on the market today (see chapter 13 for a list of other writing tools), *The Children's Writing and Publishing Center/ The Writing Center* is the most versatile. Believe the age rating. Kids should have a good awareness of writing and spelling to use this program well. And they will be ready by the time they reach the third grade. There are other programs that introduce younger children to the same concepts. (If you want to start writing early, investigate something like Davidson's *Kid Works*, their *Once Upon a Time*, or the storybook section of First Byte's *Dinosaur Discovery Kit*.) *Kid Works* doesn't get very sophisticated in terms of page layout, for example, but it does allow children to incorporate all kinds of drawings in their stories and even includes speech digitized playback that reads the finished story back to the child. There are other packages, really marketed for adults, that older children may feel comfortable with. We will discuss these shortly.

The Writing Center for the Macintosh is more complete and better integrated than the PC version. Instead of beginning with a choice of five functions, *The Writing Center* opens a blank document in the column format of your choice. All tools and options, including fonts, graphics, and page layout are available at all times. *The Writing Center* also includes a 100,000-word spelling checker and an offer to purchase the Word Finder thesaurus for $19.95.

Quick Tour

The Children's Writing and Publishing Center/ The Writing Center is easy to master. The extensive documentation barely needs to be opened. The entire program revolves around a main menu, where your child finds five icons that take him to all the publishing tools he needs. The Mac version has no main menu. Instead, all functions are integrated into the Menu Bar and are available from within any document. Kids can use a mouse or the function keys to make selections from the menus. Here's a quick look at the tools you'll find:

- Word Processing. Word processing may be the most fundamental computer skill. With this set of tools, kids can cut and paste text and undo mistakes without "messing up the paper." Word processing frees children from worrying about mistakes. It's a liberating concept for most children. Adult word processors include features like spellcheckers and thesauruses that you won't find in *The Children's Writing and Publishing Center*. *The Writing Center* comes with a 100,000-word spell checker and an offer for the Wordfinder thesaurus. But *CWPC* focuses on a minimum of tools to introduce the kids to word processing. In essence, the word processing component in this program simply allows you to enter and delete text and to reorganize thoughts by cutting and pasting sections of the text. This in no way diminishes the program. As a matter of fact, many educators don't like programs that include spellers and thesauruses because they feel it hampers efforts to get children to spell correctly and learn new vocabulary words.

- **Fonts.** Fonts are styles of type. By changing type styles to give words an Old English or modern, bold appearance, children can add drama to their words, phrases, headlines, or captions. Fonts even come in different sizes to provide additional emphasis.

- **Graphics.** *The Children's Writing and Publishing Center* shows children how they can enhance their stories by choosing color pictures from a library of more than 150 pictures. *The Writing Center* comes with over 200 pictures. As the saying goes, "A picture's worth a thousand words." Children become adept at matching relevant pictures with their stories. The library offers a wide range of artwork on kidcentric topics like sports, holidays, and animals. They can choose a picture from the library, place it in the document, and watch the text automatically adjust to make room for the picture. On a Mac, you can edit pictues in a paint program and paste them back into your document or paste any PICT format picture in.

- **Page Layout.** *The Children's Writing and Publishing Center* lets kids choose different types of report layouts and page designs: a single page, a single page with a headline, or a multicolumn "newspaper" style page. Children soon learn which design is most appropriate for the type of story they have to tell.

As versatile as all this is for kids, *The Children's Writing and Publishing Center* is no substitute for adult desktop publishing programs. If these features sound like what you need to publish flyers for a garage sale or a monthly bridge club bulletin, think again. Adult information requires different treatment than children's, and *The*

Children's Writing and Publishing Center isn't designed for adult needs. The artwork that comes with the program addresses themes that are of interest to kids, and the print quality of the final published document isn't up to what entry-level adult desktop publishing packages can produce. (Mac printing is high-quality.) But for kids, there's a positive side to limitations like these—simplicity.

The Children's Writing and Publishing Center delivers a functional subset of full-fledged desktop publishing programs, along with a kid-sized word processor. Children can use it to become acquainted with the underlying principles and jargon of desktop publishing without getting lost in the myriad options that are packed into adult programs.

The downside of the limitations is that there's a point at which the program stops growing with the child. Just as adults won't really want to use *The Children's Writing and Publishing Center*, neither will growing kids, once they master what they find here. As your young publishers reach their teens and become involved in newspaper and yearbook activities in school, they'll begin to want something more. And when that happens, there are adult entry-level programs that fit the bill for both you and your growing children. These include Timeworks' *PublishIt!* or Spinnaker Software's *PFS: Publisher*. Windows users will enjoy Microsoft's *Publisher* and *PublishIt! Easy* from Timeworks. Mac users will enjoy *Aldus Personal Press* from Silicon Beach Software.

Tip

Teaching a child about desktop publishing can be tricky. And in *The Children's Writing and Publishing Center*, the creation, editing, art, and layout processes are all intertwined. It isn't always easy to identify just where to begin. You can set the proper tone at the outset by giving your child a quick Journalism 101 lesson.

(continued)

Tip (continued)

Pull out a magazine to help illustrate your points. Show your child that a publication is really synergistic, greater than the sum of its parts. The parts, of course, are the stories, illustrations, captions under the illustrations, headlines, and even the ads. You can underscore the point by cutting apart pieces of the magazine and letting your child reassemble them puzzle-fashion. Or play mix-and-match by putting different headlines over different stories and different illustrations next to different text. In this way, you can show how an article loses meaning when the picture that accompanies it doesn't complement what the story says. For instance, you might swap an illustration of a Sopworth Camel from an article on early aircraft with a picture of a cow in a milk ad. Point out what happens. Cows have nothing to do with airplanes. The article just looks silly. After a few turns at this nonsense, your child will begin to understand how illustrations lend context to words and vice versa.

Make sure that after your discussion your child can distinguish and identify the headlines, columns, captions, and illustrations. Older children can be shown how a story can begin on one page and then "jump" or continue on another page. Explain that this allows the newspaper to put more headlines on each page, making it more exciting to read.

Tell your child about the different types of jobs that people do to create a publication: writers write; editors edit; typesetters decide which type styles to use; illustrators come up with pictures to convey ideas; and layout artists figure out how all these things should come together on a page. As you work through *The Children's Writing and Publishing Center*, show your child how the computer program lets him be all these people.

(continued)

Tip (continued)

Take the same newspaper article you just worked with and see if your child can identify who did what. Who made the decision to use a certain size and style of headline? Who did the art image? Who decided how the images and text would be placed on a page?

You might want to involve older children in a discussion on advertising in newspapers and magazines. Certainly advertisements are some of the most thought-provoking and clever combinations of text, art, and layout in a publication. Give your child an apple, orange, or maybe a canned food from your pantry and ask him to create an advertisement for it.

Step-by-Step Tour

The Children's Writing and Publishing Center turns your child's efforts into a one-person show. But which act should come first? Writing? Art? Layout? That's a tough question. And it's one you'll probably have to help your child answer, unless he is inclined to dive right in and think about what typeface to use as he types his stories into the word processor.

The easiest thing to do is to encourage your child to wear one hat at a time. Tackle each role individually beginning with the general layout, focusing on editorial content, and then tweaking and tuning the document layout.

This starts your child down a path that parallels the learning curve for most professionals and provides a structure for completing all the tasks involved in producing a published document. When the kids are adept enough to work with all the elements at once, turn them loose and let them explore.

Before loading the program on your PC, be aware that many of the more advanced commands in *The Children's Writing and Publishing Center* are hidden from view. You won't find them on the main menu. And kids, if left to their own devices, may never find them. The commands are mentioned in a help file that pops onto the screen when you press F1. Show your child how to use this key to get additional information about the program. There's also a quick-start exercise in the manual, which walks children through writing and publishing a letter (sample report in *The Writing Center*). Make sure the kids do this exercise. It helps introduce them to the functions.

Figure 8.1 The tools for publishing are in *The Children's Writing and Publishing Center*'s menus.

Our own exercise, the one you see below, takes them further down the path. In it we ask them to publish a journal. Not only does this prompt them to write and publish, it encourages them to think about the things that happen in their daily life. Try out the following exercise after you've installed the program. It will give your child a head start in using *The Children's Writing and Publishing Center* for all sorts of things: creating invitations to a party, posters for a backyard carnival, or a neighborhood newsletter of kids' news.

Publishing a Short Daily Journal

Journals and diaries offer a great way to introduce children to writing. Unlike a homework assignment, writing in a journal isn't a chore. As your child records thoughts and activities, a journal can become a personal refuge where he can write what he wants. These brief thoughts will come to be treasured. By using a desktop publishing program to add graphics, visual interest, and form to what they write, children can be even more creative. *The Children's Writing and Publishing Center* offers all the tools to get them started.

Select a Story Type

The program's main menu lets children choose between two types of writing: *Report, Story, or Letter* and *Newsletter.* When you select New from the File menu there are three choices in *The Writing Center*: Report or Letter, Newsletter, or Custom. To create a journal, choose the former. This tells *The Children's Writing and Publishing Center* that you want to write in a standard single-page format, such as what's normally used in a book or letter; you don't want the multicolumn newspaper style.

Select a Format

The next menu you'll see on screen is the Report Layout dialog box with two choices: Heading and No Heading. Select *Body without Heading.* This gives your child a blank page on which to write. If you had chosen to use a heading, the program would have opened an area at the top of the page in which you could create a headline or letterhead insignia. But that's not what you want for a journal. *Body without Heading* gives your child a completely open page on which to type. Now it's time to use the program's word processing features.

Type the Entry

Don't worry about whether your child has touch-typing skills. For now, any hunt-and-peck method will do. Simply have your child type in the following paragraph:

> Today was terrific. Weekends usually are. First, my best friend Nancy and I went roller-skating. Next, we worked on our homework for awhile, but it was fun because it was a report we are doing on the World Olympics. Then my Dad came home and took us out for ice cream sundaes. Finally, Mom said Nancy could sleep over.

The child may balk at writing a paragraph about people he doesn't know and activities he didn't do. Ask him to type it anyway. Later in this exercise, you'll show him how to edit the text and customize it to reflect his own interests.

We like this boilerplate approach because it gives your child something to work with right away. Children, when first called upon to record their thoughts, frequently have trouble thinking up things to say. Our little paragraph gets them started. It also gets the imagination moving. Once the kids see how the program works, they'll want to explore it and will begin to let their imaginations run wild.

Add the Date

After typing the paragraph, use the arrow keys or mouse to move back to the beginning of the paragraph. Add a date:

August 24, 1992

Give It Form

Press the Enter key five times to insert lines between the date and the body of the text.

Edit the Text

Now you'll introduce your child to simple word processing concepts. Use the arrow keys (or mouse) to move across the text. Show your child how the cursor highlights the letters it touches. The Delete key removes the character that the cursor is on. The Backspace key removes the character to the left of the cursor. On a Mac there is a flashing vertical line called the insertion point. The delete key removes the character before the insertion point. There is no backspace key on most Mac keyboards. You can highlight a selection of text by holding down the mouse button and dragging over the text. You can highlight a word by double-clicking on it (clicking the mouse button two times in rapid succession).

On a PC your child can use the delete and backspace keys to transform the text in our paragraph into one that tells a story he is familiar with. Use Delete and Backspace to erase Nancy's name and substitute the name of your child's best friend. (Make sure you use the Shift key to capitalize the name.) Don't forget to change the name of the friend the second time that it appears in the paragraph. If you are using a Mac, select the name, Nancy, by double-clicking and type in the name of your child's best friend.

1. Delete *roller-skating* and substitute the name of his favorite activity.

2. Delete *ice cream sundaes* and type in your child's favorite food.

Add a picture

We'll add a picture called *Pals* to illustrate this journal entry. Here's how:

1. Press F4 to bring up the Picture menu. Select Choose a Picture from the Picture menu.

2. Choose *Select Picture by Name* from the choices on the Picture menu. This brings up a list of the different pictures to choose from. Open the Pictures folder, choose a subject folder from the list, and when you find a picture you like click on the Place in Document button.

3. Select *People* from the Picture list. Another list of pictures appears on screen.

4. Select *More* from the pop-up menu to move to the next list. Use the arrow keys to move up and down the list, from one picture name to the next, until you find *Pals*. Highlight the name and press Enter to select it.

5. Use the arrow keys to move the picture across the screen and position it at the beginning of the paragraph. Press Enter to place the picture when you have it where you want it. Notice how the program automatically moves the text, readjusting it to accommodate the picture. The picture will apear in the upper left corner of your document. You can drag it anywhere you like with the mouse. If you leave the picture on top of your text, the words will automatically reflow around the picture.

6. Repeat what you did in Step 5, but select a picture from the *Sports* collection. Place this picture at the end of the document.

Connection

As kids use the program, they quickly learn that they can put pictures on a page before they even start writing. At first, it might be fun to concoct stories around the pictures. But, for the long term, you'll want to encourage the kids to write first and then illustrate. This frees their imaginations from the limitation of writing to a picture and lets the picture augment the writing, instead of the other way around. Keep in mind, too, that pictures take up lots of space in a document, so you may want to use them sparingly. Also note that the text wraps around the picture on the page. In many adult desktop publishing packages, you have fine control over this text-wrapping feature, but in *The Children's Writing and Publishing Center* the text wrap is preset.

Change the Typeface

Now it's time to explore the different designs, styles, and sizes of type. We'll begin by changing the typeface and size of the date. Here's how to do it:

1. Using the mouse or arrow keys on the keyboard, move the cursor to the beginning of the line that contains the date. Select the date by dragging over it with the mouse.

2. Simultaneously press the Alt key and F. Then press Enter. This activates a highlighting function where characters on the screen appear in reverse video. Choose the Font command from the Text menu. This lists all of the fonts installed in your system. (Your Mac comes with many fonts and this is a good opportunity to find out what they look like.) Select the font, size, and style you want from the Font dialog box—try New York, 12, Plain. Click on the Ok button and your date will have a new character format. The PC version has a few built-in fonts.

3. Use the arrow keys or mouse to move the cursor and extend the highlight to the end of the line that contains the date. The line will now appear as light text on a dark background. Press Enter to end the highlight. When a selection of text is highlighted, you can do any number of things: move it, copy it, delete it, or, as we'll do in this case, change the font.

4. Press F3 and the Font menu pops up. Here, you'll see a list of different type styles that you can apply to the highlighted text. Let's select the last font on the list: *Old English.* When you select the font, it is automatically applied to the highlighted text. If you know in advance you want your font to be a certain style, then you don't need to bother with this typing and highlighting. (Just select the font before you start typing your text.)

Sign the Entry

Let's put your child's signature at the end of the text, this time using another font. Here's how to add the signature:

1. Using cursor keys or mouse, move to the bottom of the page.

2. Press F3 to bring up the Font menu and select the fourth font down. Press Enter.

3. Type Your friend, and insert your child's name. As you type the words, every letter in the line appears on screen in the new font . This way, your child can use one font for all the text and have the program apply the typestyle automatically as he types.

If you're using a Mac, move the insertion point to the end of your text by clicking there with the mouse. Use the Font command from the Text menu and change the Style to Italic. Click Ok. Now type "Your friend," and then your child's name. All of this will be italicized.

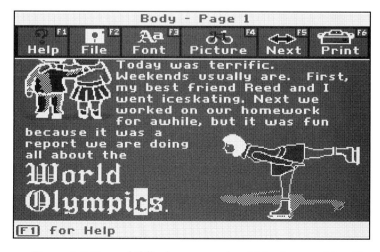

Figure 8.2 Your child's document should look something like this.

Save the Document

This stores the document as an electronic file that your child can recall and revise later. To save:

1. Press F2 and select *Save on Storage Disk*. Press Enter. The program prompts you to save the document to the storage disk that The Learning Company provides with the program or to a directory on your hard disk. If you don't specify a directory path, the program will save the file to the directory that the program is in. On a hard disk, this is the CPC directory.

2. Type a one-word name for the file. You can use any name with up to eight characters. Press Enter.

On a Mac, choose Save from the File menu. Give the letter a name and click the Save button. (If this is new to you, review the section on the Macintosh file system in your Mac manual.)

Tip

If there are several kids in your family, it's a good idea to make each one a separate subdirectory below the CPC directory on your hard disk. If you don't have a hard disk on your system, give each child his own floppy disk. In this way, your kids will have their own personal disks or directories. If you're using *The Writing Center* on a Macintosh, you might want to create folders for them. To create subdirectories on your PC-compatible hard disk:

1. Make sure you've saved your child's journal entry, so you don't lose the work.

2. Exit *The Children's Writing and Publishing Center*. You find yourself in the C:\CPC directory. At the prompt, type the command MKDIR (it stands for *make directory*), followed by your child's name, for example:

```
mkdir linda
```

(continued)

Tip (continued)

3. After creating the directories, type dir at the C:\CPC> prompt to see the new subdirectories.

4. Type cd (which means *Change Directory*) followed by the name of the directory, for example:

```
cd linda
```

to get into that directory.

Remember, on PC-compatibles you can only use directory names that are no longer than eight characters. If your child has a long name, you'll have to get creative with abbreviations.

On a Mac, you can put a folder anywhere you like. To put one in The Writing Center folder, open that folder and choose New folder from the File menu. A new folder named Untitled Folder appears in the Writing Center window. The name is selected, so you need only type your child's name to title the folder. Mac file names can be 32 characters long, but there is only room to display 18 letters in the file dialog box.

Print the Journal

Your journal file now exists in electronic form. But the magic of publishing is seeing the work on paper. You can easily get a printout from *The Children's Writing and Publishing Center*. If you exited the program to create subdirectories, you'll have to first reload it.

Connection

Have crayons handy to keep the kids interested and involved. The pictures you see on screen may be full-color images, but, unfortunately, few of us have color printers, so you should explain to your child in advance that the color won't show up on the printed document. Children are often very disappointed when they see the black-and-white printout. But you can turn disappointment into a fun exercise by passing out crayons or markers when the dull document appears. Then the kids can color in the pictures to make them even prettier than what appears on screen.

1. Press F6 or select *Print*, from the main menu. This brings up the Print menu, where you are given three options: *Print Your Work, Change System Setup*, and *Test Printer.*

2. Before you actually print the work, you'll need to make sure you have the right printer setup. Select *Change System Setup* by moving the cursor highlight to it and pressing Enter.

3. Select *Change Printer Model.*

   This brings up a list of more than 40 printers that you can check to make sure that the program knows about the one on your system.

4. Move the cursor down the list of available printers to highlight the name that matches your printer. Press Enter.

   The Children's Writing and Publishing Center makes necessary changes and returns you to the original Print menu.

5. Now it's time to actually print the journal entry. Select *Print Your Work* from the Print menu.

   If you have not saved the document CWPC prompts you to do so. The program presents you with another menu and asks you to *Choose Printout Options.* This menu first asks if you want to *Print Now* or *Change Options.* Under *Change Options*, you'll see all the options you can use to tell *The Children's Writing and Publishing Center* how to handle the printing process.

6. Move the cursor over *Change Options* to use different options than the ones in the menu. For this exercise, let's change the options.

7. Use these options to tell the program you want two copies (one for your child and one for you), a border on the page, no bold print, no stopping between pages, and no page numbers. Press Enter.

8. The highlight returns to the Print Now option at the top of the menu. Press Enter to print the journal.

On a Mac, choose the Page setup command from the File menu. There are many options to set that you should explore later. If you are using computer paper, click on that button. All the other default options are fine, so click the Ok button. Choose Print from the File menu to bring up the standard Mac printer dialog box. There are several printing options including one that allows you to use a color ribbon on an ImageWriter printer. You can read about them in your hardware manuals. For now, just use the default settings and click on the Print button.

Congratulations! You have just published a simple diary.

Tip

Use meaningful names when you save documents. They will be easy for your child to remember. For instance, you could use *Journal 1* for the journal entry we created above. Document names on PC-compatibles, like directory names, can be no longer than eight characters. But, you can also add a three-letter extension. A name might look something like this: *journal.ext*, where journal is the name and ext is the extension. Extensions for the names on the Mac are not particularly useful since you can use spaces and long descriptive names. You can use the extension to indicate categories of documents and make it easier to identify different types of writing.

(continued)

Tip (continued)

For example, you could use the extension, *new*, for news-letters and save monthly newsletters as *january.new*, *feburary.new*, and *march.new*. For book reports, you might use the extension *.rep* and the book name: *heidi.rep*, *blbauty.rep*, or *ninjatur.rep*. Or, you can use extensions to categorize the documents according to who wrote them, *diary.sue*, for instance. Work out a naming scheme that suits your child. In Robin's family, *klet1.doc* is Kari's first letter. Or, if you're saving the file with the extension as the identifier, you might use something like KSue.let (Kari's letter to Susan).

Advanced Features

Like many adult programs, *The Children's Writing and Publishing Center* uses a number of key combinations that either serve as short-cuts around the menus or do things that the menus don't do. (In *The Writing Center* on the Mac, all keyboard shortcuts are listed in the menus.) These can be a little hard to find in the documentation, so we've listed them here for you. After you've successfully printed your diary entry, go back to the document and experiment with these key commands to get used to how they work. Here are the ones you should try out and practice. To use them hold down the Alt key while you press the letter.

Alt+V This combination lets you view up to four pages of the document in an on-screen preview. It positions thumbnail images of the pages side by side before you actually print them. In desktop publishing terminology, the view you see on screen is called *greeking* because the text is only representational, not readable. Instead of ac-tually seeing the words you wrote on each page, you'll see dark blocks where every line of text is and shaded squares where the pic-tures appear.

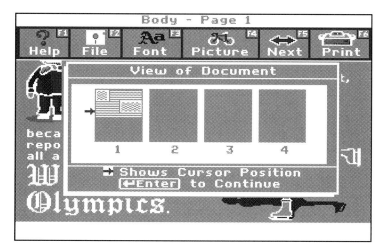

Figure 8.3 The greeking view lets you preview your work.

Connection

When we do large documents, such as family newsletters and reports, we often draw a thumbnail sketch of the project. We simply use greeking to indicate where headlines, images, and text will appear on paper and how the story will flow from page to page.

Alt+E This key combination lets you see where you've inserted carriage returns by pressing Enter. The carriage returns show up as little arrows, bent back to point at the text. Show your child how to toggle this key combination on and off to be sure he hasn't inadvertently inserted a carriage return where one shouldn't be.

Alt+M You can center a line of text in the middle of the page by moving the cursor to the beginning of the line and pressing this key combination.

Alt+L This moves text to the left.

Alt+C The *C* stands for *Cut*. This key combination performs the first part of the two-part cut-and-paste operation that's commonly found in adult word processing and desktop publishing programs. This key combo offers a fast, easy way of removing, (cutting) a block of text from a document. Simply highlight the text you wish to remove and press Alt+C.

Alt+P The *P* stands for *Paste*. After you've cut text from a document, move your cursor to the place where you'd like to insert it and press Alt+P. The cut-and-paste process is an important editing function that makes it easy to make big changes in a document. You should practice it with your child; once he masters it, he'll use it often.

Alt+F This is a shortcut that starts a highlight and then takes you to the Fonts menu to change the appearance of text. You can use it instead of F3.

Alt+U Use this to start underlining. After you press Alt+U, any text you type will be underlined.

F After you've selected a picture for your document but before you place it in the document, the F key is transformed from a key that types a letter of the alphabet into a key that does something special. Before you place the picture, you can press F to flip it so that it faces the other way.

Activities

Once the kids master the basics of *The Children's Writing and Publishing Center/ The Writing Center*, encourage them to explore and experiment. Below are a just a few of the things you can prompt them to do.

Newsletters

Create a multipage newsletter. This can be a bit tricky, since the program only provides a space for headlines on the first page of a document. On subsequent pages, your child can use large fonts to create headlines. Prompt your child to think of the Page 1 headline as a title box, to create a banner name for the newsletter, rather than a place to write an actual headline.

> **Tip**
> To change the number of columns, choose the Page Setup command in the File menu and choose the appropriate button on the columns box.

Connection

Printed information is part of daily life, and a desktop publishing program can be used to produce leaflets and literature for all kinds of children's activities. We like *The Children's Writing and Publishing Center/ The Writing Center* because it offers enough to give children a diverse publishing environment (eight different type styles in six different sizes, plus 150 clip-art images) without overwhelming young desktop publishers. Many schools also use this program. The school where Robin's children go uses *The Children's Writing and Publishing Center* to publish a monthly newsletter that the kids create and carry home. If your kids use *CWPC* at school, you'll forge a great home-school connection by using the program at home. At home, we use *The Children's Writing and Publishing Center* to let the kids publish a newsletter we distribute to family members.

Expand the Journal

Ask the kids to write down a little something about their daily activities each night for four nights and use the pictures in the program to augment their stories. At the end of four days, print the four-page document.

If the kids enjoy the process, they can keep writing a journal and even make a book out of it by creating front and back covers for it. They can use *CWPC* to create covers or make their own out of heavy construction paper. Another good idea is to use a colored folder as the covers, then paste a *CWPC*-published cover page on the front. The journal books can be stapled together, or the children can punch holes in each page and tie the book together with colorful ribbons or string.

Create Awards and Certificates

Work with your kids to create a series of certificates you can print and hand to them when they complete their chores, lose a tooth, or graduate to higher classes of expertise in their swimming, gymnastics, or karate classes. Host a little awards ceremony around the event and make it special by fixing and serving a favorite snack or dessert.

Ask the kids create awards for family members and friends: A Best Friend Award, Thanks for Coming to My Birthday Party Award, Best Grandmother, Best Mom (nice on Mother's Day), and Best Dad (ditto, but for Father's Day).

Older siblings can reward younger ones for good works: Tooth-brushing, garbage collection, and so forth. In classrooms without computers, you can ask your children's teachers to designate your family as the makers of certificates for accomplishments like Best Citizen and Least Days Absent.

For Mother's Day, Robin's children invariably surprise her by publishing some coupons that are redeemable for household chores. They give her sister some free-babysitting coupons.

Create a Comic Strip

Use the illustrations in the program to create a comic strip, laying down the art side by side and then adding dialogue. It's a good idea to first clip a comic strip from the newspaper and keep it alongside your child as he works. This shows him what a real comic strip looks like and gives him a form to follow as he works. You will have to hand draw any word balloons, since *CWPC* doesn't have drawing tools. When the strip has been printed out, your child can use markers to color in the pictures, *CWPC* doesn't create borders, so let your child use a ruler to put boxes around each picture.

Send Invitations and Well Wishes

Upcoming holidays or special events offer good reasons to publish. Have the kids print birthday cards and valentines, invitations to your Thanksgiving Day feast, thank-you notes, congratulations when someone graduates or goes on a nice vacation, For Sale signs for a garage sale, or talent show signs.

Create a Treasure Hunt

We often print clues (if you print four or five clues on a page and then cut them into smaller strips, you save a tree) to make home-grown treasure hunts. We often put a piece of *CWPC* clip art into the document to make it more attractive. After carefully cutting our clues into strips, we can hide them as appropriate.

Moving on

But perhaps the most important guidance we can give are tips on when to move on to other programs. This profile of how *The Children's Writing and Publishing Center* differs from adult programs will help you decide when the time has come.

Layout options in *The Children's Writing and Publishing Center* are limited and the pictures come in one rectangular size only. You cannot enlarge, shrink, or crop them as you can in adult-level programs. You cannot import pictures from other programs. The new version, which is already underway at the Learning Company, will be more versatile and not a moment too late, since we believe that even the youngest desktop publishers need not be confounded by sizing and cropping artwork. We've seen kids as young as eight master sizing tools in other software applications. Using a Mac and *The Writing Center* you can resize to any size, but you can't crop. You can also import any PICT image.

The Children's Writing and Publishing Center's provisions for newsletters are also limited; you cannot create newsletters with more than two columns, winding columns, or variable-width columns. You can't change the size of the headline block. Adult desktop publishing programs do this, and they often include simple box and line drawing tools to let you create frames around stories. They also give you the ability to write captions under illustrations, to edit those illustrations, and to adjust line spacing. If your child becomes a real publishing pro and begins asking why the printouts don't look more like real magazines and newspapers, it may be time to move up.

With *The Writing Center* on a Mac, you may have any number of columns on a page, but they all must be the same width. The Headline block automatically changes size to fit the type that your child enters.

The editing capabilities of *The Children's Writing and Publishing Center*, although limited by adult standards, provide plenty of opportunity for young editors. But kids cannot search for and replace specific words or italicize type. There's no spellchecker to identify and help correct misspelled words. And there's no thesaurus.

Kids must rely on a hardbound dictionary or the help of their parents to avoid misspellings. But manual dictionary practice is good;

children should learn to spell and look up words before they begin depending on an electronic spelling checker. We've found, too, that children's spelling is so inventive that many times a dictionary or spellchecker is no help at all. If the kids don't get the first two letters right, it's nearly impossible for them to find the word in a dictionary or for a spellchecker to divine what they're trying to spell. Mom and Dad must prompt them. *The Writing Center* does include Find/ Change capabilities and a spell checker.

Kids find the editing process empowering. Educational research tells us that children enjoy writing with computers because revisions and modifications are less tedious than with a #2 pencil and eraser. For years, children have told us stories and illustrated them using crayons. Desktop publishing gives them a new means of expression and gives us something different to post on the refrigerator door.

CHAPTER
9

PLAN V: KIDS ACTIVITIES FOR WINDOWS

The software you'll need: Windows, version 3.0 or higher

What it costs: $99.95

Why it's special: Windows puts a Macintosh-like look on a PC screen, which makes it easier for children to use. It allows your child to run her programs from a central, visual system of menus. Windows is often deeply discounted and comes free with many IBM PC-compatible computer systems. Even better, Windows is packaged with its own set of applications: a clock, calculator, simple database program, note-writer, word processor, calendar, games, a paint program, and more.

Ages it appeals to: Ten and older to use the programs, three and older as a graphical environment

Activities: Learn to use simple versions of adult applications like word processing, painting, and information management. Create a school calendar and an easy-to-use phone book, play games, and more.

Introducing Windows

Windows is a program for users of IBM or IBM-compatible personal computers. To run Windows, you should have the type of PC-compatible hardware we recommend in Section I of this book. If your computer system is more powerful, great! If your system is less powerful than what we suggest, you may find Windows sluggish or even unusable. Macintosh users don't need a program like Windows, because their computer system already provides a friendly, visual face—and this face (called a *user interface* in computerese) is exactly what Windows gives your computer.

In Chapter 4, you were introduced to Windows as an environment where your child, even if she's as young as three years old, can get easy access to her applications. You learned how to childproof Windows and customize it for kids. Before you read this chapter, you should make sure that you've followed our recommendations in Chapter 4.

In this chapter, we'll show you how your older child can learn to use the applications that come with Windows, and we'll fill you in on some of the details of this important program. We'll also explore some entertaining activities that can make Windows a special place for the older child and get her on the road to using adult software. As parents who own a PC, you'll find the instructions in this chapter helpful for your own purposes—Windows is a powerful force in the PC world and is becoming a standard in business and professional workplaces, where PCs still dominate. We don't try to give you a full Windows tutorial, because that would require a whole book by itself. (For an excellent Windows introduction, read *Van Wolverton's Guide to Windows 3.1*, by Michael Boom and Van Wolverton, published by Random House; for an overview of adult software applications designed to run under Windows, read *Using Windows Products Together* by Joseph Fournier III, available in Fall/Winter 1992 and also published by Random House. The latter also comes with valuable discount coupons to help you start your collection of Windows software.)

Despite the frightening label of *Graphical User Interface* (*GUI,* pronounced "gooey"), what Windows gives you is really quite simple. It does many of the same things that DOS does, like helping you move around your hard disk and print your files. But it doesn't replace DOS, it works *with* DOS to make your computer easier and more fun to use. Windows creates an environment from which you can manage your software programs; this environment is based on an obvious metaphor, yes, *windows*. Different programs appear in different windows on the screen. You can focus on one window at a time or use several programs at once. (How well Windows works with several programs running at one time depends on the power of your computer system, but for kids we suggest running one at a time.)

Our description of Windows in this book is based on Windows version 3.1, the latest version at the time of this writing. There is some variation in different Windows' versions, but they are not significant for our purposes here.

Moving around Windows

To use Windows, you really must have a mouse, even though it's not strictly required. The mouse lets you shift easily from one program window to another, and to quickly choose icons that stand for different files and programs. There are four important things you do with a mouse:

- **Roll** Move the mouse on your desk to control the position of the pointer (an arrow or other symbol) on your screen.

- **Drag** Hold down the left mouse button (or the only one, if your mouse has a single button) and roll the mouse at the same time. Dragging is generally used for moving the pointer and doing something else at the same time—making a rectangle bigger or smaller in a paint program, for example.

- **Click** Press the left mouse button (or the only one, if your mouse doesn't have another button) to choose something from the screen at the pointer's location.

- **Double click** Press the mouse button two times in rapid succession to choose something from the screen at the pointer's location. Double clicking is generally used as a shortcut, when otherwise you might have to select from a menu or click an item followed by a confirming button.

Some software programs are especially designed to be managed by Windows; these programs all look and work alike, which makes learning new software easier. Other programs simply coexist with Windows; you can run them from Windows, but they don't use Windows' standards for operation. *Kid Pix*, discussed in Chapter 7, can either be run from Windows or purchased as a real Windows product. Other programs, like many discussed in this book, don't work with Windows at all. Programs created to work with Windows are clearly labeled. However, you can be fairly certain that new versions will be Windows-compatible, because millions of copies of Windows have already been sold, and millions more will be found in homes and businesses in the next few years.

Windows comes with several adult-level software programs, for example: *File Manager* for organizing your files and directories; *Print Manager*, for controlling the way different files are sent to your printer; *Control Panel*, for handling the way Windows itself works. To find out more about these Windows features, you'll have to look at one of the books we suggested earlier. The only adult Windows program you need to know about now is *Program Manager*, which is both the core of Windows and its main window.

Figure 9.1 shows the *Program Manager* window, set up and organized as we recommend for older children. In addition, it shows a window for Windows' *Notepad* program, which we'll talk about later. It also shows some of Windows' key elements that help you navigate within a window and organize your applications. We also describe some of these elements, just to get you started on the jargon that comes with using the Windows environment. Don't worry if these terms seem strange now. As you perform the exercises for the different Windows applications, refer back to this figure, and you'll soon find out how easy it is to learn Windows. (That's why so many copies have been sold!)

Desktop This is simply the "background" in Windows. It contains windows and sometimes the *icons* (symbols) for programs that are currently set aside (minimized) but still running. If you double click on the desktop, Windows presents a menu called Task List, which lets you work with the various programs on your desktop. We'll mention Task List later on.

Title bar This line of text at the top of each window tells you what program window you're looking at. In this case, we're looking at Program Manager. Title bars can give you a bit more information too, for example, the name of the file you're using at the moment and where on your hard disk that file is. You can move a window around the screen by dragging on the title bar.

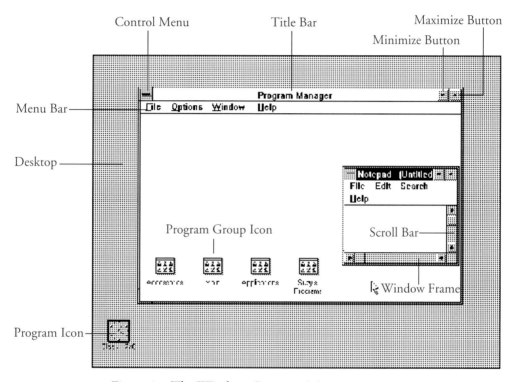

Figure 9.1 The Windows Program Manager

Window frame Windows have frames. You can click on a frame, or any part of a window, to place the window in front of other windows on the screen. If the frame is visible, you can drag on a corner of it or any side of it to make the window bigger or smaller. There are several ways to size and arrange windows on the screen. We suggest that you look at the Windows manual or at *Van Wolverton's Guide to Windows 3.1* for more information.

Menu bar All Windows programs place a menu bar across the top of the screen that contains lists of commands or activities you can perform. Click on one of the words in the menu bar and a pull-down menu appears. Click on one of the words in the menu (called a *command*) to perform an activity.

Minimize button Click on this button to make the window smaller, maybe even turn it into an icon like the Clock icon on the screen.

Maximize button Click on this button to make the window fill the screen. If the window is already filling the screen, you see a different button here, one that shows both the minimize and maximize arrows and shrinks the window.

Control menu icon Click on this icon to bring up a menu of basic activities you can perform on the window. Double clicking on this icon closes the window; if you are running a program, you can stop the program this way.

Scroll bars When you use a program in Windows, you look at it through a window. The picture or document you are working with may be bigger than what you can see through the window. The scroll bars allow you to adjust what portion of the document or picture is shown in the window. We'll show you how to use scroll bars later, when we try out some Windows programs.

Program Group icon This icon (a symbol) hides a group of applications. (We talked about program groups in Chapter 4.) This one is titled *Suzy's Programs* and it holds the programs that a child might use. Double click on a program group icon, and a window opens up, revealing another group of icons that stand for the programs that Suzy needs.

Program or application icon. This icon stands for a program. Double click on a program icon, and a window opens up that contains that program.

Program workspace. Program Manager's workspace contains other programs. A word processor's workspace contains a document, and a paint program's workspace contains a picture.

What Comes with Windows

Windows comes with a lot of smaller programs. Some of these control how Windows works and some are rather complex to operate. But others are good starter-programs or games for older children and can provide hours of fun activities. Here are the programs we're going to discuss in this chapter:

- **Paintbrush** A paint program, good for artistic forays at the keyboard. You can use *Paintbrush* art in *Write* documents.

- **Write** A simple word processor with most of the basic features that children need to learn about. *Write* is great for reports and other longer documents

- **Notepad** A quick and easy program for writing short notes.

- **Calculator** You can guess what this does

- **CardFile** A rudimentary program for organizing collections of information, a good way for a child to keep simple lists

- **Calendar** A rich and entertaining tool for making schedules and to-do lists.

In addition, Windows comes with two games: *Solitaire* and *Minesweeper*. These entertaining games help a child get a feel for Windows while providing hours of play. We aren't going to discuss these games in detail, because their online help tells you all you need to know.

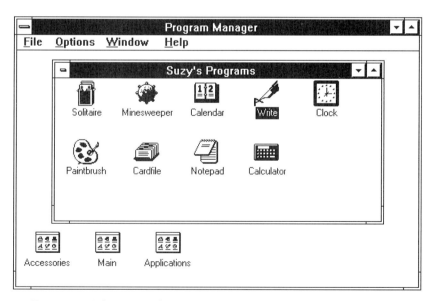

Figure 9.2 These Windows "accessories" come free when you buy the Windows environment.

All the programs that come with Windows include online help. When need help using a menu or a command on a menu, just click on Help in the menu bar or press the F1 function key. A help window appears, letting you select a help topic or a menu and command that you want to read more about. Windows' help is simple and easy to use. If you need to learn more about getting help, look at your Windows manual.

Quick Tour

Spend some time with Windows by yourself first, then give the kids a walking tour of the programs before they explore on their own. Load one of the Windows applications listed above and use the mouse to position the pointer on different parts of the screen. We'll start with Windows *Notepad* for this tour. When you first start Windows, *Notepad* and the other programs in our list above are located in a *Program Manager* program group called *Accessories*. If you followed the directions in Chapter 4, you placed *Notepad* and the other programs in a new program group labeled with your child's name. Now, double click on the program group where *Notepad* is located. (Remember, to double click an icon, you position the pointer on it, then click twice in rapid succession.)

To start *Notepad*, double click on its icon, a little pad of paper. Point out to your child that this is how you start all Windows programs. You don't have to know how to spell the program's name; you just have to pick out the icon.

A window opens for *Notepad*. The title bar shows *Notepad - (Untitled)*—the name of the program and the name of the file; files only get titles when we name them, hence the label we see on the screen now. Under the title bar is the menu bar, which begins with the word *File* and runs across the top of the window, above the workspace. (The workspace is empty now, because we haven't started typing yet.) Show your child how she can drag the *Notepad* window around the screen, by holding down the mouse button while the pointer is positioned on the title bar, then rolling the mouse. Point out the scroll bars on the bottom and sides of the window. In a few minutes, we'll practice using them. Menu bars, scroll bars, and title bars are common to all Windows applications.

Now that your kids have had a quick look at some of the basic elements of a window, let's start practicing with the applications that come with Windows.

Calendar

Let's close *Notepad* for the moment. Show your child how to do this by double clicking on the control menu box in the upper lefthand corner of the *Notepad* window. Now, double click on the *Calendar* icon. *Calendar* opens to the daily view, shown in the figure below.

As soon as children become aware of the passage of time, they want to mark it on calendars. Windows *Calendar* lets your child mark the hours in a day or the days in the month. She can mark appointments in the daily view and use the monthly view for special occasions like birthdays and holidays, where you don't need too much detail. As you work with Windows, you can set *Calendar*'s built-in alarm clock to go off at a certain time. We've used it to signal the end of music practice.

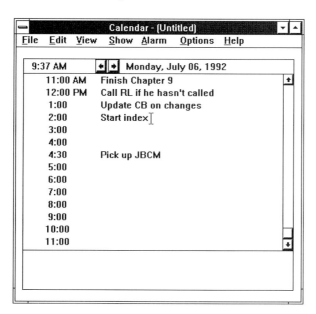

Figure 9.3 Calendar in daily view

One of the easiest ways to expose your child to scheduling is to keep track of the hours in the day. Look at the daily view that's on your screen now. It shows today's date and then lists the hours of the day, with space next to each hour where you can write in an event. Let your child fill in today's activities by the hour. Just point to the hour you want and click. A cursor that looks like a vertical line appears; this is the *insert cursor*. It shows where the letters you type will be inserted. Use the arrow keys to jump up or down to another hour.

Click on the right arrow by the date at the top of the window to move to tomorrow. Do you need to mark any special appointments or other events that are coming up tomorrow? Maybe your child would like to fill in her school calendar for each school day? Try it now. Don't forget about lunch and recess. After school, block out time for homework, recreation, and computing. (She might want to set an alarm to tell her when it's time to stop computing and move on to the bath or bed; we'll try that in a moment.) When her schedule is complete, let your child click on *File* in the menu bar, then click on the *Save* command. Have her type in an eight-letter name for this schedule—*thisweek* might be a good name.

Now your child can start *Calendar* at the beginning of each day, use the File menu and the Open command to choose *thisweek.cal*, consult her calendar for the day, and make any changes that are necessary. If Tuesday is gym day, for example, she'll know to wear sneakers to school.

If your child needs to add a new time, such as a half-hour interval for a music lesson, she can go to the Options menu and click on *Special Time*, type in the time, and select *AM* or *PM*. When she clicks on *Insert*, the time is entered into the calendar for the day. You can increment the time in minutes, whether you simply want to show *4:30 PM* or something more precise, like *11:18 AM*.

To get a monthly view, click on *View* and then on the command Month. The screen changes to show a calendar for this month. Notice that today's date is highlighted. Pick a special day this month, a birthday, holiday, or other important event. Then click on the day to highlight it. To mark the day, choose *Options* from the menu and then click on *Mark*. A list of five symbols appears. Click on the box next to the symbol you want to use. (You can mark a day with more than one symbol, if you want.) When your child clicks on *OK*, the monthly calendar is again displayed, and the special symbol marks the day.

Now that you've explored this monthly view a little, create a birthday calendar for special friends and family.

1. Use the File menu and select *New* for a new calendar. Your child can save *thisweek* before the new calendar is opened.

2. Click on *View* and then *Month*.

3. To go from month to month, use the arrow keys above the calendar. From the Options menu, *Mark* the birthdays.

4. When you are finished, save the file as *bdays*.

Let's try a few more exercises. Have your child open *thisweek.cal* again. Now, choose a time for an alarm to go off or enter a special time from the Options menu, if necessary. Just enter a time that's coming up in the next couple of minutes. Choose *Alarm* and then *Set*, with the pointer positioned on the time. Now, look at the Alarm menu again. See the check mark next to *Set*? To turn the alarm off, you would click *Set* again.

While you're waiting to hear the alarm, review this week's appointments. Do you want to change any? If you want to remove just one appointment, use the arrow keys to position the typing cursor on it and then press the Backspace key to erase. You can position the typing cursor to just remove or add a word if you wish. If you want to remove all the entries for a day, choose *Edit* and *Remove*. *Calendar* asks you to fill in a range of days where you want appointments erased.

Has the alarm gone off? When it does, you hear a series of beeps. You don't have to turn the alarm off—it just stops.

Connections

Now that you've played with *Calendar*, we'll mention some ways that you and your kids can use it. Depending upon your child's age and abilities with scheduling, you may want to help out.

(continued)

Connections (continued)

- Enter the school schedule into a calendar. The easiest way to get to a day of the month is to call up the monthly view. Then highlight the day you want and choose the daily view. Urge the kids to come up with special markers for things to remember, like a *0* for days when they need to wear sneakers or a dot to mean *bring violin.* Older children can learn to copy and paste (from the Edit menu) from one day to another, so they don't have to type in repetitive schedules; they simply drag the mouse pointer over the line of text to copy, then select *Copy* from the Edit menu. Next, they go to the new day, position the typing cursor at the correct time, and use the Edit menu to to *Paste* the schedule there.

- Have the kids set the alarm to tell them when it's time to start their homework or come to dinner.

- Type in a to-do list with the scheduled times for all the tasks involved in preparing a special event like a birthday party, a dinner, or a garage sale. When you're done, click on *Print* in the File menu to create a checklist.

- Have the kids print out their schedules each day or week to carry in their school bags. Or post the month's birthday calendar on the bulletin board. (If they want to add words to the monthly calendar, they'll have to write them in by hand.)

Calculator

Every child should learn to use a calculator—Windows' *Calculator* looks and acts pretty much like a real one. And, it's easy to keep it on the screen, minimized and ready for use when kids need it for homework assignments or reports. Open *Calculator* and try it now. When you see the window open, click on the minimize button in the upper righthand corner of the window. *Calculator* turns into an icon. Drag the icon to a convenient spot on the desktop and double click the icon to display *Calculator* again.

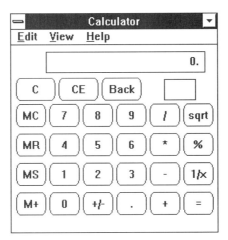

Figure 9.4 The Calculator window

The numbers appear in the center of the panel, set off in their own color. Have your child enter a number. Click on an operation: + (plus) for addition, − (minus) for subtraction, * (star) for multiplication, or / (slash) for division. Now enter another number and click on the equals sign (=) to see the result. (Older children can use the scientific calculator to figure logarithms and averages. They just click on *View* and then *Scientific*.)

Notice the *M* functions on the left side of the calculator. These let you store values in memory. Older children may want to read the Windows manual to find out more about how they can use the memory functions to run subtotals and multiple calculations to achieve a single result.

Connections

Hold competitive races to help the kids get used to the calculator. Two kids, one with a pencil and paper, one with *Calculator*, can race and then switch places, or you can race against your child. You can even use *Calendar* to set alarms so a single child can race against time to perform a series of calculations.

(continued)

Connections (continued)

Get the kids in the habit of using *Calculator* to add lists of numbers for budgets, perhaps the cost of favors for a birthday party. Or maybe your child wants to create a savings plan in order to accumulate allowances or other money for buying herself or someone else a special gift by a certain date. Both *Calendar* and *Calculator* can be used together for such planning.

Clock

There's a handy little clock in Windows. Click on it and then minimize it. Place it in a convenient spot on the screen to keep track of all the time you're spending playing with these Windows applications! Just double click the icon to play with the display. The Settings menu gives you the opportunity to use the clock as a learning tool for smaller children, because you can set the clock to look like a regular clockface or a digital readout with numbers. Your child can read the digital clock, then switch to *Analog* to see what the time looks like in a standard, old-fashioned clock display. Play a game with the analog view; let your child guess the time, then switch to digital view and see if she's correct. Choose *Seconds* to see a second hand. Let your child practice some basic Windows operations to drag at the sides and bottom of the clock and make it the size that's right for her. Then point out that she can drag the clock by the title bar to position it in a convenient place.

Cardfile

Cardfile is a fine way to introduce your child to the principles of *database management*. Although it isn't powerful enough for really "fancy" work, it's a good starter tool. A *database* is a collection of information, just like a real card file of names and addresses, a phone book, or a library catalog. Each item of information, a person's name and phone number, for example, is called a *record*. If you have twenty people in your phone book, you have twenty records. Each record contains blanks, sometimes called *fields*, for pieces of information about the person or other item. For example, the first blank in your card file might be for a name, and the second blank could be for a telephone number. Each record would use the blanks the same way, always including the name on the first blank line and the number on the second. After you enter information in your database, you can quickly search for a particular record. And speed is the big advantage of databases like *Cardfile*. It takes less time to find what you need with your computer than it does by "letting your fingers do the walking."

Open *Cardfile* and look at the window. You see a blank card for your first record. Notice the double line. Above the line goes the information that you can search on; this is called the *index line*. In a real card file, you'd sort your cards by what was written on this line. Let's get started by creating a simple telephone book for friends. First, have your child decide whether she wants to search the phone book by last name only, first name only, or just the whole name. Having made that decision, click on the Edit menu and choose *Index*. Let's say your child wants to be able to find Gina Clark by her whole name. She types in Gina Clark as the index and clicks on *OK*. Now we see *Gina Clark* above the double line.

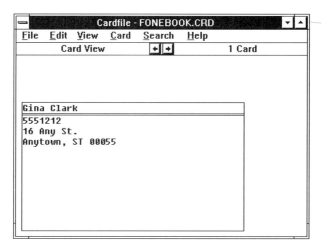

Figure 9.5 Windows Cardfile lets your child keep computerized lists.

It's time to enter Gina's phone number. If you have a modem and are using it with Windows, have your child type in the phone number just as she would dial it. It's okay to include hyphens (-) to separate the numbers, but she shouldn't include the area code for a local number. For a long-distance number, include the area code (and *1*, if necessary). On the second line under the double line, she enters Gina's street address—if this phone book is to include addresses as well. Next, she should add the town, state, and zip for Gina.

To add another record or card, click on *Card* and then *Add*. *Cardfile* automatically brings up the box where she enters the index. For the next record, she can type in the name of another person. Maybe your child can't remember the last name; that's okay, she can just enter the first name. As she continues to add cards, the cards appear in a stack on the screen. To see an alphabetized list of the records by index line, click on *View* and *List*. Now she can highlight a name and click on *View* and *Card* to look at the whole record.

Tip

You may wonder why we placed the phone number before the address. There's an important reason for this. If your modem is connected and set up to work with Windows (see your Windows manual), your child can dial a friend right from Card view. She just brings up the card she needs and chooses the Autodial command from the Card menu. *Cardfile* searches for the *first* number on the card and dials it. That's why we don't want any house numbers before phone numbers. As soon as your child hears the line ringing, she picks up the handset on the telephone. If she waits too long to pick up, and her friend picks up the phone with the modem "still talking" on your end, her friend will hear an earsplitting screech from the modem!

You can also add other information to the cards, like birthdays, notes about where you first met, pets' names, and so on. Explore the program a little and learn with your child to delete or duplicate cards. If, for example, two friends are in the same family, you may want to duplicate one card and just change the index line for the second family member.

Your child should get into the habit of using the File menu to save her card file at frequent intervals. This sample we've just created might be called *fonebook*. When you've completed a few entries, re-view them in Card view, using the arrow keys to go from card to card. Have your child click on the index line of a card she wants to see. To print out a displayed card, choose *Print* from the File menu. To print out all the cards, choose *Print All* from the File menu.

When you have a lot of cards, you might want to use the Search menu to find the card you need, rather than selecting it from List or Card view. This way, you can also search for text that isn't displayed on the index line. Say, for example, that your child wanted to locate that old pen pal from Normal, Kansas and can't remember his name. To find him, your child chooses *Find* from the Search menu. She types Normal to find all the records that contain that text. If she just types No, she may not get to her pen pal right away; *Cardfile* may find words like *Orono* or *North*. If she checks the box labeled *Match Case* (referring to upper- or lowercase), *Orono* won't be found. But the easiest way to search for text is to type in as many letters as you can that will correctly match the letters in the record.

You can't use the Find command to locate records by the index line information. Instead, you use *Go To* from the Search menu. It works much like *Find*. You can type in any letters from an index line—they don't even need to be the first letters. So, she could enter Clark to find Gina; or, if she has another Gina on her list, she could just enter Gina C or even cl for *Clark*.

Cardfile isn't as powerful as database programs you can buy sepa-rately from Windows. You can't, for example, print out a list of all the people in *fonebook* who have phone numbers beginning with *310*, or zip codes starting with *85*. The only sorting you can you can do is alphabetic, by index line. You have a choice of printing out one record or all records. However, *Cardfile* is an excellent introduction to database management and helps a child think in terms of data-bases.

Connections

In addition to the phone book we used in our example above, there are many other ways your child can use *Cardfile* to keep track of:

- **Recipes** The index might be the name of a recipe, for example, *Kimberley's Famous Brownies,* while the text would be ingredients and measurements. Your child can search using the index, or browse through recipes that contain, for example, the word *chocolate.*

- **Records, Tapes, or CDs** These can be indexed by artist or by the name of the recording.

- **Baseball Cards, Dolls, Stamps, or Coins** Hobby or toy collections can be easily tracked using *Cardfile.* A child can tell in an instant what she might like to trade for another item missing from her collection.

- **Software** Have your child keep track of a software collection —maybe all the software at your house. She can index on the product name, but also record the version number, the company phone number (this is a quick way to call for technical support, if you have a modem) and address, and even the serial number.

- **School Reports** For assembling facts to be used in school reports, *Cardfile* provides easy, quick access. The children can print these notes and use them during oral presentations too. A report on the Middle Ages might feature cards with index lines like: *Joan of Arc, Plague,* and *Unicorn Tapestries.*

- **Kids' Business** Robin's children keep track of their babysitting contacts using *Cardfile.* They include the name of the family, the phone number, the number and names of the children, and any notes as to the children's likes and dislikes. *Cardfile* works just as well for paper routes or a lawnmowing business.

Notepad

Windows *Notepad* is a very simple word processor. Just as its name says, it's for quick jottings and notes. *Notepad* doesn't work for long reports, but it's a nice introduction to typing text at the keyboard. And, it has a special time and date logging feature that makes it ideal for noting phone calls. Have your child practice by typing a phone message, perhaps a funny, imaginary message destined for you.

1. Choose *Time/Date* from the Edit menu. *Notepad* enters the time and date at the beginning of the message.

2. Ask the child to press the Enter key and point out how this places the typing cursor on a new line.

3. Now have your child take down a message, maybe something like,

   Aunt Mabel called and said that you should come right over. Her tabby cat has got his head caught in the fishbowl, and Aunt Mabel can't get it unstuck by herself. She says you have to come over now or she's going to go crazy.

   without pressing Enter. Point out how the text just stays on one line, and she can't see the beginning of that line. Now practice using the arrow keys, Home, and End to look at different parts of the text.

4. Show her how she can also use the arrows and box on the bottom scroll bar to move around the text. Click on the right pointing arrow to see more of the text. Now, have your child drag the box in the scroll bar all the way to the right. Notice how the end of the message is displayed.

5. To explore the principles of word wrap, where the lines of typing adjust to the size of the window, choose *Word Wrap* from the Edit menu. Look, you can see the whole message now, without using the scroll bar.

6. Now, make the *Notepad* window much smaller by dragging it on a couple of sides. Look at how the lines of text change. Use the righthand scroll bar to move the text up and down under the window.

7. Try out the Search menu and choose *Find* to move the pointer instantly to the word *you.*

The date- and time-stamping feature in *Notepad* makes it perfect for recording a short daily journal or quick messages like the one above. If you type the word .LOG at the beginning of a *Notepad* file, in uppercase letters, it records the time and date each time you open the file. That makes it easy for your child to keep track of phone calls as she works within Windows.

Children can also use the logging feature to track hours of music practice, household chores, or an exercise regime. Parents can log in their jogging or keep a diary of children's medical records.

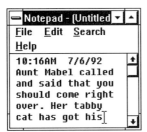

Figure 9.6 Here's a small *Notepad* window.

Kids can use their imaginations and pretend they are starship captains, with *Notepad* keeping a record of their experiences. Several kids can join in on the fun, adding entries and looking at new entries as they work with Windows.

Brothers and sisters can entertain each other by setting alarms for each other in *Calendar*. When the alarm goes off, the child at the computer consults the calendar, which might say, *Time to open Notepad and look at the jenny.txt file.* When the child opens the *Notepad* file, she sees a message (or a treasure-hunt clue) from a sibling.

Write

When your child has learned the basics and had some fun with *Notepad*, she'll be ready to try out *Write*, a more full-featured word processor that comes with Windows. *Write* is good for longer reports and schoolwork. And, your child can add pictures to her *Write* files. *Notepad* doesn't offer much control over paragraphs and typefaces, but *Write* can handle these features, as well as headers and footers, indents, tabs, and fonts. It can search, like *Notepad*, for a word or phrase but can also replace the searched-for text with new text that your child types in. We can't present a comprehensive tutorial here —there are too many features—but we will give you a brief overview, and after we discuss *Paintbrush*, we'll show you how your child can combine words and pictures.

Have your child start off by writing a letter to a friend or family member, keeping in mind that she is going to add a simple picture later on. If your child has started a phone book with *Cardfile*, urge her to pick someone whose address is in that file. After she's written a few lines, show her the ruler, which she can turn on from the Document menu. The ruler can be used to justify the current paragraph, so that all the lines are the same length, or so that the text is lined up on the right or left side of the page. When your child wants to start a new paragraph, she can just press Enter. Don't let her indent the first lines of paragraphs with tabs or spaces; we'll do that later, automatically.

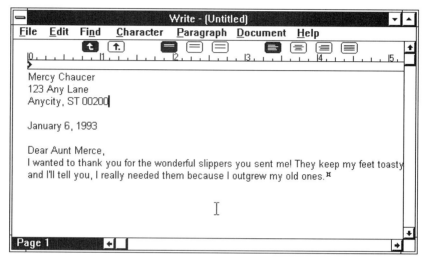

Figure 9.7 This is *Write* with the ruler turned on.

Have your child enter a headline, on its own line, to set off the picture she'll be putting in later. Now, show her how she can drag the cursor over the headline text to highlight it. When the text is highlighted, have her center it using the ruler above the workspace.

Tip

The ruler works the same way for making text double- or triple-spaced, especially useful for school reports. Often it's easiest to write a report single-spaced, then double-space it before printing it out for the teacher to read.

With the headline still selected, explore the Character menu—there your child can experiment with boldface, italics, and other styles. She can change the size or font of the headline until she finds a pleasing look.

Don't have your child leave more than a line or so for the picture. On the line where the picture will go, have her insert a marker by typing in the word baba. Later, she can use *Write's* Find command to locate the spot.

Continue with the letter, perhaps relating some interesting events from the past week or so. To try out *Write's* find feature, have her write a paragraph about another family member or pet. But ask your child to enter a silly, wrong name for the person or animal. Then, let her use the arrow keys to position the cursor at the beginning of the paragraph. Your child already knows what searching for a word is like, she tried it out with *Notepad.* So go one step further now, choosing *Replace* from the Find menu. Now, your child can explore the possibilities of the replace feature by typing in the wrong name and then the correct name in the blanks in the Replace window. She'll enjoy watching *Write* do its magic, and she can keep searching and replacing until she's discovered all the possibilities.

Point out to her how useful this feature can be when she discovers a misspelling in a school report and wants to make sure all the wrong spellings are replaced with the correct spelling. (*Write* doesn't have a spellchecker, and this may be just as well for younger children, who really need to know how to use the dictionary.) Show her how she can specify whole words only to avoid finding word fragments. For example, if you search for the word *mind* and don't specify the whole word, you'll find words like *reminder* and *mindless* as well.

You can create games with this feature by letting kids search for words within words—kids love to find the little words within bigger words, and often, this game will open their eyes to new facts about our language.

Finally, have your child try out the Windows Clipboard, using the Cut, Copy, and Paste commands from the Edit menu. The Clipboard is a place to keep text or pictures that are copied or cut from a file. Only one picture or block of text is kept at a time, and it disappears when you end your Windows session or cut or copy another item. You can often use the Clipboard to move or copy items from one program to another; you can always use it within the same application to move items from one location or file to another. Before using the Clipboard, your child should save the letter. Yes, you guessed it, she uses the File menu.

1. Your child should move to the beginning of the letter by using the righthand scroll bar or the arrow keys, or by holding down the Control key and pressing the Home key.

2. If your child has a phone book card file, have her open *Cardfile* now and find the address card for the person she's writing to. Now she can use *Copy* in the Edit menu to capture the address for the person she's writing to. (Since the name is probably used as the index, she can't copy it.) She just drags the typing cursor over the address information.

3. Have your child close *Cardfile* and return to *Write*. She simply chooses *Paste* from *Write*'s Edit menu, and, voila, the address information is inserted.

If your child hasn't started a *Cardfile* phone book, just let her try cutting, copying, and pasting some text within the letter, using the Edit menu.

You can also set tabs in *Write*, just as you can with a typewriter, so perhaps your child would like to include a short list in her letter. Maybe she'd like to describe each of her best friends, for example, or her pets, or her activities on a typical day. Choose an interesting subject that your child enjoys writing about. First, make sure the ruler is displayed. We'll use a sample list just for the purposes of this exercise.

1. First, type a title for the list:

My Best Friends

2. Now, use the ruler to center the title on the page. Next, choose the Character menu and pick a new font with the Fonts command.

3. With the title still highlighted, choose *Bold* from the Character menu to add emphasis. (Notice that the menu tells you that you can also use Ctrl+B to boldface selected text.)

4. Now it's time to start the list. Type:

Mary Ann

leaving the typing cursor after the last *n*.

5. Move the mouse pointer to the first Tab symbol on the ruler, the up arrow with the curved stem. Click on the Tab symbol.

6. Click beneath the measurement line on the ruler in the spot where the first tab should go. Try 1.5 inches, midway between the 1 and the 2 on the ruler. Now press the Tab key. The typing cursor jumps to a point 1.5 inches from the left margin. Your child should type a short description of Mary Ann, like:

Enjoys swimming and math.

7. To enter the next person's information, she presses Enter and repeats the steps. When she is done, she might have a list like this:

Mary Ann	Enjoys swimming and math
Joe	Likes to read murder mysteries
Danielle	Plays a mean piano

If your child wants to adjust the tabs to make the columns closer together, for example, she can just use the mouse to move the tab symbol on the ruler line to the left. After she lifts her finger from the mouse button, all the text in the second column moves too.

The ruler can control paragraph indents also. Now is a good time to point out the dot in the right arrow that starts the ruler line. If you drag that dot to the right, maybe to a half inch or so, the first lines of all the paragraphs in the letter are indented a half inch. After the first lines have been indented, you can grab the arrow itself and drag it a little to the right. The right margin then moves over. (By using the bottom scroll bar, you can also locate the right margin arrow beneath the measurement line. Sometimes its fun to set off special text by indenting it within a letter or report.) Using the ruler, you can control text simply and visually.

By now, saving a file frequently should be second nature. Use the File menu to save this letter. Next, minimize *Write* to an icon. We're going to check out another exciting Windows program, but we'll be coming back to *Write*.

Paintbrush

Like *Write*, *Paintbrush* is one of the more capable programs that comes with Windows. And, it works hand in hand with *Write*, so that your child can quickly and easily merge words and images in her documents. Plus, *Paintbrush* pictures can be used with other word processors as well. Furthermore, *Paintbrush* loads several different types of images, so your child can take a picture she's created in *Kid Pix*, for example, and work on it with *Paintbrush*.

Start your child out with a simple picture, maybe one of a house (your house? her dream house? the house where an imaginary character lives?). For our example, we've chosen the house of the witch, Baba Yar. A good way to learn *Paintbrush* is to take a picture like this and to try duplicating it using *Paintbrush* tools. The toolbar is located in two columns at the left of the window. At the bottom is the palette, where you click on a color of your choice.

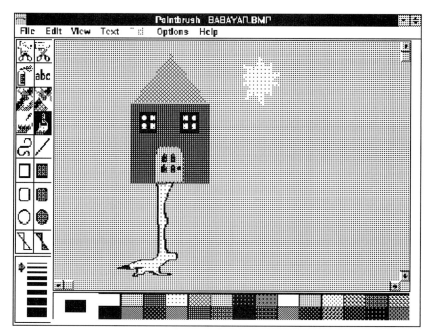

Figure 9.8 Paintbrush is packed with tools and colors that helped us make Baba Yar's house.

Before you start, maximize the *Paintbrush* window. For the sake of simplicity, the picture you and your child create should be no larger than the size of the workspace you see on the screen.

To draw the outline of the house, she chooses the hollow rectangle tool, the one with no fill. Click on the tool. Now she positions the cursor where you want the upper lefthand corner of the house to be. The cursor changes to a crosshair. Drag out a rectangle. You now have a black outline for the main part of the witch's house. But we want to use a color for the house, so your child should click on the Rectangular Scissors tool and drag out a dotted rectangle that encloses the one she's drawn. Try it now. When the rectangle is enclosed by the dotted lines, choose *Cut* from the Edit menu to erase the shape. The Scissors tools make it easy to get rid of mistakes.

Now your child should choose a color for the witch's house. That decision made, she's ready to use the filled Rectangle tool and hold down the Shift key as she drags out a square shape for the house. Next, she can use Filled Rectangle tool to draw a window, perhaps in black this time. But don't let her do it yet! To quickly and easily draw windowpanes, use the Edit menu. First, she can draw one pane. Then she should outline it with the Rectangular Scissors tool. When the shape is outlined, she chooses first *Copy* and then *Paste* from the Edit menu. The copied pane appears in the top lefthand corner of the workspace. Now she can drag that pane down to the position next to the first one. Finally, she can use the Rectangular Scissors tool to outline both panes, copy them, and paste them below the first pair.

If there are white lines left on the window rectangle, have her choose *Zoom In* from the View menu and position the block that appears over Baba Yar's window. Now she can fill in the white lines with the colors of her choice. First, she selects a color from the palette. Then, she can click on individual blocks of color shown on the screen or, to work more quickly, drag the mouse over the blocks. When the window looks the way she likes, she should copy and paste it to make a second window.

Now your child is ready to place the triangular roof on the house. She should first pick a color, maybe green, and click on the Filled Angled shape tool at the bottom of the tool bar. First, she clicks at the top left of the house, where the roof should start; then she drags a line up to the point where the roof peak should be. Next, she clicks at the right top of the house square—a line connects the two points—and finally, she clicks again where she started. When the roofline is complete, the triangular shape fills with green.

To create the chicken's foot that Baba Yar's house sits on, your child is going to use the Paintbrush tool. First, she can select a shape for the Paintbrush by double clicking it. When she has a shape she'd like to use, she's ready. Now she should carefully draw outline of the foot, dragging the paintbrush cursor. If she makes a mistake, she can erase the problem, using the righthand Eraser tool from the tool bar. (Also, point out the Undo command at the top of the Edit menu. It remembers the last thing you did and undoes it.) Complete the foot by closing off its shape entirely, so there are no breaks in the line of the limb.

Now, she should choose another color to use to fill the foot. She should choose the Paint Roller, which fills a closed shape with a color. When your child clicks inside the foot, it is flooded with the new color.

To create the yellow sun she should start by making a circle, holding down the Shift key as she draws. This is a guide only; now she uses the Filled Angled shape tool again to create a closed series of spikes around the circle.

The door in Figure 9.8 was first created away from the body of the house, using the Rounded Rectangle tool; then we cut the shape off at the bottom. The outline for the door was drawn in Zoom view. The door panels were made using the Filled Circle tool to create an ellipse, which was then cut off at the bottom to form an arch shape. When a panel is complete, it can be copied to make the others.

We've chosen a simple picture for our example, but your child may want to add some special flourishes, like roof tiles and a chimney, or the ground where the house sits. She can try using the Paint Roller to color the background.

When the drawing is complete, use the File menu and choose *Save*. Give the picture a meaningful name: *babayar* would make sense. Now, your child is ready to combine words and pictures in a *Write* document.

Using *Write* and *Paintbrush* Together

It's easy to add pictures to your *Write* files with the Windows Clipboard. We've already used the Clipboard to copy parts of windows in the house. Now, we'll show you how you can take copying and pasting one step further.

1. Make sure the whole picture fits in the *Paintbrush* workspace. Maximize the window, if it isn't maximized already.

2. Have your child select the Rectangular Scissors tool and draw out a rectangle to enclose the whole picture.

3. She should choose *Copy* from the Edit menu.

4. Double click on the desktop background. The Task List window appears. To switch to *Write*, have your child double click on its name in the list. Point out that this is just another way of switching among the programs on the desktop.

5. The *Write* window opens, displaying the letter that your child was just working on. Does she want to include Baba Yar's house in this document? If not, choose *New* from the File menu. For our example, we'll assume that she does want this drawing in her letter.

6. Use *Find* to locate the word *baba*. Cancel the Find window and highlight the word; press the Del key. Now the cursor is on the line where she'd like to add the picture. Have her choose *Paste* from the Edit menu. And there it is!

7. Let's center the illustration. Have your child click on it and point out how it changes to show that it's selected. Now, choose *Move Picture* from the Edit menu.

8. Roll the mouse (now shown on the screen as a double block) to center the picture and watch how the outline shows the new position of the picture. When you or your child clicks, the image is placed.

You can't move the picture up and down this way. Instead, you must add or erase lines to change its vertical position. Try pressing Enter and few times to watch the picture move down the page. Your child may also want to try the Edit menu's Size Picture command to make the picture smaller or larger. This process works much like moving. You size the picture from the right or left side, or from the bottom. As you move the mouse, the outline gets larger or smaller. If you position the pointer at one of the two bottom corners, you can change the length and width at the same time. When you click, the picture resizes to fill the new outline.

When your child saves her letter, the picture will be saved with it. Windows allows you to link pasted items with their original applications, so that when you change the picture in *Paintbrush*, it is also updated in the *Write* document. But this is an advanced feature; if you and your child are interested, take a look at the Windows manual for more information.

This completes our look at *Paintbrush* and *Write*, two of Windows' most useful programs.

CHAPTER
10

PLAN VI: COMMUNICATING WITH OTHERS—PRODIGY

The software you'll need: The Prodigy Service

Why it's special: Prodigy is not a computer program. It's known as an *online service* on a faraway mainframe computer. For a monthly fee, you can use your phone line, a modem, and Prodigy's software to access as many services as you like.

Ages it appeals to: Five and up

Activities: Make friends; find a pen-pal; exchange letters; talk to a group by leaving messages on a bulletin board; play games.

What you'll need: Prodigy software, modem, and a telephone line that does not feature call waiting.

Introducing Prodigy E-Mail

We tend to think of computing as a solitary experience. And we tend to think of kids who compute as antisocial nerds. You know the stereotype—the under-athletic, brainy type who sits alone, pecking at the keyboard all day.

Well, that may be the stereotype, but the reality is very different. Computers open the door to a vast community of friends and colleagues. A computer is also a way to get the most current information about a wide variety of topics. When you connect a modem to a computer and dial an online service, you are connected to people all over the country. You can hone in on those who share your interests, those who are mentors in a given field, or on those people who want to share a bit of their lives with you.

For a child, this telecomputing experience is liberating and exhilarating. Suddenly he is part of a virtual community with other computer kids. If his hobby happens to be butterfly collecting, and there are no other butterfly collectors in town, then the computer becomes a way to share that experience. Or, he can use the vast reference materials available online to explore his hobby. If the child is experiencing a tough social situation in school, then conversing with an electronic penpal can help vent some emotion. And if the child is an urbanite, finding a rural electronic penpal offers a view of a different lifestyle. And through it all, the child is writing—communicating thoughts and emotions. Since the feedback is much more immediate than that from a handwritten letter, there's a real incentive to keep communicating.

By coupling the computer with the telephone, you usher your child to new computing horizons. The magic that makes this kid/computer/telephone relationship work is an online service. An online service is basically a bank of mainframe computers in a distant city; you access it from your PC, using a modem and a telephone line. Some services offer 800 numbers, but most have local access numbers in many cities. If you live in a rural town, you may have to pay for a long-distance telephone call to use an online service. Once you're connected, everything on the mainframes is available to you —just as if you were working on a local terminal. The best online services feature a variety of services—everything from stock quotes to electronic mail.

The best online service for families is Prodigy. Unlike other services, which offer few options for children and boast plain-text screens that reveal their mainframe connections, Prodigy is graphical. The graphics are not entirely state-of-the-art. What you get doesn't rival a Saturday morning animation fest, but the screens are interactive. An online version of *The National Geographic* may take your child on a tour of the Serengeti Plain or the Black Forest using maps, as well as pictures of the landscape, animals, and people. Your child can explore the territory at leisure or move to a different screen and join The Club, a corner of Prodigy where kids can get acquainted and talk about their interests, concerns, and problems. (Adults who talk down to them seem to be a favorite topic).

Be aware, however, that one reason that Prodigy looks so pretty is because it is trying to sell you something each time you use it. Prodigy is the only online service that features graphical advertising on every screen. You can click on those ads and move to screens that tell more about the products. From *those* screens, you (or your child) can place an order. Prodigy offers its customers the option of storing a credit card number online and using it to make purchases. Many adults with children prefer either to enter the card number only when making a purchase or to store the number under a parents' password, so that the kids cannot help themselves at random.

Not surprisingly, the ads are Prodigy's least celebrated feature. Just as people complain about television commercials, Prodigy users complain about the ads. But even if you're not inclined to shop online, don't let the ads turn you off on Prodigy. They're almost as easy to ignore as the ads in the Sunday newspaper. But they are there if you need them and, like newspaper advertising, they keep the price of the media low. With advertising revenue to subsidize the service, Prodigy can offer the service to families at a dynamite price. A family of six can spend as much time as they want on Prodigy for a monthly fee of $12.95. That compares to $12.80 for just one hour on online competitor CompuServe!

Don't let the idea of another recurring monthly cost sour you on Prodigy. Where else can you find subscription entertainment offerings at this price? Compare the $12.95 to cable TV or the cost of the videos you rent in a month. Prodigy's legions of offerings for kids and families vastly outnumber what comes across your TV cable.

And, because it's interactive and PC-based, Prodigy presents kids with possibilities no cable channel ever could.

Think of Prodigy as the Disney channel of the online world. The Prodigy staff works hard to keep it wholesome. The service has drawn fire from First Amendment defenders for its habit of censuring strong language in messages and on bulletin boards. But the practice does insure that children of any age can log on and browse the service at their leisure without happening into discussions their parents would find inappropriate. Services for kids are structured with fun and learning in mind. So much so that quite a few schools subscribe.

And lest you think that you, the parents, are being left out in the cold, take another look. Prodigy offers a variety of services that helps kids and parents. For instance, if either is plagued by the problems of growing up, they can Jump to *Ask Beth*, a kind of "Dear Abby" for modern families. Parents can also see what the experts say by Jumping to the parenting center and reviewing articles by noted experts on childrearing. There they can also post questions on the Homelife Bulletin Board. And, if information on family fun and nutrition is what you're looking for, Jump to *Vacation*. The Prodigy Vacation Guide features travel information about Hawaii, Florida, New England, and the country's major cities. For tips on nutrition and medical concerns, Jump to the Consumer Reports Health Guide.

And Prodigy keeps the service fresh with new offerings. As we were preparing this book for print, Prodigy announced The Baby-Sitters' Club for teens. This service, which follows the adventures of the members of the Baby-Sitters' Club from the book series by children's author Ann Martin, carries a monthly membership fee. (Prodigy allows parents to control access to extra-cost services.) Members can chat with one another via e-mail and a bulletin board, follow special online stories about the Baby-Sitters' Club characters, and even leave messages for Ms. Martin. New services for preschoolers will be added this fall. Nowhere will you find so many online services for kids.

To check into Prodigy, you'll first need to install the service's communications software on your PC or Mac. Startup kits sell for $49.95, but you find them for less in the PC departments of large merchandisers. And, of course, you'll need a modem to link your PC to a telephone line. You shouldn't even think about using Prodigy if you don't have a 2,400-baud modem. Prodigy will work with slower modems but not well. You really won't be able to enjoy the service if you have to wait a long time—and with a 1,200-baud modem you will wait a long time for Prodigy's graphics to move down the telephone line to your PC.

For those who lack modems or the determination to set one up, Prodigy offers a special $179.95 startup kit that bundles the software with a plug-and-play Hayes 2,400-baud modem. And, like the software-only package, you can often find the modem startup kit priced much lower at discount merchandisers.

Quick Tour

It's easy to log on. On a PC-compatible put the Prodigy disk into your A drive, type install, and answer the questions in front of you. The software prompts you to enter information about your computer and where you live. Once it knows, it presents you with a list of local access numbers, and you select the one you'll normally call.

If you have a Mac, copy the Prodigy software to a folder on your hard disk. Click on the Prodigy Service icon to start the program. The first time you use the software, you will be asked several questions about your computer configuration and asked for your local access phone number which you look up in the guide provided.

Then it's time to log on. Enter the Prodigy Service ID and password that comes with the software. Once you're on the service, you can change your password to whatever you like and assign passwords to your kids. You'll want to give each child his or her own password, so that friends they make online will be sure to send messages to them and not to you. This also serves the purpose of keeping the kids away from your bank account and credit card number if you're in the habit of using two of Prodigy's more convenient adult features— online shopping and banking.

After you log in, Prodigy greets you with a screen called *Highlights*, showing headlines at the top, followed by a list of ads and promotions. Each item bears a number, which you can enter or click on to go directly to a screen that gives you more information on the subject.

At the bottom of the screen is the command bar: *Next, Menu, Find, Jump, Path, Tools, Help, Exit*. On all Prodigy screens, you can click on an item with the mouse, tab through items, or type the number or first letter of an item to select it. You can click on *Menu*, type m, or Tab over to it and press Enter or Return to bring up a menu of general topics you'll find on Prodigy. This brings up three screens of Choices: *Guide, News and Features,* and *Information.* These include: *News and Features, Living, Shopping, Money, Travel,* and *Computers.* Under each one lies another menu with many options. For instance, click on *Living,* and up pops another menu with the options: *Information, Entertainment, Funhouse, For Kids, Lifestyles, Health, Travelog, Computing,* and *Food.* And from there you can access a wealth of information on any one of those topics.

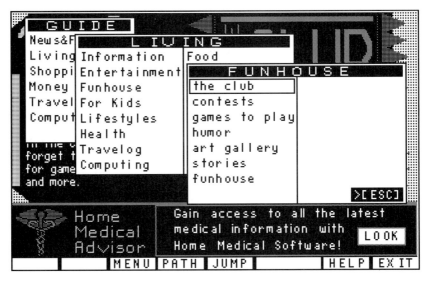

Figure 10.1 Prodigy's menus cover a wide range of family topics.

It's easy enough to find your way around Prodigy by clicking your way through the menus. And why not? You're paying nothing extra for the time it takes to do it. But once you become familiar with Prodigy's offerings, you'll want to use some shortcuts to get directly to the options you use often. And Prodigy offers these too.

After you and your child have explored Prodigy and picked your favorite haunts, each of you can set up a personal path to go directly to them in the sequence you specify. Or you can use the Jump command to go directly to one point from another, bypassing the menus in between. Prodigy also features a series of shortcut keys that help you move efficiently through the service.

Before starting, you should know a bit about the commands and shortcuts you can access from the primary screens. Once you're on the service, you'll find that some screens have their own set of commands and shortcuts that you'll also want to explore.

Figure 10.2 Prodigy's Jump menu is a shortcut to fun.

The Jump Command

The Jump command is important. Learn this command. You'll use it in the exercises that follow. You'll find the Jump command at the bottom of the screen. Click on it to bring up the Jump menu. This is one menu that you and your child should become familiar with soon after you join the service. From here, you can view a list of topics to jump to and then get to them by using the Find, Guide, and Index commands you see listed on the menu. *Find* allows you to enter a subject you want to look up, and Prodigy will identify the areas of the service that can accommodate you. *Guide* gives you a description of where to find things. *Index* brings up an index of Jump words that you can use to get directly to the service you need.

You'll also use the Jump command to get printouts of Prodigy screens. Simply click on it or Tab to it and press Enter. The Jump menu pops up in the upper left of your screen. In this window, click on *Print a Copy* or Tab to it and press Enter. You'll see Prodigy's miniature wristwatch come onto the screen, indicating that you should pause while Prodigy takes action. In a moment, you'll hear your printer printing out the text.

Your Personal Path

A Prodigy *path* is exactly what the name implies—a path you follow through Prodigy whenever you log on. Like *Jump,* the Path command appears at the bottom of every screen. Whenever you click on *Path,* Prodigy takes you to the next feature you listed as a favorite in your personal path. Click again and you go to the next, in whatever order you specified.

It's a marvelous feature for adults and older children, who generally lack patience to roam through the menus. But we've found that young children prefer to explore. It's up to you and your child whether to use it. If you wish to customize your own path, here's how:

Select *Tools* from the main menu. At the Tools menu, choose *Personal Path* (or *Change Path* on the Mac), and you see a list of items on a path that Prodigy has created for you. When you join the service, Prodigy assigns you a default path, which you then edit to include the features you want.

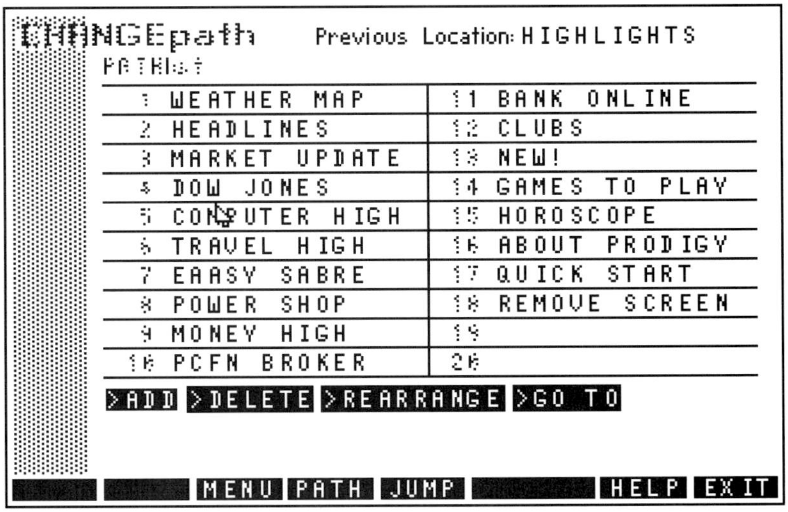

```
CHANGEpath        Previous Location: HIGHLIGHTS
  PATH list:
    1  WEATHER  MAP        11  BANK  ONLINE
    2  HEADLINES           12  CLUBS
    3  MARKET  UPDATE      13  NEW!
    4  DOW  JONES          14  GAMES  TO  PLAY
    5  COMPUTER  HIGH      15  HOROSCOPE
    6  TRAVEL  HIGH        16  ABOUT  PRODIGY
    7  EAASY  SABRE        17  QUICK  START
    8  POWER  SHOP         18  REMOVE  SCREEN
    9  MONEY  HIGH         19
   10  PCFN  BROKER        20
   >ADD >DELETE >REARRANGE >GO TO

        MENU PATH JUMP        HELP EXIT
```

Figure 10.3 Prodigy's Change Path screen lets you chart your course.

We recommend that you not bother with the path until you've fully explored the service and know what you want. If you immediately set one up for you and your child, based on what you think you will be interested in, you risk missing many of the delightful services that Prodigy offers. Take some time to look around.

The Shortcut Keys

If you lack a mouse and tire of tabbing over to the commands at the bottom of the screen, you can get around by using Prodigy's shortcut keys. Here's a list for PC-compatible users:

PgDn	Invokes the Next command to get to the next text screen in whatever area you happen to be
PgUp	Invokes the Back command to return to the previous screen if you want to review what you just read
F9	Invokes the Menu command to go to the last menu screen you were on
F4	Invokes the Path command to go to the next location on your personal Path
F2	Invokes the Action command on ad screens to bring up an order form to purchase the product. (Don't tell the kids about this one!)
F1	Invokes the Help command to bring up online help
F6	Invokes the Jump command to bring up the Jump menu

To see more shortcuts, choose Jump and type "Help Hub" Select "Shortcuts" from the menu.

Now that you know how to get around Prodigy, it's time to introduce your child to it. The service features many options for kids. Here we'll show you how to use just a few. By mastering these, your child will gain the skills to become a Prodigy adventurer and begin his own exploration.

And because it is a national service that is used by parents and children across the nation, you and your child can begin using Prodigy to communicate with people across the country, make friends, find pen pals, and send letters that arrive at their destination in minutes.

In fact, there's so much to be said about Prodigy that we're devoting two chapters to it. This chapter stresses the communications part of Prodigy. We'll show you how your child can use Prodigy as a homework helper and electronic penpal. The next chapter will introduce your child to the marvelous resources for research and information-gathering that exist online.

Step-by-Step Tour

We begin our excursion through Prodigy with an introduction to the online community, the universe of people who become acquainted through their keyboard. With a modem and your Prodigy software, your child can dial up the service and communicate with other members, meet children of the same age, compete with others in online games, exchange notes about hobbies and mutual interests, and even find mentors to help them advance with their skills and schoolwork.

But to do this, they must first connect to Prodigy and get to know other users while they make themselves known. The best place to do this is a *bulletin board.* An online bulletin board is the computerized equivalent of the kind of bulletin board your kids find at their schools and in their classrooms, or you find in a grocery or community building. It's a place to post public messages. Often, those who respond to messages find that they have interests to share, become friends, and begin exchanging mail. The online equivalent of mail is *electronic mail,* sometimes called *e-mail.* It's much like real mail, but these letters don't go in a big blue mailbox. Instead, they're sent via your PC and across a phone line to an online service that serves as a kind of electronic post office where the person you're writing to can retrieve them.

Prodigy offers a number of bulletin boards where adult members can exchange information about special interests. But there is a special one just for kids. It's called The Club. If you and your child are new to Prodigy, it's a good idea to explore The Club together. Below we describe the choices and options The Club makes available to kids. Point them out and show your child how to use them. Once the kids get the hang of it, they don't need you there. And, they probably won't *want* you there. This is, after all, their haunt.

The Club is for kids under 18, and it offers a variety of bulletin boards geared to the things that interest kids in particular age groups. From within The Club, your children can access bulletin boards devoted to various subjects. To get to The Club, click on the Jump command at the bottom of the screen and enter the club in the space in the menu that appears.

Figure 10.4 The Club offers a variety of activities for children.

Prodigy takes you to The Club's main screen. From here, you can access a variety of interesting activities. Most are for kids, but you can also get to some other family activities from this menu. The first two options on the menu relate to the bulletin board that we are interested in. Click on the first option to go directly to the bulletin board. Click on the second item to learn more about how to use them and about Prodigy's expectations that the messages posted there will conform to general standards of good taste.

Beneath those two options are other options which change from time to time. These take your child to a host of other activities. One option is Stories, which is just as its name suggests. Clicking on *Stories* takes your child to a virtual library, where kids can call up stories and read them online.

Games carries your child off to an area where both kids and adults can access games to play. You'll want to steer your kids to the online *Carmen Sandiego* game. This one is similar, but not identical, to the *Carmen Sandiego* software we discussed in Chapter 2. It's a special adaptation for Prodigy. But because the game coming to your computer over a phone line, instead of from your hard disk, the play is slower and not quite as engaging; you also have to provide your own almanac.

Many of the other games on this menu are for adults. *CEO*, for instance, is a business simulation game that might interest kids in Junior Achievement clubs but could cause young children's eyes to glaze over. Baseball Manager is a fantasy baseball league that carries a steep additional fee of $119 per year. Best to keep the kids away from that one unless you're willing to foot the bill!

Also on The Club's menu is *Science Center*, a section of Prodigy sponsored by the Public Broadcasting Service's *Nova* program, where the kids can engage in graphical, interactive, science excursions. And, you'll find an online encyclopedia, perfect for research. We'll discuss both these options in the next chapter.

Our first foray into The Club will be to the bulletin board, so click on *Bulletin Board* to go to a screen where you're given more options. Click on *Bulletin Board* again to go directly to the bulletin board. Notice that the next option alerts Prodigy sysops (system operators) to problem notes. If you see something that's offensive to you, you can click on this option and send a note to Prodigy. System operators will consider your complaint and remove a note from the boards, if they agree that it violates Prodigy rules.

When you click on the Bulletin Boards option, you see a large fill-in-the-form options screen. The form is designed to take kids quickly to the kinds of messages that interest them. Since you're new here, don't start with the form right away. Select the *Write a Public Note* option at the bottom of the screen to post a message and introduce yourself.

Figure 10.5 Children choose the topics they wish to get involved with on a Prodigy bulletin board.

After you click on *Write a Public Note,* you'll see a list of topics on the righthand side of the screen, identifying the subject matter already under discussion on the bulletin board. These include such subjects as: Schoolwork (6-12) (12-14) (13-18), College Prep, Lit (where young readers and budding writers can talk about books), Music, Fashion, Sports, Games, Film/TV/Video, Hobbies, and Wheels.

The kids can pick any topic here that interests them by simply clicking on it. We'll start with *Hobbies.* Click on it, and another menu pops up on the lefthand side of the screen. This one lists different hobby topics that a child can write about. If you have a pet in your house, look for a pet related topic like *About Animals* to write a short note about life with pets.

Up pops a memo form where you'll compose your note. Let's leave the top line, the one addressed *To:,* blank to indicate that we're writing to everyone who reads messages on the board. Notice that Prodigy has filled in the *Subject* line; it automatically says *About Animals.* In the space below, you'll compose your note. Click in the upper lefthand corner of the space to move the cursor there and begin typing. Your kids can personalize their notes in any way they want. But it's a good idea, when starting out, to type a short introduction, giving your name, age and interests, so that others who share your hobbies will be better able to respond. It's also a good idea to prompt other users to respond by asking questions and requesting information. That way, the kids connect to one another quickly. An example would be something like this:

Hello everyone on Prodigy. My name is Lisa. I am 10 years old and live in Cincinnati, Ohio. I have a pet dog named Riney. She is a black-and-brown German Shepherd. We also have an aquarium, but we only have guppies right now. I would like to hear from anyone who has tropical fish because I am thinking of getting some and would like to know which ones you recommend.

Thanks,

Lisa

If your child writes a long message and fills the page, simply click on *Next* to bring up a new page and continue writing. When you've finished with the letter, click on *OK.* A menu pops up. Here you should click on *I have finished writing. Submit my note and return to Main Menu.* Prodigy will do exactly what you request and take you back to the Read Public Notes form.

If you've never before checked into Prodigy, you'll have to change the date in the See Notes Added Since box to a few days before the current date, so you can see what others have been talking about recently. If this isn't your first time on Prodigy, note that Prodigy remembers the last date you checked in and displays it in the box. All you'll have to do is pick a topic and then click on *OK* to see messages that were posted since the last time you logged in. You can simply browse the notes by reading them and clicking on *Next Note* when you reach the end. But if the subject of one of the notes interests you, you can click on *Read Replies* to see how others responded and follow the train of thought. In the online community, this train of thought is often called a *thread* because the conversation threads from one related idea to the next, kind of like a conversation. When you've finished with a thread, you can click on *Next Subject* to go on to the next topic.

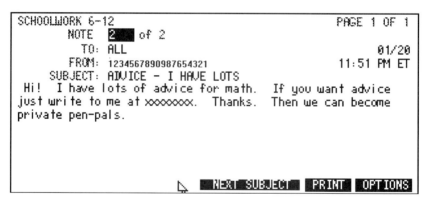

```
SCHOOLWORK 6-12                                  PAGE 1 OF 1
        NOTE  2  of 2
         TO: ALL                                    01/20
       FROM: 1234567890987654321              11:51 PM ET
    SUBJECT: ADVICE - I HAVE LOTS
 Hi!  I have lots of advice for math.  If you want advice
just write to me at xxxxxxxx.  Thanks.  Then we can become
private pen-pals.



                              ▷ ■ NEXT SUBJECT ■ PRINT ■ OPTIONS
```

Figure 10.6 Children can read notes addressed to everyone on a bulletin board.

If you tire of a subject, you can click on Next Subject to move to the next subject on the Prodigy menu. The option simply moves you to the next in order. To get to a particular subject, click on *Options*. This brings up a menu that allows you to select mail options from a menu.

After your child posts notes on the bulletin boards, it won't be long before he starts to get responses. Some kids will post replies on the bulletin board for all Prodigy members to see. Others are likely to answer with electronic mail (e-mail). E-mail offers a fun way for kids to develop writing skills. Once kids find one another online, they often become pen pals and swap mail regularly.

Prodigy offers an easy way for your kids to record the user numbers of their pen pals. Whenever they receive electronic mail from another child, the Options menu offers an opportunity for them to record the person's user number in the address book. After reading the mail, simply click on *Options.* Then click on *Add User # to Your Address Book.* Prodigy records the user number and lets you assign a nickname to it. We like to use the person's first name as the nickname.

Whenever your child wants to write to someone whose user number they recorded in the address book, they only have to jump to Mailing List to look up the number and make sure they're addressing their e-mail properly. As your child composes his e-mail message, he need only enter the number in the *To:* field. Prodigy presently has no way of automatically entering numbers from the address list, so your child will have to type it in manually.

CHAPTER

11

PLAN VII: ONLINE RESEARCH WITH ONLINE SERVICES

The software you'll need: Prodigy

Why it's special: The Prodigy online interactive service features graphical learning games that take kids into the archives of *The National Geographic* and the PBS science program, *Nova.*

Ages it appeals to: Five and up

Activities: Take a tour of a country or travel back through history to visit some of your favorite characters.

What you'll need: Prodigy software, modem, and a telephone line that does not feature call waiting.

Introducing Prodigy's Library

The Hapless Homework Hour. You know what we mean. It's that time in the evening when you pull out all the stops to help the kids through homework problems and school assignments that even you do not understand. How many times have the kids' questions stumped you more than they did them? "Mom, if the square root of 9 is 3, what's the square root of 27?" Or, "What is air made of?"

How many times have you packed up the kids and hauled them off to the library in the hope that they could find the answers there? Or turned to the dated encyclopedias on the bookshelf in the family room only to find no listings that could help? Parent-child puzzlement over homework has been an evening malady in American homes for generations. And the fast pace of today's world isn't making it any easier. Or is it?

The fast pace, after all, is what brought the PC into your home. And did you know that with a PC and a modem you can link into some of the finest, most up-to-date, information sources? Information databases of all stripes live on the giant mainframe computers that play host to online services. And the Prodigy service is no exception.

Prodigy, with its home-and-family orientation, is an especially good information source for kids. Not only does it offer an online encyclopedia, it also offers interactive learning programs that bring children closer to the subjects they are studying in school.

In this chapter, we'll show you how the kids can use Prodigy's online encyclopedia to research topics for school reports. And how they can interact with special online versions of *The National Geographic* and *Nova*, the Public Broadcasting Corporation's award-winning science program. Prodigy's treatment of these two outstanding educational resources is nothing less than exceptional. Kids not only view the offerings, they interact with them. It's much more fun than structured study, and what better way to reinforce what the kids are learning? And you can use the real magazine and TV show to further the connection.

Quick Tour

To get to Prodigy's Kids menu, click on *Jump* and type kids at the Jump menu. You'll be taken to a screen with a colorful graphic menu that's much livelier and more visually interesting than the blue-and-white pull-down menus that characterize Prodigy's adult-oriented offerings.

Figure 11.1 Children have their very own menu of options on Prodigy.

There are six regular options from the kids main screen: Activities, Stories, Reference, Games, The Club, and Custom Choices. There is also a seventh choice that is changed often.

This screen greets you with different story characters, quizzes, and references to new features, depending on what Prodigy's up to at the time you log on. On the day we checked in, Prodigy offered kids a little riddle before taking them to other features. From here, you can access all the features you saw on the screen: Exploring, Stories, Reference, Games, The Club, and Current Events.

Step-by-Step Tour

For our look at the *National Geographic/Nova* features, we use the Activities section. In this exercise, we'll focus on *The National Geographic* because we happen to be travel fanatics. However, you must promise to explore the *Nova* offerings as well. They're structured much like the Geographic's, giving children a chance to interact with a graphical science lesson, instead of geography. WGBH, Boston's public television station, teamed up with Prodigy to bring this science series online. Like the National Geographic's offerings, it features a new exploration each month and an archive of all previous lessons. Every Thursday, the *Nova* section offers a different lab experiment the kids can try on their own (great for schools and often even convenient for home). And on Mondays, Wednesdays, and Fridays, kids can turn to the section to read the latest science news.

The *National Geographic* section can take you on tours of places of interest throughout the world. And the magic of the PC makes the subject much more palatable than those geography lessons we endured—the ones where the teacher forced us to memorize vast collections of states and their capitals—often on hideous-looking and severely outdated maps. In contrast, the National Geographic "tours" are tours-de-force that introduce children to fascinating cultures, people, and traditions. And, as such, they offer all sorts of opportunities to let you make connections that help the world of reference come alive for your child.

To launch this excursion, click on *Activities*.

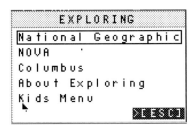

Figure 11.2 Many adventures await children on Prodigy's Exploring menu.

You're whisked to another menu. Here your options are *National Geographic, Nova, About Exploring*, and *Kids Menu*. Select *National Geographic*. (*Nova* takes you on a science expedition; *About Exploring* tells you how to use the features listed on the menu; *Kids Menu* takes you back to the title screen.)

Tip

If this is your first tour of Prodigy, click on *About Activities* and on *National Geographic* at the next menu to find out what to expect from the online magazine and how to use outside resources to enhance your child's learning and enjoyment. The text screen you'll see offers basic information: current features change at the beginning of each month; the *National Geographic* magazine of the month features an article related to the Prodigy tour; your child compares her views on the topic by using the Viewpoint option on the *National Geographic* title screen. This information offers all sorts of options for you to connect the online *National Geographic* with library references, further reading, maps, and the like. We'll show you how later.

The *National Geographic* title screen shows a graphic from the Geographic's tour or story of the month. In our example, the tour happens to be a graphic of a car tooling through the Black Forest. By the time you read this, the Black Forest lesson will be in Prodigy's archives and you'll look at a new lesson. (If you want, you can take the Black Forest tour by clicking on *Other Features*. This brings up a screen like the one in Figure 11.3 below, and you can click on next until you find the entry for the Black Forest. It's the one from September 1991. That tour will be about the same as the one you're about to experience—though not exactly. Once a story is in the archive, kids won't be able to express Viewpoints, which they do by selecting the second option on the title screen of the month.)

Translate what you learn in this Black Forest example to whichever tour is current when you log on to Prodigy. Fasten your seatbelts because we're embarking on our adventure.

From the title screen, click on the top option, the one that begins this month's story. In our example it's *A Day's Journey*. The Black Forest tour takes us first to a picture of a cuckoo clock with no text on screen. Note how Prodigy makes the Next command flash. That flash is Prodigy's polite way of suggesting what you should do. Click on *Next* to continue.

Our tour actually begins on the second screen, where we are taken to a map. Depending upon the tour or story you're using, the graphics and sequence will differ. But maps are a signature of the *National Geographic* section. And maps are great educational tools.

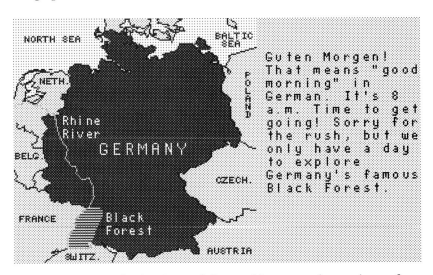

Figure 11.3 Prodigy's *National Geographic* tours make good use of maps.

A map launches the adventure. From there, the child romps through descriptive screens and scenes. Depending upon how long your child lingers over the information on screen and how quickly they click on the Next command to move ahead, this adventure will consume fifteen minutes to the better part of the afternoon. Make sure you can spare the phone for that long!

Connections

Have a world or national Atlas on hand as your child roams the subject country. If your child is young and needs some help, look up the area and point out such things as nearby towns. Compare your printed map to the one on screen. Chances are yours will contain more detail but it may also be out of date.

Discuss the legend on the map and point out such facts as how inches on a map are really miles in real life. If your child is a teenager, prompt her to explore the paper maps on her own. And, if you're lucky enough to have a subscription to *National Geographic*, look up the article that the Prodigy lesson relates to and see if it includes a map. Many of the magazine's articles do. And *National Geographic's* magazine maps often features wondrous items of interest you rarely find in atlases—with pictures of local wildlife or native tribesmen, arrows mapping historic voyages, and significant dates called out.

As the kids click through the tours and stories, they'll encounter all sorts of interesting information about the locale, its customs, and culture. Screens, like the one illustrated in Figure 11.3, which focuses on the Cuckoo clock as an innovation and form of industry in the Black Forest, are typical of what they'll find.

Connections

Here again you can turn to the pages of *National Geographic* magazine to find photos that supplement the on-screen tour. But an even better way is to help bring the lesson alive for your child. Here's just a few of the things you can do:

Serve a food from the country. It may be Thai or Chinese takeout. If you're fortunate enough to travel to or live in a city with a variety of ethnic restaurants, treat the kids to something like an Ethiopian sit-on-the-floor lunch. But don't overlook opportunities if your town doesn't. Po' Folks and Dutch Pantries are fast food chains that offer fares of regional interest.

And then, of course, there's the history-and-literature link. Geography affects history. History is the record of human events, and human events are often determined by human thoughts and motivations. And those are the stuff that great literature is made of. *National Geographic* is well aware of this. Often their Prodigy stories bear names like "Sherlock Holmes' London," which links the great literary mystery hero to the landscape of his mother country.

Even in our tour of the Black Forest, we learn that the area was the site of many of the great German folk stories, such as "Little Red Riding Hood" and "Hansel and Gretel."

Connections

These online references cry out for a trip to the library after the kids log off Prodigy. Use your judgment here and point your child to whatever is most appropriate for his or her age group. Older kids love mysteries, and who hasn't heard of the great Mr. Holmes and his lovable Dr. Watson? But as reading material, they're more for the junior high to high school set. If the kids are too young to handle the books that the Geographic's stories suggest, you can always read to them— a parental pastime too often lost in the rush of everyday activities.

When the story of the month has ended, or the tour is complete, make sure the kids click on *Express a Viewpoint*. Here, they are taken to a series of information screens that tell them something about the events of the day. In our Black Forest tour of Germany, many of these screens focused on the new-found freedoms in East Germany and reunification.

Here your child can read about controversies that plague the lands they just discovered and then post their thoughts on the subject in an opinion poll. At the end of the month, Prodigy edits the answers and posts a representative sample, which the kids can review to see how others responded.

Connections

The *National Geographic*'s stories are generally very topical. Chances are your kids are learning about these events on the evening news even as they're reviewing the stories on Prodigy. Use any of the topics in the *National Geographic* stories that pop up in the news as fodder for good dinner table conversation. This gives the kids a chance to show off their knowledge and converse with adults on an adult level. You may often be surprised to learn they know more about what's happening than you do.

Finally, click on Bibliography, the last option on the National Geographic title screen. Here you'll find a list of the references that *National Geographic* used to assemble the story. Once again, this suggests a trip to the library. If your child was particularly intrigued by the *National Geographic* tour, you'll want to extend her interest by seeing that she follows up with a good book.

The last item on the menu, *Other Features*, will take you to The *National Geographic*'s online archives. We've found that kids love to roam through the archives, go on tours that have already been conducted, or repeat their favorites.

But travel can be exhausting. The *National Geographic* tours reward a child's imagination only as long as a child is willing to work through them. Don't urge your kids to complete a tour at a single sitting. If they tire of a tour, let them stop along the way and return to it when their interest is renewed. There are plenty of other things on Prodigy to keep them busy in the meantime.

> **Tip**
>
> With older children, it's a good idea to read the stories during your own session on Prodigy. Young adults tend to be protective of their Prodigy haunts and don't particularly care to have Mom and Dad reading over their shoulder. And you shouldn't. After all, your child may be composing e-mail or swapping opinions with a friend in The Club. Teens value their privacy, and they're likely to turn off on the service if they think parents are using it to snoop on them.

Homework Helpers

Many parents never think of the computer as a homework helper. Instead, it becomes the game machine to be used after the homework is done. But Prodigy, thanks to its electronic encyclopedia, is an ever-patient, well-informed, homework helper. It helps train your child for this complex world, where information-gathering is a survival skill. It's your job to structure and enhance the child's quest for information.

If your family is like mine, you inherited an ancient encyclopedia that's most useful if your child is studying Mesopotamia, not the U.S.S.R. Prodigy's encyclopedia is constantly up to date. No longer do you need to set aside a substantial pool of cash, not to mention space on the bookshelf, for an encyclopedia. Prodigy brings one of the best right into your home.

In the following exercise, we'll show you how to use the *Grolier's Academic American Encyclopedia*. The beauty of this online encyclopedia is that it uses the kinds of resources you can only get from a computer to ease the chore of finding information. No longer will you have to haul the kids to the library on stormy winter nights. No longer will they have to puzzle through volumes of information to find cross-references. With a little coaching from you, the kids will soon learn to let Prodigy flip the "pages." And the best part is that they'll be honing their spelling and reference skills as they go along.

So let's use Prodigy's encyclopedia to find out everything we can about eagles. Click on Jump and enter encyclopedia. This takes us where we need to go. Prodigy prompts you to enter the name of the subject you wish to look up.

The best way to structure a search is to type in just enough characters to arrive close to the alphabetical sequence of the word you're looking for. In this case, if you type only ea or, better, eag, you'll get a whole list of words that begin with those letters. Then, you can simply click on the word you need, and Prodigy will find it in the encyclopedia.

So go ahead. Enter *eag* in your search field, then click on *Eagle*.

This takes you to a table of contents, which tells you how the reference is structured. You can click on *Beginning of Article* to read the whole article. You can click on one of its subsections to focus on a specific aspect of the subject. Or you can click on *Bibliography* to learn the sources of the encyclopedia's information.

Click on *Beginning of Article* and read the article with your child.

Tip

At this point, we could enter EAGLES, but if Prodigy's referencing mechanism can't find an exact match for what we type, it will take us to its best guess, which isn't always what we want. To structure a good search, you'll need to know how Prodigy looks up words. It first finds a match for the first letter, then the second, then the third, and so on until it's matched all the letters. In this case, if we entered EAGLES, Prodigy would take us to the encyclopedia entry, *EAGLES, THE*—the pop group. But we're looking for a bird. The proper reference, *EAGLE*, is just above *EAGLES, THE* on Prodigy's reference sheet. But we can't see it, because Prodigy brings the reference it "thinks" you want to the top of the screen page. The reference we want is on the previous page (you see, people really are still smarter than computers); we'll have to click on *BACK* to find it.

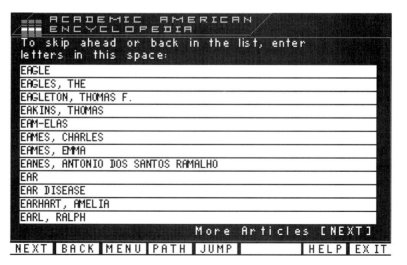

Figure 11.4 Prodigy's encyclopedia features a table of contents.

> **Tip**
>
> As you read, note that some words appear in all caps; in the Eagle article the word *HAWK* is fully capitalized. The caps are the keys to unlocking Prodigy's electronic cross-referencing feature.

To find out more about this related subject, click on the box next to *Cross-Reference* near the bottom of the screen, and enter hawk in the blank. Prodigy jumps you to the table of contents for the Hawk reference. Once again, you can choose to read the entire article or any of its subsections to learn about the eagles' place in the hawk family.

Once you've called up the articles, you can get printouts of them. Simply use the Copy command. Prodigy will ask whether you want to print only the "page" you see onscreen or a selection of pages. We want to print the entire article, so we click on *Select*. In the next menu, Prodigy asks you to specify the pages you want to select. Note how the service automatically detects the total number of pages in the document (six in our example). If we wanted only the information in the top half the article, we'd change the *6* to a *3*. But we want the whole thing. So, click on *OK* to select the number of pages Prodigy detected in the document.

Your child now has a printed reference she can carry to her desk— with information she can weave into a report or essay.

Other online services let you save text from the service to a file on your hard disk. Once there, it can be loaded into a word processor, where it can be edited and revised. Prodigy does not. On a technical level we'd normally fault the service for this. It's one bit of flexibility you lose by subscribing to Prodigy instead of another service. But, in matters of schoolwork, Prodigy has the right idea. By forcing kids to print the references and then to rewrite and summarize appropriate information in their own notebooks, it discourages them from plagiarising.

If you're going to spend inordinate amounts of time with an encyclopedia, then you might want to consider a CD-ROM version. You will have to buy the CD-ROM software and a CD-ROM player, which could cost a couple of hundred dollars, but after that, there are no costs, and the access time to information tends to be faster. The best volume for children is *Compton's Multimedia Encyclopedia*. Compton's mixes sound and graphics with text to make the research experience a compelling one.

CHAPTER

12

PLAN VIII: LOGO—
A TASTE OF PROGRAMMING

The software you'll need: *LogoWriter*

What it costs: $89

Why it's special: *LogoWriter* is an introduction to computer programming that's both playful and provocative.

Ages it appeals to: Eight to adult.

Activities: Create your own computer games, greeting cards, and designs. Create programs to draw a geometric design, play a musical birthday greeting, and create an adventure game.

What you'll need: *LogoWriter* software; a printer.

259

Introducing *LogoWriter*

LOGO is a computer language that was designed at MIT in the late 1960s. (Its originator, Seymour Papert, created the language to help introduce children to computer programming.) Since then, LOGO has become the computer language that's most often taught in elementary schools.

LOGO is unique because it uses an on-screen helper, a friendly little turtle, to help children visualize the spatial concepts involved in programming games and simple tasks. It makes something as abstract as programming a simple task for kids. LOGO is also a very graphical language, so the children can actually use it to draw.

In this chapter, we will show you how to use LOGO at home to introduce your children to the language or to reinforce what they are working on in school. We'll create programs to draw a geometric design, play a musical birthday greeting, and create an adventure game.

We, as authors, feel strongly that programming is an exercise in logic and a skill that kids should know. Creating a program that lets other kids play a game gives children a terrific shot of confidence. If the instructions (the program your child creates) aren't logical, the program won't work. The child must find the flaws or what he left out and make corrections. Getting a program to run becomes a self-correcting process that builds self-esteem. It's an empowering process. Once he has written a successful program, your child will have no doubt that he, not the machine, is boss.

True, most children won't grow up to be computer programmers, but children should be exposed to programming, regardless of career path. In all likelihood, your child's school curriculum features LOGO, and working with the same tools at home can only help reinforce the knowledge he gains at school.

Programming also forces your child to become organized and direct his efforts at a series of individual goals. If you want to write a program, the only way to do so is to break the larger task up into much smaller, discrete tasks. This idea of breaking up a large project into more manageable sub-projects is fundamental to a child's academic success. And, programming teaches precision. Computers don't understand subtlety and nuance, nor can they infer what you mean. Precision, exactitude, logic. These are qualities that will help your child grow, regardless of what field he chooses to enter when he grows up.

In 1968, when Seymour Papert created the LOGO language, he passionately documented his ideas in a book called *MindStorms*. The book is now considered a classic among computer educators. It explains how the LOGO language can be useful in all areas of academics. Papert's original LOGO language has been expanded upon by many people. Today it uses commands that let kids write procedures to generate animations, create geometric designs, play music, and do simple word processing.

One of the most important features of LOGO, and one that is especially pleasing to kids, is the Turtle. Papert's idea was to use the Turtle as a physical representation of the abstract ideas of programming. The Turtle is a small, turtle-shaped cursor that acts as a pen. Kids direct the Turtle to move around the screen and draw computer graphics. They have to tell it where to go, how to get there, how fast to get there, and what to do once it's there. These Turtle instructions become the program that kids create with the LOGO language.

Figure 12.1 This is what the LOGO Turtle looks like. Children learn to direct this critter across the screen to create programs.

Children use English-language-like commands to move the Turtle around the screen. For example, the command FD 10 tells the turtle to go Forward 10 units. PU (Pen Up) and PD (Pen Down) tell the Turtle to lift and drop the pen so it can move with or without drawing a line.

Once your child masters simple drawing commands such as FD 10 (go forward 10) or LT 90 (left turn 90), he can use more advanced features of the language to make the Turtle repeat *procedures* and create routines. (*Routines* are made up of simple procedures.)

Simple procedures become more powerful when your child applies rules to them. The turtle can respond differently based on a set of decision points or criteria that your child writes into the program. So, for example if the Turtle receives the words "go to the forest" as input, it would react differently than if it received the words "pick up treasure." These sorts of decisions can become the basis for creating your own adventure game.

As a matter of fact, a very common project in the schools is for children to teach the Turtle enough procedures to create LOGO-generated poetry. A procedure can be an advanced exercise that involves "teaching" the Turtle parts of speech (nouns, verbs, etc.) and rules of sentence construction. LOGO projects also often involve the creation of complex geometric shapes using command sets that start with the simple Pen Up and Pen Down instructions and advance from there.

Today there are a number of different versions of LOGO, each with somewhat different features. In this chapter, we use *LogoWriter* from LCSI. We chose it because nine times out of ten, *LogoWriter* is the version of LOGO found in schools. (It runs on Apple, IBM, and Macintosh computers.) But, most importantly, we chose *LogoWriter* because LCSI makes a special home edition available to parents at a very reasonable price. Finally, *LogoWriter* is appealing because its documentation is chock full of interesting projects and ideas, with chapters that feature everything from building your own games to writing an animated adventure story.

LOGO is not a state-of-the-art program. The graphics are primitive compared to most of the paint programs and desktop publishing programs available today. But it runs on just about anything. Even if you have one of the oldest PCs in existence you can probably run some version of LOGO. Most of the things you can create with LOGO—animations, drawings, stories—can be created elsewhere with less trouble. But LOGO is to kid's software as handstitching is to the sewing machine. There's a handicraft and sense of pride in mastering the process as well as the product.

Quick Start

When you load it, LOGO greets you with an opening menu. To get quickly into the program, select *New Page* from the main menu. Before you turn your child loose with the program, you might want to point out the components of a page: the Turtle, the blank area, and the command center. The command center, which is the lower section, is the place where he'll enter his instructions telling the Turtle what to do.

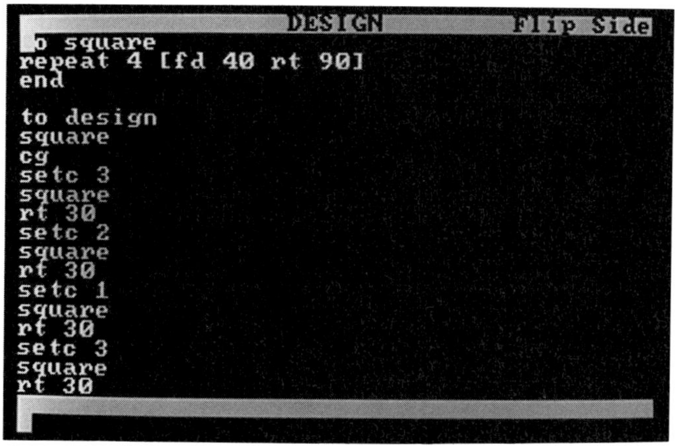

Figure 12.2 By entering commands in the command center, your child trains the turtle to move across the screen.

You begin a *LogoWriter* program by specifying that you are creating a new page or program. Next, you give the program a name. Now, in the command center, enter the following code:

```
np "design
fd  30
rt  90
fd  30
rt  90
fd  30
rt  90
fd  30
rt  90
*
```

In the commands you just entered, *NP "design* tells *LogoWriter* that you are creating a new page called Design, *FD 30* tells the Turtle to move forward 30 units, and *RT 90* tells the Turtle to make a 90° right-angle turn.

> **Tip**
>
> Teachers often use graph paper to familiarize their students with the concept of moving the Turtle across specific units. You can do the same thing. Have the children practice moving the Turtle on their graph paper.

But there are easier ways of getting the Turtle to go where you want it to go. *LogoWriter*, like most computer languages, uses something called *primitives* or procedures to help young programmers avoid entering lines and lines of tiny instructions that yield very little in the way of tangible results. And it's a good thing that they have more advanced commands. Machine language programming is much more picayune.

Basically, a procedure is a list. It allows your child to make a list of commands like the ones he just used to create a square and give it a name. The lines of code that we wrote can be saved as a procedure called *SQUARE*. Now the computer understands your definition of a square. That definition can be used over and over again. It's much faster to enter the word *square* in the program than it is to type out all of the commands each time you need a square. Here's how to make a procedure called SQUARE:

We use a piece of electronic scratch paper that you don't see on screen unless you call it. To call the scratchpad and write a procedure you type the word flip (it flips from the program to the scratchpad).

To get to the Flip screen with a shortcut you can toggle over to it by pressing Ctrl+F or click on the flip icon at the top right of the window.

After pressing Ctrl+F, you're on a blank screen. Simply enter the phrase *to square*. The word *to* tells the computer that you are defining a procedure.

To make your work easier, you can copy the make-a-square commands you've already entered in your original square example. To do this:

Press Ctrl+F to move back to your main page.

1. Move your cursor to the first occurrence of FD 30 and press F1 to select a block of commands.

2. Move cursor to last occurrence of FD 30. This selects all of steps you used to make your square.

3. Press F3 Copy to indicate that you want to copy the commands.

4. Press Ctrl+F to return to your Flip page.

5. Press F4 to paste the copied commands onto your flip page.

6. Then type *end* to end the procedure.

If you're using the Macintosh version, follow these steps to copy your square procedure:

1. Drag the mouse from the first FD 30 through the last RT 90. All the commands should be highlighted.

2. Select Copy from the Edit menu.

3. Press Cmd+F to flip back to the scratchpad.

4. Select Paste from the Edit menu.

5. Type *end* to finish the procedure.

Here's what you should see on your Flip page:

```
TO  SQUARE
FD  30
RT  90
FD  30
RT  90
FD  30
RT  90
FD  30
RT  90
END
```

Now, any time you want to draw a square on your main page, all you need to do is to type the word square. The program now knows that the definition of SQUARE can be found on the procedures (Flip) page. Now that wasn't too hard was it?

> **Tip**
>
> A procedure is only applicable to the current page or program. So, if we teach the program what a square is in this program, we have to do it again if we want to use a square in another program. To save time, you can use the Copy and Paste commands between programs.

Step-by-Step Tour

The best way to show kids what they can do with LOGO on a computer is to have them start in the real world, away from the keyboard. So to introduce you to LOGO, we'll give you a real-life exercise that's easy to do at home.

Have the children take their favorite stuffed toy and plunk it down in the middle of your living room floor. (Children ages four to adult can benefit from this exercise.) Then pose this question to them, "Suppose your toy understood four words: *forward, backward, left,* and *right.* What would you say to your toy to get it to draw a square?" Ask your child to tell you what he would say and let him move the toy across your floor as he supplies the answer. He'll probably tell the toy (though he may need a little coaching):

FORWARD
RIGHT
FORWARD
RIGHT
FORWARD
RIGHT
FORWARD
RIGHT

Now, tell your child that he has to specify a number of units for the toy to travel, so that it is always pointed in the proper direction. In this case you are employing simple right-angle geometry, and a square might be:

FORWARD 10 (steps)

RIGHT 90 (angle)

FORWARD 10 (steps)

RIGHT 90 (angle)

FORWARD 10 (steps)

RIGHT 90 (angle)

FORWARD 10 (steps)

RIGHT 90 (angle)

Have your child walk through this exercise, using the toy to pace out the units and turn right 90 degrees, until he understands the type of movements that have to occur to get the toy to draw a square. These commands with their units and angles are precisely the ones he'll use to communicate with the Turtle in *LogoWriter*.

Let's take the real-world "floor" and move it to the computer display. It's time to draw a LOGO square. The Turtle cursor on the screen moves just like the stuffed animal on your living room floor. But on the computer you can watch it draw its path as it moves along.

Tip

You can make this little shortcut even shorter by using the Repeat command. You can put a command or a set of commands inside brackets and use the Repeat command to tell the LOGO Turtle how many times to perform the action in parentheses. So, to create a square using this shortcut, you would write:

```
to square
Repeat 4 [fd 30 rt 90]
```

Can you see why this works? Try it with your stuffed animal or your graph paper. It works the same way.

Now that you have a procedure called SQUARE, it's easy to make a geometric design by repeating the square pattern. Here's a deceptively complicated design that's really just a bunch of overlapping squares.

SQUARE
FD 30
SQUARE
FD 30
SQUARE
FD 30
SQUARE
FD 30
SQUARE

This draws a square, moves the Turtle 30 units, and draws another square. This is what it should look like when you are done.

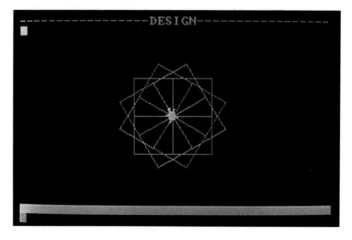

Figure 12.3 This design is a simple program that draws overlapping squares.

See how you are using the square in an overlapping pattern to create a geometric shape? Can you think of a way to use Repeat to simplify the procedure even more? You could enter:

```
repeat 5 [square fd 30]
```

Now you're really keeping things short and powerful! And, of course, you could turn this pretty design into a procedure called SQUARES, and use it in other designs whenever you feel like it. To do it, you'll go to the flip page again and list the procedure:

1. Type Ctrl+F to go to the Flip page.

2. Type *to squares* to name the procedure you are about to list. (Make sure that each to square procedure finishes with an *end* before you start the next procedure.)

3. Type *repeat 5 [square fd 30]* to tell the turtle to draw a square, move ahead 30 units, and repeat the action five times.

Tip

To run your procedures after you create them, you need to return to the main LOGO page and type the name of the procedure "SQUARE", "DESIGN" or whatever. LOGO knows to look on the Flip page to carry out your procedures.

That is the essence of LOGO programming. Just by using this simple language, children can record their work, step by step, play it back, and refine it. They can also take the little baby steps of their work and turn them into powerful procedures.

Connections

LogoWriter can be used to make pretty designs, such as the pinwheel made of squares that we showed you in our previous example, but *LogoWriter* also combines the elements of simple word processing, music, and animation, which can be used to breathe life in your child's graphic creations.

The next example uses more complicated LOGO commands including:

- **Pen Up and Pen Down Commands.** To turn the turtle's drawing capabilities on and off
- **Text-Writing Tool.** To let you put text on screen
- **Stamp Tool.** To let you use shapes that come with *Logo Writer* to make up parts of the screen in your program
- **Music Writer.** To let you play notes on screen.

Now you're ready for some more advanced activities. Here's a program the Raskin kids use at home to create musical birthday cards. On a new page, type:

```
NP "Birthday
```

HT (This command hides the Turtle)

Ctrl+UP (this one moves you onto a page to let you enter text)

```
Happy Birthday to you !
    Happy Birthday to you!
    Happy Birthday dear Reed
    Happy Birthday to you!
```

Cake (this command draws a cake)

Happy (this command plays Happy Birthday)

But the program isn't finished yet. CAKE and HAPPY are procedures your child will have to write. Here's the procedure for drawing a cake. Remember you'll have to move to the Flip page to list commands in the procedure. You can put all the procedures on one page, but you'll have to make sure there's a blank line between each procedure.

```
To Cake
```

PU (Brings pen up)

Setpos [-65-40] (Sets position of the turtle on the screen beneath the text)

PD (Pen down)

rect 15 50 (draws a rectangle with 15 and 50 units as its measurements. *Rectangle* is another procedure you'll need to write)

fd 15 (moves up to draw the upper rectangle on the cake])

`rect 15 50` (draws a second rectangle)

`pu`

`fd 25` (Moves the turtle forward without a pen trail)

`rt 90`

`fd 5` (positions the turtle for the candles)

`setsh 31` (selects the vertical line tool from the stamp kit)

`setc 3` (changes the color of the candles)

`repeat 4 [candle fd 12]` (draws four candles each spaced 12 units apart, which makes good sense, since the length of the rectangle was 50 units)

And for drawing a rectangle, the following procedure moves the Turtle to the height of the birthday cake, has him make a right-angle turn, and makes him go to the left. If you repeat this twice, you wind up with a square.

`to rect :h :l` (lets you put in variables for the height and length of the rectangle)

`repeat 2 [fd :h rt 90 fd :l rt 90]`

A *variable* is a placeholder for a value that you enter when you actually use a procedure. Now you have what you need to draw the cake. Your Birthday cake should look like this.

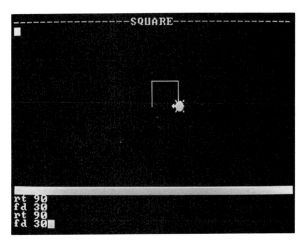

Figure 12.4 In LOGO, a cake can be two rectangles placed on top of each other.

Now it's time to add the candles. To do that, add the following procedure to your list:

```
to candle
pd  (Pen down)
stamp  (uses selected stamp)
pu end
```

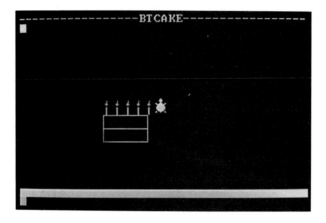

Figure 12.5 A cake with candles, the words to "Happy Birthday," and a musical accompaniment by your computer are all relatively simple when using LOGO.

And finally for playing "Happy Birthday," add this procedure on the Flip page (Ctrl+F)

```
to happy
tone 523 10
tone 523 5
tone 587 15
tone 523 15
tone 698 15
tone 659 30
tone 523 10
tone 523 5
tone 587 15
tone 523 15
tone 784 15
tone 698 30
```

Now, go back to your main page and type happy. You hear the song.

LogoWriter's music-making capabilities are logical, but they are very primitive. The first number in the birthday example refers to the tone, and the second refers to the duration of a note. The way you write music in *LogoWriter* is by listing both of these items for each note you want to play. Procedures can make writing music considerably easier. For example, you could write a procedure that would give a name to each note you assigned a frequency and duration. The procedure for a C would be:

```
to c
tone 523 20
end
```

This is not a very long procedure, but it is a very useful one. And your child could assign letter names to all the notes on the scale so that, in the future, he only has to type the names of the notes to create music.

Figuring out which number goes with which tone can be tricky. So here's a list of LOGO's numeric tones to go with each note:

Note	Tones
B	62 123
A#	58 117
A	55 110
G#	52 104
G	49 98
F#	46 92
F	44 87
E	41 82
D#	39 78
D	37 73
C#	35 69
C	33 65

Keeping this chart of the music notes and their respective tones in *LogoWriter* should make it easier for your child to compose music.

To make the language even more succinct, you can do what we did in the Birthday Card example above. Turn the notes into a procedure called happy so that each time you want to hear the birthday music you can just type happy.

You've seen two examples of how *LogoWriter* can be used to create practical applications. They look pretty complex, compared to the types of activities we did with programs like *Playroom* and *Carmen Sandiego*. Programming can make chess or bridge look like child's play, so the best way for your child to work on LOGO problems is in groups. Together, the children can try out commands and procedures and see how they work. They can discuss what's happening with one another and collaborate on finding higher levels of procedures to try out.

Your child will probably be using shapes, music, and text for the bulk of his LOGO experience. So, before we go further, we should go into a bit more detail about them.

As you saw with our birthday candles, *LogoWriter* has a shape-maker, which is really nothing more than a simple paint program. When you typed the Setsh command you were transported to a display of all shapes. This is the shape-maker, as shown in Figure 12.6. Each shape has a corresponding number, which you can use in your programs to identify that shape. But, you can also make shapes of your own by selecting from the shape list a number that shows no assigned shape next to it and then creating the shape you want to go with it.

When you select a number that has no shape associated with it, you are transported to a shape editor, where you can create shapes by "coloring" in the squares on the screen, the same way you might color in the squares on a piece of graph paper. As a matter of fact, it's a good idea to use graph paper and sketch out your shape ideas before entering the editor to do it in LOGO. Your child can create shapes to do all sorts of things. Robin's children have made shapes of their initials so that they can "sign" the drawings they do in *LogoWriter*.

On the Macintosh, you type *shapes* to bring up the Shapes Editor. This is a major enhancement to the Mac version of *LogoWriter* which makes the creation and editing of shapes much easier.

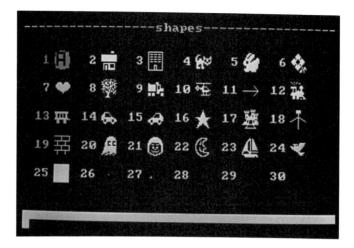

Figure 12.6 The shape editor is like a little stamp set where you can design the stamps.

Using the illustrations from the Setsh list, you can also create procedures to simulate animations. For instance, you could make a rabbit jump by writing a JUMP procedure that would go like this:

```
TO JUMP
SETSH 5 (a bunny rabbit)
FD 30
Wait 10 (tells Logowriter to pause so the jump looks more realistic)
BK 30
Wait 20 (tells LogoWriter to wait at the bottom)
```

And then you could have the rabbit jump six times by entering *repeat 6 jump* in a program.

If you're really feeling inspired, you can use the shape editor to create two rabbit shapes, each with paws in different positions, then simulate a rabbit's walk by switching between rabbits on the forward and backward portions like this:

```
setsh 22 wait 5
fd 30
setsh 26 wait 5
bK 30
```

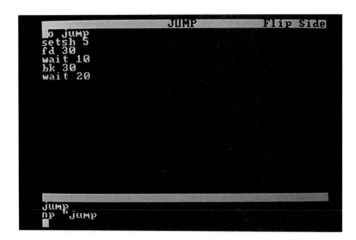

Figure 12.7 Animating stamps like this hopping rabbit is an amusing LOGO activity.

LogoWriter gives you a command or primitive called Choice, which you can use to create different plots in electronic games. You can use this, for example, to write a test-based adventure game by entering text that reads:

```
You are standing at the edge of a cliff. Do you:
a. jump
b. climb down with a rope
c. head back down the mountain
```

Within the program you are writing, each choice gets a new page of its own.

Target Practice is a game you can help your child create and, at the same time, improve his skill at using LOGO's directional commands. Using *LogoWriter*'s stamp command, create a circle on screen. Then have the kids try to move the Turtle to the edge in the fewest number of moves by letting them approximate how far forward, right, left, or backward the turtle will have to travel to get there.

Hopefully, we've only whetted your appetite, and now you want your child to explore the much larger world of LOGO. There are many good books on LOGO. Two of the better ones for parents include: *Learning with LOGO,* written for kids and their parents by teacher Daniel Watt, (McGraw-Hill, 1983); and, *Turtle Geometry* by Abelson and diSessa (MIT Press, 1980), which is written for more advanced students and their parents who want to use LOGO to explore geometry. We've looked at *LogoWriter* because it is so well entrenched in the schools and because it's got a particularly full set of tools for kids. But there you may want to investigate other versions of LOGO. *LogoExpress* from Logo Computer Systems, Inc. is also available in a home edition. It is a LOGO-based telecommunications package that adds an e-mail option to *LogoWriter*. Call 1-800-321-LOGO for more information.

Ladybug LOGO is for bargain hunters. It's a freeware package (which means the generous author of the program encourages you to download it from online service and not pay for it). It also means you'll need a modem to get to it. *Ladybug LOGO* can be found on the CompuServe online service in Library 11 on the LOGO Forum. (If you have a friend who uses CompuServe, you might want to ask him if you can watch as he logs in and downloads the program for you. CompuServe is an enormous service and, unlike Prodigy, it is not graphical. Its screens of text and menus can be confusing to newcomers but, if you like what you see—many databases of information (good for high-school and college-age kids)—you might think about signing up.) *Ladybug LOGO* is more limited than *LogoWriter*. It doesn't have many of the higher order functions that *LogoWriter* has. (It isn't even written in LOGO, it's actually written in a language called BASIC, which makes it much less flexible). In the same CompuServe forum, you'll also find the documentation for Ladybug's Discovery Book, a family activity book.

LOGO has actually found its way into other games and forms of play. Imagine playsets that combine the abstract concepts of LOGO, combined with the practice Lego gives a child at manipulating objects in the real world and building dexterity. Lego and LOGO and both building blocks designed to enhance a child's understanding of the ways objects and ideas fit together. When teamed up, they can delight children for hours at a time.

Lego LOGO does just that. It's an amazing game that lets children build real life devices that are controlled by the LOGO language. In addition to LOGO, you get special Lego pieces with touch and light sensors. Using these, a child can build robots that are controlled by the programs they write using LOGO. The *Lego LOGO* play set is pricey. It starts at $450 for the basic kit, so it may not be the sort of thing your family budget will justify. But you can and should pressure your local school or PTA to purchase this wonderful teaching tool so that your kids can use it in classroom activities. For information on the set, call LEGO DACTA at 800-527-8339.

If you want more information on LOGO, there's a LOGO Foundation that will be happy to provide it. You can reach it through its director, Michael Tempel at LOGO Foundation, 250 W. 57th St., NY, NY 10107-2603, 212-765-4918, 212-765-4789 (FAX).

Terrapin Logo has infinite, multiple turtles, supports arrays, and includes debugging tools that make writing longer programs more practical. The Mac version has multiple, resizable windows which is a big advantage over *LogoWriter*. Contact Terrapin, Inc., 400 Riverside St., Portland, ME 04103, 207-878-8200.

And if you're equipped with a modem, you can download information on LOGO from a number of bulletin boards. The largest and most accessible is Compuserve, which sponsors a forum for LOGO fans. You post electronic notes on it to share insights, questions, and problems with other users. And you can also download interesting games like *Ladybug LOGO*, or read through information about what's going on with LOGO in schools. To get to the forum, log onto CompuServe. Select *Software* from the main Compuserve menu and then choose *LOGO* from the sublist.

SECTION III

SOFTWARE CLASSICS FOR KIDS— PREVIEWS OF YOUR FAVORITE PRODUCTS

The computer industry is dynamic, which is both good and bad for parents. It means that you have more choices than ever in quality software at increasingly better prices, but all the movement can leave you breathless. The ever-changing software frontier can be frustrating when you are trying desperately to keep pace, and it means that writing a book like this one is like aiming at a moving target. By the time the ink dries on these pages, there will be new software packages on the market. Long after this book is in its first edition, you will still be making software buying decisions.

Thus far, we've shared our knowledge about kids and computers in order to empower you—to make you good consumers and users. We've shown you some of our favorite software and activities. The software packages we looked at in Section II of this book are especially broad-based and important.

In this last section we give you an idea of the larger world of software that lies waiting on the shelves. Rather than bore you with details about games that you wouldn't want to own because they just aren't very good, we've chosen just to tell you about the classics, the programs that stand out and have staying power. Software classics have the right combination of content and technology. They endure the test of time. They are the best of breed. And so, in this final section of the book we offer mini-reviews of the best and ignore the rest.

We divided the reviews into four categories: Reading and Writing, Math, Logic and Thinking Games, and Creativity. We may have missed a few programs that you're interested in. And, chances are, many other good ones will have come to market between the time we write these words and the time you read them. At this writing, software developers are racing to take advantage of many new developments in computer sound and animation.

Also in this section, you'll find Tips and Connections, as you did in the other sections. These will help you get the most from each program.

Most of the reviews focus on traditional disk-based software. But at the end of this section, you'll find reviews of programs that are available on CD-ROM, a new and emerging technology that is like the computer equivalent of CD-audio disks. It makes heavy use of sound, color, and animation in software that is stored on a high-capacity CD.

This last section may be one that you'll skim on first reading. But you should return to it again and again, whenever you want to go shopping for children's software. It's then, we suspect, that you will be poring over every word. And we think you'll agree that our software picks will stretch your kids' minds, as well as the dollars you have to invest in them.

CHAPTER
13

READING AND WRITING:
THE ESSENTIAL SKILLS

Introduction

Teaching reading and writing to children is one of the most challenging yet rewarding tasks that we face as parents and educators. In part, this is because children have different styles of learning. The process is evolutionary and children are ready to tackle different aspects of reading comprehension at different stages in their development.

Children learn to read in different ways. Some learn to recognize whole words after seeing them again and again. Others respond to the more phonetic approach popular in schools. There are software packages with both orientations and, in fact, exposing children to both may be the best route you can take as a parent.

Of course, computers don't do a very good job when it comes to teaching penmanship, but some of the packages, like the *Children's Writing & Publishing Center* (reviewed earlier in this book) do concentrate on the writing process. When learning to write, some children learn better in a creative environment; others prefer the structured approach of recognizing parts of speech in sentence construction.

An abundance of pre-reading software teaches children to link a letter with a particular sound, or a written word with its picture. But there are only a limited number of software packages that tackle reading comprehension and a child's ability to decode complex words. As multimedia computing matures, reading software will be better able to address more conceptual material.

Computers are not the only way, and certainly not the finest way, to teach children to read and write. As a matter of fact, some educators insist that computers will ultimately result in greater illiteracy because they tend to expose children to short pieces of work instead of books, and because word processors have spellers, thesauri, and even grammar checkers, which relieve children from having to learn fundamental skills. Others claim that kids at computers will happily press keys with abandon instead of reading for meaning. We, however, believe that computers can play an important part in a multi-solution approach to reading.

Helping a child learn to read by purchasing good reading software can supplement the reading instruction your child receives in school. It won't replace it. Software is an adjunct, but it's an important adjunct. Reading and writing software is heavily focused on given tasks, but it can also captivate children. When the written word is accompanied by animation, sound, and positive reinforcement, the child has an agreeable, self-motivating, and entertaining environment to explore.

So here are the reading and writing programs that we consider to be the best on the market.

Bank Street Writer Plus

Broderbund Software (PC-compatibles)

Scholastic Software (Macintosh)

Ages: 7 to 12

Skills taught: Word processing

No one has come up with the ideal word processor for young children, and this one is only significant in that so many schools still use it. If the home-school connection is high on your list of priorities, you may want this program.

Bank Street Writer's menu structure and features in the PC-compatible version are beginning to appear a bit antiquated. The Mac version from Scholastic has been updated and streamlined. It has more formatting power and the ability to use graphics. Although it is still widely sold and widely available, *Bank Street Writer* was created to offer students a more or less full-featured word processor with a manageable set of commands that children can input. It allows them to cut and paste text and do simple page formatting, and it sells for somewhat less than most adult word processors. But, more graphical word processors make text editing easier for kids as well as adults.

For home use, you might consider other options. One might be Microsoft's *Word for Windows,* for older children especially. This is a full-featured program, and you would only introduce a child to a limited subset of its capabilities. *Word for Windows* is expensive (you can buy it on sale for just under $200, but the list price is $495). It also requires Windows. So you would only proceed in this direction if you're buying for the whole family. A second option would be to use an adult integrated software package, such as *Microsoft Works* or *Lotus Works.* Integrated packages include several programs—usually word processor, spreadsheet, and database modules—but none of

the modules have quite the depth of features that standalone programs have. However, integrated programs sell for less. An integrated package costs about $129 (you can often find them for $99)
—a bargain, considering how much software you get. MacWrite II
($129) or Microsoft Write ($125) are good basic word processors for
the Mac that offer easy upgrade paths to professional-strength word
processors.

Figure 13.1 Davidson's *Kid Works* lets kids produce talking picture
books.

Davidson's *Kid Works*

Davidson and Associates, Inc.

Ages: 4 to 10

Skills taught: Writing, Illustrating, Storytelling, Desktop
Publishing

Kid Works is an integrated software package for juniors. It combines
simple word processing, a paint program, an icon maker that can
create picture symbols, and the ability to digitize speech and record
it in a story. With all this in one tidy package, kids can create clever
talking picture storybooks.

Like some other Davidson games, *Kid Works* uses First Byte's speech technology, which lets the computer speak the text that's written on the screen. So, a child can enter text into the word processor and have the computer read back the text, even if there is no specialized sound hardware.

Tip

With the First Byte speech technology in *Kid Works* for IBM PC-compatibles you can play sound through your regular speaker, even if you don't have a speech accessory. (The program also supports a number of add-on sound boards). To make the speech sound a bit better on a system without a sound card, select the Version 3 speech setting in the program. It reads the speech faster, so that it sounds more natural.

The program has a graphical user interface. Press on the Mouth button and your story gets spoken; press on Pen and Paper and you go to the word processor; press on the Television button and you play back your talking book.

Kid Works comes with more than 200 icons, or small pictures, that kids can put into their documents. The pictures include illustrations of nouns like "man," "baby," and "computer," and verbs like "laugh," as well as adjectives. Kids can plop these ready-made illustrations into their stories, or they can create icons of their own and give their icons a name. They can also put background pictures behind their stories. Or they can write a rebus-style sentence such as, "Today I went for a bike ride," showing the "bike ride" as a picture instead of text.

Connections

You can use *Kid Works* to create a rebus game. Have your child make puzzles for her friends by combining words and pictures, as in the TV game *Concentration*. For example: Sp + (picture of an eye) +A + (picture of a lady) + (picture of a bug) = I Spy a Ladybug.

The word processor is simple. It lets your child cut and paste text to move it elsewhere in the story. But, when it comes to publishing and printing the story, there are only two sizes of type to choose from. The large text looks rather crude, like letters scrawled on primary school paper. The smaller text looks more grownup and sophisticated. The icon editor is like a very simple paint program that lets you draw dots of color to form a picture. It is also not as full-featured as most paint programs, so it's tough to create serious works of art.

The program is too limited to be used as a traditional word processor, but there are tons of things your child can do with it, from publishing her own picture books to learning to associate pictures and words or training the computer to recognize phonetical spelling.

Kid Works 2 is a step beyond the original PC version. It has four modes: Story Writer, Story Player, Story Illustrator, and Icon Maker. The Story Writer is like a simple word processor except that you can use pictures instead of words—*Kid Works* comes with over 250 and you can add more—and it will read your story back to you. The Story Player lets you put stories and illustrations together and play them in tape recorder fashion. The Story Illustrator is a very good painting module. It's not as silly as *Kid Pix*, but it has a good set of painting tools and is very easy to use. The Icon Maker let's you add speaking pictures to *Kid Works'* word bins. On Mac LC's and IIsi's, you can use the built-in microphone to record your own sounds to add to your icons. Everything in *Kid Works 2* is graphical. Even the dialog boxes use thumbs up and thumbs down icons instead of the words yes and no. *Kid Works 2* also takes advantage of the Mac's built-in sound, graphics, and font capabilities. You can use any font installed in your System Folder, though *Kid Works 2* still limits you to two font sizes—18 and 36 points.

Shopping for Sound for PC's

Any time the sound in a store demonstration is really magnificent, you can bet your bottom dollar that the computer where the demo is running has some kind of sound accessory. Ask the salesperson what kind of sound quality you can expect if you have no sound accessory, so that you are not disappointed when you get home.

The lucky Macintosh owner has sound built in. But IBM PC-compatible owners will have to add accessories to get sound. For them, there are three good products for a home computer.

1. **The Sound Source from Disney Software.** Unlike other accessories which fit as cards into the computer, this is an external speaker box. It is also inexpensive and can usually be found for about $20, which makes it an ideal purchase for kids. Its sound isn't the same high quality as the other two listed here, but it is easy to install. All Disney software supports this device, as do a growing number of others, but, in general, it is not as widely supported as the SoundBlaster or Ad Lib cards.

2. **The SoundBlaster Card.** This is a widely supported audio card for children's software and it is priced at about $199 for the basic card. The SoundBlaster supports both sound and voice and fits inside the computer.

3. **The Ad Lib Card.** As widely supported as the SoundBlaster, you'll find several versions of the Ad Lib card on the market. Early versions, which can still be found in many discount organizations, listed for $120 and were sold for much less. Only the latest board, the AdLib Gold, supports voice and music. It can be found at prices ranging from $200 to $400. Ad Lib is a card that fits inside the computer.

There are other sound boards that cost more and deliver higher quality sound, but these are not geared to home computing, unless you plan to compose and play music from your computer.

The Mickey Mouse Series

Walt Disney Computer Software

Ages: 3 to 7

Skills taught: Pre-reading and concepts

Disney's line of software is geared to the very young—preschoolers. It includes several programs, each sold separately, that feature Mickey Mouse. And, often, you'll see these programs bundled together in stores. The characters in the software—Minnie, Mickey, Goofy, Pluto, and the gang are memorable—the music and animation are top-notch. The games are simple. There's no wrong answer. You click on a key, and something happens on screen.

The games each work with the Disney Sound Source, an inexpensive (usually about $20) device, which hooks directly into your parallel port and provides voice and sound. Without the Sound Source device, the games are relatively boring; voice is an important part of the play. We're constantly surprised at how much kids enjoy hitting the keys and watching the Disney characters do their stuff. For me, these games don't have much staying power. After two minutes of Mickey chirping in my ear, I've had enough. Yet, children will spend hours reviewing shapes, colors, letters, and numbers with Mickey and friends.

Connection

Disney also sells a series of *Fun Time Print Kits* that are very much like Broderbund's *Print Shop* (reviewed in this chapter), except that they intersperse Disney characters in your documents. You can print greeting cards, posters, banners, letterhead and place mats using the *Fun Time* kits.

In *Mickey's ABCs*, you'll find two scenarios to teach the alphabet. In Scene One, Mickey is asleep in bed. When you wake him, he travels around four household rooms doing various things that correspond to different letters of the alphabet. In the second scenario, Mickey goes to the fair and meets up with his friends, Minnie, Goofie, Donald, and others. In either case, every time you press a key on the keyboard, it's associated with something in Mickey's world. So pressing V, for example, puts the word *violin* on the screen, says the word aloud, and displays one of the Disney characters playing a few notes. Cute little touches (the violin string pops, for example) abound. The program tackles both uppercase and lowercase letters, and, since something happens every time you press a key, there's really no way to give a wrong answer.

Mickey's 123s is similar to *Mickey's ABCs*. The theme in this number-recognition game is a party that Mickey is giving for a friend. Again, any number key that you press makes something happen on screen. The various scenes involve inviting numbers of guests, shopping for numbers of favors, preparing numbers of food dishes, and finally hosting the big surprise party.

In *Mickey's Colors and Shapes,* Mickey is a magician performing magic at a theatre while Minnie assists. In the first act, Mickey juggles shapes of various colors, as you select them. In the second act, he builds scenes made of objects that you select. In the final act, he pulls animals out of a hat, the animals hide behind a shape of a particular color, and you hunt for them. This game uses a plastic keyboard template that you overlay on top of your own keyboard. It replaces your keys with keycaps that have shapes on them. (Beware, these templates are easily misplaced.)

Tip

Early versions of these games were copy-protected with a dreadful copy protection scheme that forced you to match one of 64 Mickey characters on a sheet of non-reproducible, barely legible, dark, burgundy paper to a picture of Mickey that appeared on screen. Your eyes bugged out of your head before you made the correct match. Disney has recently removed the copy protection. Sometimes software shops try and unload old software on unsuspecting customers. Make sure you have a new version of the software—one without the copy protection.

In *Mickey's Crossword Puzzle Maker,* you'll find a novel approach to teaching spelling and word meanings. We don't know about your kids, but Robin's are crossword puzzle-holics. In addition to enjoying the play, they're often asked to create puzzles for homework in school, and since we remember doing the same thing in our own formative years, we doubt this is simply a passing fad. *Mickey's Crossword Puzzle Maker* lets you play eight puzzles on a disk or create your own puzzles by entering words and clues from a supplied list of vocabulary words. There are three varying degrees of difficulty for the game, and because the easiest level mixes pictures and words, it's well suited to the beginning reader. Puzzles can be saved and solved on screen, or they can be printed to dot-matrix printers with a variety of handsome Disney-esque backgrounds and borders. Older children may be disappointed because they can't make a puzzle from their own vocabulary words.

Figure 13.2 **Mickey's Crossword Puzzle Maker** features familiar friends.

Tip

All of the Disney Games, only available for IBM PC-compatibles, can take advantage of a device called the Sound Source. The list price of the device is $39.95, but most stores carry it for about $20. Consisting of a speaker box, a nine-volt battery (we find it's good for about a month of fairly regular play), a cable, and an adapter plug, the device is an economical no-brainer to use and a pleasure to install. To hook it up, you plug the adapter into the parallel printer connector on your PC and the back of the speaker box on the Sound Source.

(continued)

Tip (continued)

Don't even think of buying the Disney games without the Sound Source—you lose too much of the play. Without the Sound Source, you see Mickey and the gang move their lips soundlessly. Disney games don't support any other sound device. The good news is that the Sound Source, in part because it is so inexpensive, is becoming more widely supported by other game manufacturers. As a matter of fact, Disney recently announced a deal to integrate the Sound Source with products from Phoenix Technologies. Phoenix makes a popular BIOS (or instructions at the most basic level of the computer), which means that computers with a Phoenix BIOS will have a sound source built directly inside the machine.

Figure 13.3 Kids face villain Morty Maxwell in *Midnight Rescue!*

Midnight Rescue!

The Learning Company

Ages: 7 to 10

Skills Taught: Reading comprehension

Midnight Rescue! is The Learning Company's introduction to a series of learning adventure games that feature the villain, Morty Maxwell, and the gang from the Super Solvers Club. In this particular incarnation, Morty Maxwell has a diabolical plan to make the Shady Glen School disappear by midnight. He is in disguise, posing as one of five robots, and is roaming the Shady Glen School.

> **Tip**
>
> Even if you're not particularly good at the arcade part of *Midnight Rescue!*, you can do very well at Super Solvers. We find the game works well when younger children take care of the zapping and dodging and the older children stick around to answer the reading questions.

Your job is to roam through the rooms at the school capturing photo facts that you can piece together. The pieces of the puzzle help you discover Maxwell's true identity. As you travel, you also spend considerable time dodging harmless objects and banana peels hurled at you by Morty's robot henchmen. You, in turn, can try and zap them in mid-air. Throughout your travels, you are hit with reading comprehension questions that must be answered correctly. Each time you get to a room and bump into a mystery spot, you must answer a question that involves reading a paragraph before responding. Each correct answer gives you another piece of the puzzle. Arcade-like elements make this a fast-paced game. And since the reading comprehension is tied in to the plot of the story, children find the questions a pleasant, information-rich diversion.

Connection

The Learning Company's Super Solvers Club is a real club with its own newsletter and active roster of children who participate as members. When you buy the software, you can send in for your Super Solvers Club membership. Make sure your child signs up, it enhances the fun.

Reader Rabbit and Reader Rabbit 2

The Learning Company

Ages: 3 to 6 and 5 to 8

Skills taught: Phonics and word recognition

Reader Rabbit was one of the first computer games designed to teach preschoolers about phonics and vowel sounds. The early version had meager graphics and sound, but a new version released in 1991 brought *Reader Rabbit* into modern times.

The four games included on the *Reader Rabbit* disk are designed to introduce simple phonics and word recognition. The Sorter presents children with a letter and asks them to match it to words that contain the same letter. A match, when it is made, goes through the "sorter" machine, and the child scores points. The Labeler game presents pictures with scrambled letters below them and asks the child to unscramble them. The Word Train game asks children to create a train of words, each word differing from the one before it in only one respect. And the Matching Game asks children to match words and pictures or vowel sounds and pictures.

Reader Rabbit 2 is a continuation of pre-reading skills; it also incorporates state-of-the-art animation, sound, and graphics. In this game, the plot thickens. Rabbit 2 lives in a town called Wordsville. From Wordsville you can click on one of four games, each set in a different locale, each teaching a different skill. The Mac version includes color graphics and sound. All words are spoken by the program and music accompanies the animation.

Tip

Keyboards display only uppercase letters, but the Rabbit games are played with lowercase letters on screen. This can be confusing to kids who are only beginning to recognize letters in the alphabet. It would be nice if the game had a toggle between uppercase and lowercase letters so that kids could choose between the two and get practice on both. And wouldn't it be nice if there were a special kid's keyboard with lowercase letters? We've seen some ambitious parents actually make "keycap labels" with lowercase letters on them that can be stuck on the keys. But this is truly a heroic effort. We recommend that you work with your children at the keyboard to point out the differences between uppercase and lowercase letters and explain to the kids that they will be working in both modes on screen.

Kids learn about compound word construction down in the Word Mine. In this crystal mine, the miner's cart shows a picture of an object with the first part of a compound word displayed (butter ___, for example). Your job is to find the crystal with the other half of the compound word (in this case, "fly").

At the Vowel Pond, kids go fishing for short and long vowel sounds. A fish, sporting a word on its belly, swims underneath the fishing net. The kids decide whether it matches the phonic on the fish bucket and opt to catch it or let it go. To play, kids must be familiar with the diacritical notations for long and short vowels.

The Match Patch is a variation on the old memory game. Carrots, buried in the ground, contain words written on them. As you click on a carrot, you reveal a word. The game lets children match rhymes, opposites, or homonyms. Match Patch is great fun, but we suspect that the youngest children would benefit more from matching a word with a picture of the word.

Finally, the Alphabet Dance, set in a barn, teaches alphabetical order. Four dancing characters with name tags must be placed in alphabetical order. Moving them involves a considerable amount of mouse or keyboard clicking, which can leave a kid lost.

Throughout all the games, the levels of play become increasingly challenging. Children are rewarded with whimsical animation sequences. All of the games have multiple play levels.

Connection

Another Learning Company program, called *Writer Rabbit*, uses the same mix of games, animation, and structured concepts to teach writing skills. The focus of *Writer Rabbit* is on sentence construction and parts of speech, and it is designed for children between seven and ten years old.

Writer Rabbit invites you to a sentence party to write fancy sentences. There's an ice cream machine, a cake maker, a juicer, and a dessert. Each offers a different milieu for exploring the parts of a sentence. The culminating event is a Silly Story Party where you can use the sentence parts you've learned about to write simple stories.

Teaching sentence construction is a bit harder than teaching prereading skills, and the game's graphics and animations are not as new and exciting as the *Reader Rabbit* version. Nonetheless, this is an entertaining game, especially if your children are learning parts of speech using the traditional who, what, where, when, why, and how constructions.

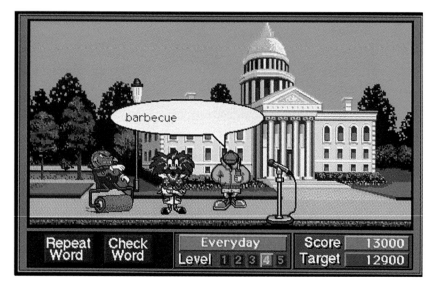

Figure 13.4 Spellbound offers four spelling games.

Spellbound!

The Learning Company

Ages: 7 to 12

Skills Taught: Spelling

A wild and wacky way to get your kids spelling properly, *Spellbound* is actually four entertaining games. The game comes with predefined spelling lists, but you can also create customized lists (great for those reviews for spelling tests). The first game is a word hunt, the second a crossword puzzle, and the third flash-card practice. All three offer practice and preparation for the fourth game, a bona fide spelling bee, where you are pitted against Morty Maxwell and his robots.

The spelling bee features an announcer's voice with uncannily good computerized speech. You can use a sound card, but the words are quite audible even if you only have a PC speaker. The Master of Ceremonies pits you against the robots. You must outspell them in order to win the game and proceed to the next level. The nicest part about this game is that you can easily customize the spelling lists to include your children's own weekly spelling lists. It is one of the best ways to study for spelling tests that we've found. And if you outspell the robots and make it to the top, you get to the White House.

Figure 13.5 StickeyBear is the star of a software series by Weekly Reader Software.

The StickeyBear Series: ABCs, Opposites, Shapes, Numbers

Weekly Reader Software

Ages: 2 to 5

Skills Taught: Pre-reading Skills

Like Disney's Mickey Mouse series for pre-schoolers, the Stickey-bear series from Weekly Reader Software takes kids through a variety of learning scenarios. These programs, which sell separately, are a delightful way for the pre-reader to become exposed to basic skills. Stickeybear is an engaging teddy character, who performs sweet animations to teach basic concepts. In each program, Stickeybear presents certain concepts: alphabet, opposites (near and far, up and down) shapes, and numbers. Again, these are games where you can do no wrong. Any key you press elicits a response. The latest Stickey-bear release which, unfortunately, is available only for the Apple II GS, uscs synthesized speech to introduce kids to spelling; it is called *The New Talking Stickeybear Alphabet. StickeyBear's Reading Room* for the Macintosh has sound input and is the first bilingual English/Spanish program in the series.

There are some other Stickeybear products for a slightly older crowd (ages seven and up). In fact, Weekly Reader markets more than thirty Stickeybear programs. You should ask the company for a catalog. *Stickeybear Math* teaches addition, subtraction, multiplication, and division. Two others available only for the Apple II are: *Stickeybear Music*, which lets you create musical pieces using timing signatures, sharps, and flats, as well as notes; and *Stickeybear Reading*, which teaches decoding skills using various games. *Stickeybear Town Builder* teaches map-reading skills as you build a town, take a drive, and find hidden keys in the town. The Stickeybear series is reasonably priced and the educational content is good, even if the graphics are not as vivid and modern as some programs'.

Talking Once Upon A Time

Compu-Teach Educational Software

Ages: 6 to10

Skills Taught: Writing, Desktop publishing, Storytelling

The game is available in a number of different volumes (Along Main Street, The Farm, and Medieval Times, for example). Your child picks a theme from one and creates a scene by using the cursor keys to move bits of artwork on the screen. Then she annotates each scene with text and prints the story.

The program has separate drawing and text entry modes, which can be confusing to small children. When they are in the text entry mode, they cannot see their drawings as they write their text, and when they are in the drawing mode, they cannot see their text as they illustrate their story. On an IBM PC-compatible, the program uses the speaker and a robot-sounding voice to utter the names of the pictures that your child uses.

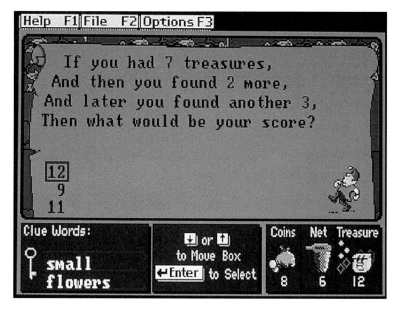

Figure 13.6 Morty Maxwell strikes again in *Treasure Mountain*.

Treasure Mountain

The Learning Company

Ages: 5 to 9

Skills Taught: Word-building, phonics

Another in the Super Solvers series, *Treasure Mountain* combines arcade-like fun with simple reading puzzles. In this adventure, Morty Maxwell, the Master of Mischief, has stolen a magic crown and is driving the inhabitants of Treasure Mountain batty. You need to reclaim the crown by uncovering all of the hidden treasure on this multilayered mountain. There are necklaces, jewels, toys, sweets, and more.

You uncover treasure by tossing magic coins that let you peer behind the scenery. To aid you in your quest, you are given nets to catch elves, who furnish you with clues as to where the treasures and where the keys to successive levels of the mountain lie. You've got to keep track of your clues and your treasures and be sure not to let your magic coin pile dwindle.

The arcade part of the game, catching elves with your net, is simple enough for even the youngest player to master. But each time you capture an elf you are given a simple reading question. For example, a question might ask you to find a word that rhymes with or sounds like another word. You may be asked to perform simple math or solve simple word problems. Each time you answer correctly, you are given one more clue that tells you where the key you require is hiding. (For example, if you amass the clues "five," "triangle," and "trees," you'd better start looking behind a group of five triangular trees for your key to the next level.)

The game gets harder as you progress. Elves turn unfriendly by throwing a special dust at you, which forces you to yield your coins. Bridges break and send you tumbling down a level; ladders end mysteriously in mid-air, as you scale the castle wall.

It's a game that you can play for hours, months even, without growing bored.

Connection: IBM's *Writing to Read*

You may have heard about IBM's *Writing to Read* program, a popular and effective computerized reading program used in schools. In fact, your school may have this novel program. The bad news is that there is no home equivalent. Nonetheless you should be aware of how the program operates and look for ways to reinforce the experience at home.

The *Writing to Read* program, begun in 1982, was started with IBM grant money. It was based on the pedagogy of Dr. John Henry Martin, a retired educator with years of experience teaching children to read. The program is designed to teach young children (ages five to seven) to read, using a very structured, prescribed sequence of writing activities.

Writing to Read was one of the first programs to combine voice and computers (early versions used the voice on the IBM PC jr., an early PC model that IBM no longer makes). The concept behind the program is simple: Children can write whatever they say. Most children enter school with a working vocabulary of 2,000 to 4,000 words.

(continued)

Connections (continued)

Writing to Read builds on this base by presenting a specific series of words phonetically and having children use them in a host of creative writing activities. To learn the words, students do all sorts of things. They type them into the computer (Martin believes this frees children from being encumbered by penmanship, which requires more dexterity). They repeat them after the computer speaks them. They play a variety of computer games with the words. They watch as the computer animates a phonetic spelling and draws a picture of a word. They even clap their hands and stamp their feet to get the rhythm of the word.

The program is interactive and filled with imaginative and varied exercises. It was one of the first programs to combine a multisensory approach to the computer—integrating sound and graphics along with the on-screen text.

The results of the early *Writing to Read* programs were very impressive. *Writing to Read* students in kindergarten and first grade typically increased their performance on standardized reading tests by fifteen points. Many educators believe that the *Writing to Read* program would be especially helpful for learning-disabled students. But the system is expensive. IBM never released a home version because the cost of equipment was high, and they felt that only trained teachers could properly administer the program.

It's ironic, and a bit sad for parents, that IBM consistently produces excellent educational software but seldom makes it available for the home user. You should keep in touch with your school to learn more about *Writing to Read* and any other IBM programs they are using. And, if you really want to get political, you can let IBM know that there's a market for consumer educational software—one that they have never addressed.

CHAPTER 14

MATH SOFTWARE— ADVENTURES IN NUMBERS

For the great majority of us, one of two things happens by the time we get around to helping our children with math. Either educators have invented a new way to teach the concept, or we've forgotten how we ever managed to master it in the first place.

Like reading, teaching math is a tough act. But math may be even tougher than reading. There are certain fundamentals, such as measurements, where nothing short of memorization will do. Other math problems demand highly evolved logic and thinking skills. And, at the most elementary level, math involves simple numeration: five apples, four balls, and so on.

Computer games can help teach math in a number of ways. They add an element of fun to otherwise dreary, routine memorization. And for the tough logic and problem-solving skills, they can supply graphics and visual aids or break a big problem into manageable components. For the very young, they can make the process of learning to count easier by combining sound and graphics in lessons that entertain as they teach. They also help individualize the instruction.

Stickeybear Numbers

Weekly Reader Software

Ages: 3 to 6

Skills Taught: Counting

Stickeybear Numbers, part of the Weekly Reader software family of educational software, is a counting and number-recognition program. In this game, even young children soon learn that pressing a number from 0 to 9 causes a corresponding number of objects to appear on the screen. Pressing the spacebar causes objects to disappear, one at a time. Cars and stars, planes and trains, ducks and trucks—and of course, bears—are among the 250 different picture combinations.

Stickeybear uses only CGA graphics and must boot from its own floppy disk, which makes it a more cumbersome program to use than others. But young children don't seem to mind.

Figure 14.1 The fun multiplies in The Learning Company's *Math Rabbit*

Math Rabbit

The Learning Company

Ages: 3 to 7

Skills Taught: Number concepts, counting, basic math operations

The Learning Company's model in many of its games is to offer four educationally sound games on a single theme, all in one package. *Math Rabbit's* four games teach young children simple numbers, counting, and addition and subtraction. There is also a talking version of the program, which uses digitized sound effects so that your child can actually hear the numbers spoken. (The Mac version also talks.)

In these games, an animated rabbit offers a sequence of problems; when the challenge has been met, the rabbit dances. The program offers customization options that let you alter the speed, numbers, mathematical relationships, and other parameters of the games to increase or decrease the challenge. The four games include A Clown's

Counting Game, where your child plays a tune using the eight numbers that correspond to notes on a scale. In the Tightrope game, she matches a set of objects (such as three fish) to the appropriate digit. The Mystery Matching game is a concentration game (a theme often repeated in the various Learning Company programs). And the Circus Train Game offers simple addition, subtraction, and number-ordering problems. When your child solves all the problems correctly, the train leaves the station.

New Math Blaster Plus!

Math Blaster Mystery

Davidson and Associates, Inc.

Ages: 6 to 12

Skills Taught: Math fundamentals, problem-solving skills

Educators often frown on using the computer as a drill-and-practice machine, but we find that most parents welcome the experience it gives their children. And the best part about it is that the computer —not the parent—acts as a learning coach. The Math Blaster programs offer drill-and-practice routines on such subjects as math multiplication tables and calculations with fractions.

Computers are terrific at drill-and-practice exercises, because they are ever-patient, add exciting game-like elements to the drill, and because the software can tailor drills to the student's needs.

Math Blaster! was one of the first drill-and-practice games to intersperse elements of video games with math exercises. And the combination works! *Math Blaster!* has seen a number of incarnations. The latest one, *New Math Blaster Plus!*, has better activities, graphics, animation, and sound effects than previous versions. It offers drill-and-practice exercises in addition, subtraction, multiplication, division, fractions, and percents.

The games have enough degrees of difficulty to make this a plausible game for first- through sixth-graders, although those in the middle stand to benefit the most. The games offer a fair degree of control, so, for example, you can choose the orientation of equations (vertical or horizontal).

The series features one robot and one Blasternaut that head into outer space. In the Rocket Launcher game, children must answer enough math drill questions to assemble a rocket and blast off. In Trash Zapper, the object is to fill in the missing value of an equation, you zap some trash. After five correct answers, you get to play the shoot the garbage in space arcade game. In a journey to a space-age recycling station, you can recycle numbers by choosing them from a slot machine-like list until you have an equation. And finally, in a holdover from the original *Math Blaster* game, your Blasternaut races against time to get to the space station with the correct answer. Problems range from those as simple as *2+3=?* to finding minuends and rounding numbers.

Math Blaster Plus! offers a fair amount of tracking and feedback. There are certificates of excellence that can be printed, an editor to enter your own math problems, and a test-maker to let you create "before and after" tests for your children. There are, however, no word-based math problems incorporated into the program.

Connections

Math Blaster is the perfect game for reinforcing the home-school connection. As children learn their various timetables and fractions in school, you can play that particular level of *Math Blaster* in the evenings. A pretest checks their knowledge before a game; a post-test assesses how well they do afterward.

Math Blaster Mystery is designed for a slightly older student (10 and up). It focuses on more advanced topics: negative numbers, factoring, and basic algebra. There are different activities, all set in a Victorian mystery house.

Decipher the Code is the mathematical version of Hangman. Weigh the Evidence is a puzzle, where children move bricks of different weights from one scale to another until they have a balanced equation. In Search for Clues, the child must figure out the mystery number by searching for clues through the rooms in the Victorian house. The game features an onscreen pop-up calculator to help the child along.

There are four different levels of difficulty. Problems can be edited and changed, so that parents can also create their own.

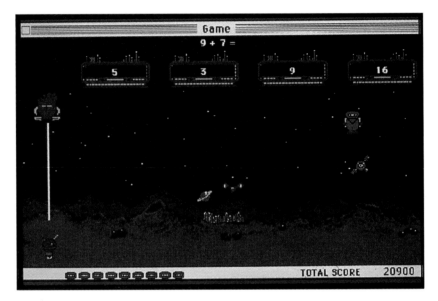

Figure 14.2 New Math Blaster Plus! combines math skills and arcade action.

Operation Neptune

The Learning Company

Ages: 7 and up

Skills Taught: Graph-reading, measurement, area, rate and distance problems, and word problems

This game is a toughy, but it is one of the more exciting math challenges we've seen. Your child guides a submarine around the bottom of the ocean, searching for data canisters that hold information that was dispersed when a spaceship crashed into the sea. The canisters are leaking a toxic substance; your child's job is to gather them up.

The game hangs together well because everything ties into the underwater adventure game theme: your child navigates the ship through all sorts of hellacious waters where he must steer clear of dangerous sea creatures. The only way to win an encounter with a dangerous sea creature is to hit it with an ink pellet. He must also attend to a finite supply of oxygen. As he collects the mystery canisters, he encounters a variety of math challenges including: calculating distances, accessing the proximity of other vessels, calculating the number of cubic feet in his volume of food, tracking the kilometers of ocean searched, toxicity graphs, and so forth. All of the math questions have a direct bearing on the game, so your child barely notices he is doing math (a much-needed improvement over The Learning Company's earlier game, *Out Numbered!*, where some of the math problems seemed extraneous to the action). Finally, he can only proceed to the next level when he picks up the data canisters and the log entry canister and solves a tricky combination-lock sequence.

There's a lot to learn and do in the program. Graphics, animation, and music are state of the art. It's a compelling game but a tough one to play. After awhile, however, children become very adept at the types of problems the game presents.

Out Numbered!

The Learning Company

Ages: 7 to 10

Skills Taught: Word problems

This game, also from The Learning Company, revisits the Super Solvers Club—a gang dedicated to outsmarting the dastardly prankster Morty Maxwell. This time Morty has a plan to take over the airwaves by capturing the local TV station. You need to find Morty, who's hiding in one of the TV station's rooms.

As your child explores the television station rooms, she'll need to use the zapper to protect herself from Morty's robot henchman, Telly and the dastardly extension cord. Each time you zap Telly you have to answer math questions to find pieces of the code. In each room of the TV station are clues that you can find by answering word problems. Match the codes with the clues to find Marty before midnight. In addition, she'll need to take photographs of the clues regarding his true identity which Morty has left in each room. She'll also be faced with various math challenges—mostly in the form of word problems. Finally, she'll use a secret code to decipher clues and figure out where Morty is hiding.

The word problems are quite challenging, and often include graphical components: bar graphs, percent pies, and money problems. A calculator is built into the game; it really helps to eliminate frustration on some of the tougher problems. And there's a terrific mix of arcade elements—the zapping and jumping that your child must do to avoid attack. There is also mystery: where in the TV station is Morty Maxwell? And math skills are needed to solve some complex word problems. Graphics, sound and animation make the play most enjoyable. The Mac version can be played in color or monochrome.

Some Tips on Out Numbered!

You can customize Out Numbered! in a variety of ways. You can tailor the supplied drill-and-practice exercises to your child's school lesson. Or you can customize the game to present only certain types of math problems, focusing on your child's particular needs.

Also, there are quite a few things to attend to in this game, which makes it ideal for group play. For example, players have a certain amount of energy, which they need to monitor during the game. One child in the group can keep track of the energy and record which rooms they've visited, since revisiting a room they've already been to wastes time. Using the zapper for no reason wastes energy, so it's important to stay near the target when zapping. You can restore your zapper's energy from the energy vending machine.

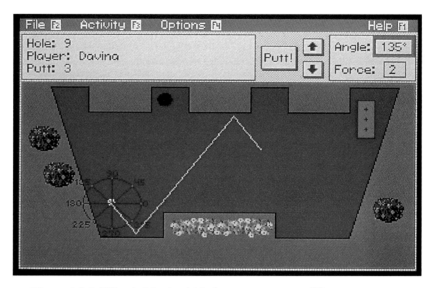

Figure 14.3 What's My Angle? brings geometry to life.

What's My Angle?

Davidson and Associates, Inc.

Ages: 14 and up

Skills Taught: Geometry

Now here's a subject that only a brave software publisher would touch! Davidson's *What's My Angle?* is a clever introduction to some rather heady geometric concepts. Five different activities help make geometry a living subject with practical applications.

- GeoBoard teaches the fundamentals by letting you create your own geometric shapes on a grid. You even get tools, like a compass to draw circles and radii. As you draw shapes on the board, you are given information about them. An interactive tutorial helps make the most of this experience.

- In GeoLife you meet a bunch of onscreen characters—each from a different profession—who demonstrate why geometry should be important to you. For example, Yvonne the Inventor gives you a tour of her flying car.

- In GeoConclusions you draw and support geometric proofs.

- And in GeoProofs you unscramble some pretty wacky proofs to make them correct.

- My favorite activity is GeoGolf, a miniature golf game that realistically shows you how important angles can be.

This is an ambitious attempt to cover some tough material, and Davidson pulls it off with style.

CHAPTER 15

LOGIC SOFTWARE— SHARPENING THE THINKING PROCESS

An ancient Japanese proverb goes something like this: "Give a man a fish, and you'll feed him for the day; teach a man to fish, and you'll feed him for a lifetime." What holds true for fish goes double for problem-solving. Solve a kid's problem and you've given him fleeting contentment. Teach him to solve problems, and you've given him lifelong proficiency. The question is, can computers help teach problem-solving?

They certainly can. Although early problem-solving software didn't make the genre very appealing, today's improved graphics have turned modern software programs into enticing and believable microworlds that can simulate all the same conflicts you'll find in history, as well as all the problems of living in the modern world. The problems in those early programs were designed to do what the computers of that era did best, which was to make pretty polygons. Kids wound up playing checker-like games ad nauseum or matching patterns in a Rubik's cube-like fashion. Those problems were uninspiring and had little relevance to the real world.

But now, in the computer world, rules can be mastered. Hypotheses can be tested. Outcomes can be predicted and victories anticipated. Like Legos or building blocks, the play in modern logic games tends to be openended and exploratory. And the computer gives children a world where they can form their own understandings and make connections between one fact and another. They see firsthand, for example, the results of any action they take on the computer.

Today, just about all computer games have the potential of being problem-solving exercises. But some have more potential than others. In this chapter, we'll give you a quick summary of the best. Generally speaking, a good problem-solving software program guides children through a series of cognitive steps. As the kids work through the program, they begin to understand more and more about the rules of the game. They can classify them, sequence them, and use them to determine the best possible course of action. And finally, at the highest level, once a child has digested the rules, he can synthesize a solution to the problem.

If all this sounds a bit metaphysical, relax. Using problem-solving software is like giving your kids vitamins in the shape of circus animals. The kids don't have to know it's supposed to be good for them. They only have to know it's fun. Play's the thing, and kids will rally to a challenge if they find it enjoyable. As the play progresses, it's all the better if they're able to sharpen their wits, don their thinking caps, and become problem-solvers.

So here are our picks for the best problem-solving programs.

Ancient Empires

The Learning Company

Ages: Ten to adult

Skills Taught: Logic and Planning

This game, which used to bear the name *Challenge of the Ancient Empires,* is a fast-paced, arcade-like game that challenges your child to use some intense logic and strategic planning skills in order to win. It's one of Learning Company's SuperSolver Adventure Series games.

Adults will find the plot a bit thin and the play a bit frustrating. But it is surely addictive. It appears to be one of those games that the kids will always play better than you do. Maybe it's because they love secret codes so much!

In Ancient Empires, pirates have hidden treasure. And you've got to wend your way through various caverns, collecting artifacts that help you get to the treasure. In order to claim the artifacts, your child must solve some pretty wild hieroglyphic puzzles in each room.

You can use a variety of strategies to navigate the rooms. For example, you can wield a light beam to attack creatures out to get you. Force fields can put an impenetrable shield around you as you move. You can also jump to various heights to capture a piece of the hieroglyph. You'll also need to learn to control the way conveyor belts rotate, or the way coded panels open.

All of these tools help your child scoot around the rooms, collecting pieces to the puzzle that she must solve to reach the next level of the game. The game is fast-paced, and players are forced to think about what seems like a million different details (their attackers, their route, and the puzzle itself). If they mess up, they are mercilessly sent back to the first room of the chamber they've entered. So, if they're not sharp, the game can last for centuries! There are two levels of play, an explorer level for novices, and an expert level for more advanced players. If you and your child get to the expert level, be sure to let us know. In our time with the game we found only one little fourth grader, Joanna Robbins, who could expertly maneuver all the passages.

If your child likes to solve puzzles and explore mazes, she'll love Ancient Empires. It's very much along the lines of another Learning Company game we reviewed here, *Think Quick!*, but the graphics and animation are much more modern.

BushBuck Charms, Viking Ships and Dodo Eggs

PC Globe

Ages: Nine and older

Skills Taught: Map and Atlas skills

BushBuck Charms, Viking Ships and Dodo Eggs is a geographical game from the makers of *PC Globe*, a marvelous electronic almanac of world maps and cultural and demographic data. *BushBuck Charms* uses the facts and maps found in PC Globe to construct an adventure similar to what you find in the Carmen Sandiego series. And the name alone is enough to intrigue children and inspire a few giggles. However silly the names may sound, *BushBuck charms, Viking ships and Dodo eggs* are or were real things. And they're just a few of the obscure but culturally and ecologically interesting items your child must search for in the game.

Players are sent on missions to find these rare artifacts. The game comes with a foldout map of 175 countries and 206 cities that players can visit to search for the items. Players catch planes from city to city to collect clues about where to look next. They can compete against their earlier scores, one another, or any of three electronic competitors in the game.

If you're looking for a computerized atlas, try *PC Globe* from the same company. It contains detailed maps, population and economic data, and more.

Choices, Choices

Decisions, Decisions

Tom Synder Productions, Inc.

Ages: *Decisions, Decisions* for Grades five through twelve. *Choices, Choices* for Grades K through six.

Skills Taught: Ethics and morals, logic and problem-solving

Here's a horse of a different color: software designed to teach ethics to groups of children in a school setting. If your schools don't offer them to children, pester your administration or parents' organization to purchase them and incorporate them as instruction in the school curricula.

Tom Synder believes that kids working individually at a keyboard may attain skills, but this type of activity doesn't help them relate to the real world. These programs are out to transform the computer into a social tool that stimulates discussion and offers a platform for dialog. Snyder's creations are designed to be played by a group of kids, a roomful of thinkers, in a one-computer classroom, where the teacher and the computer guide the enterprise for the entire class.

In each of the games, the computer poses some issues related to different scenarios. For the younger crowd, the subject under discussion is how to make wise choices. Should a kid tattle when his friend accidentally shatters the teacher's favorite flowerpot, for example? For the older crowd, the focus is on more content-oriented social studies. Should a snack-food company sponsoring a controversial TV show stop backing the show when special-interest groups start hollering? Should a sleepy little town impose restrictions on growth and industry, in order to avoid urbanization?

Next, the children are presented with goals, and, as the children discuss their goals and make decisions based upon them, the computer moves through the scenario and identifies the outcome that would occur, based on their answers. Computer animation brings the scenarios to life. In all of the games, a variety of additional course materials (handbooks, story cards, and others) stimulate further discussion.

The only prop which is a bit hard to swallow is a mysterious friend, who pops in and out and acts as a kind of narrator, providing insight and commentary and reminding the students of their original goals. At the end, when they see the consequences of their decisions unfold, students debrief one another and take stock of where they've been.

The most successful problem-solving game in existence, *Where in the World Is Carmen Sandiego?*, hit upon a magic formula for group participation. Synder takes this concept one step further. Synder's games reinforce what's important, making it fun by getting a group involved. Teachers can bring other sources of information into the game. Problem-solving software is at its best when children can carry away what they've learned. And with this software, they can.

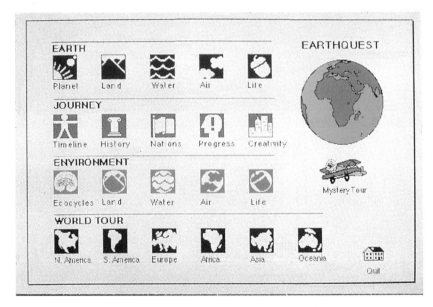

Figure 15.1 EarthQuest turns geography into an adventure.

Earthquest

Earthquest, Inc.

Ages: Ten to adult

Skills Taught: Understanding ecology, geography, cultural geography

Earthquest, from the company of the same name, is a HyperCard stack that uses icons and information cards to explore the world's resources. You navigate four main areas: Earth—where you study planets, land, water, air, and life; Journey—where you study the the history of the world; Environment—where you study endangered species and natural resources; and World Tour—where you travel to the continents and their countries. It's certainly an ambitious undertaking. The main screen houses some other selections, including Ecology, History, and the Arts, but these are for other EarthQuest knowledge bases. Time Treks and Ecology are available and others are promised.

There are numerous ways to navigate through the plentiful information. On any Mac or an IBM PC-compatible with a Sound-Blaster card, you can hear speech blurbs to accompany the programs graphics; if not, you read the on-screen text. The information combines text, graphics, charts, quizzes, and some animation. For example, you can view tables of information such as water cycles, or watch a movie (there are only a few movies included, but the company is planning a CD-ROM version that will include more) about the earth. You can click on a lightbulb icon to take a quiz about what you've learned.

Navigating through *Earthquest* is tricky. You can point at maps, use an index, or click on icons. A number of games (50 to be exact), including a mystery tour and a searchquest, are added to give a child some additional motivation.

The program seems a bit disorganized. Many of the charts and diagrams have too much information, and their presentation could be better. However, *Earthquest* is the perfect adjunct to a social studies curriculum or an Earth Day-related study. There's lots to explore.

Connections

If you're a Macintosh owner and you enjoy *Earthquest,* you'll want to check out EarthQuest, Inc.'s other two programs: *Earthquest Explores Ecology* and *Time Treks.* The first takes an ecological look at cultural geography, with such games as The Renegade Tour, in which rengede vegetables run to save the planet. *Time Treks* takes you as an archeologist into a period from 3,400 BC to the present to close time doors that allow tyrants to slip through the eons and change history. Unfortunately, there are no IBM PC-compatible versions of these two products at present.

Facemaker

Queue Inc.

Ages: Five to Ten

Skills Taught: Logic and pre-programming skills

This one is truly a classic, although it's certainly begun to show its age. We mention it because many schools are still using *Facemaker* with young children, and it's always nice to have some of the same programs at home that children use in school. *Facemaker* was first introduced in the early '80s and is now in its revised "Golden Edition."

Children of all ages are fascinated by the human face, so it was a clever idea to make face-making central to a child's first computer graphic activity. Actually, what Queue has done is make face-making a part of pre-programming skills.

The game has four different activities. Your child initially builds a face from primitive components. Each category of features—eyes, ears, nose, mouth, hair, body, and accessories—has eight whimsical variations. Your child selects a feature by using the spacebar to cycle through a visual menu of choices, and then he presses enter when he reaches the one he wants. With all this variety, your child can create an endless number of comical faces.

And, he can use the program to animate his creations, making the faces wink, smile, or frown. There are nine different movements to apply to the finished picture. Your child can do this by simply typing a single letter, W for Wink, for example. By combining as many as sixteen movements, your child can create a face that displays all sorts of expressions. And each contortion is accompanied by a unique sound effect, which adds another element to the fun.

From this basic activity, your child can move to a more advanced memory game. In it, the computer animates the face, and your child must mimic the sequence of movements by typing the letter that represents the movement, in the sequence that the movements are performed. Initially, he must duplicate two movements. That's manageable enough. But, every time he reproduces a sequence, the computer adds another movement to the string (up to a maximum of sixteen movements) As adults, we eventually found this game difficult and resorted to taking notes in order to pass the seven-movement mark.

Finally, the package includes a simple word processor that allows your child to type and delete text. With it, he can write captions for the funny faces and print them out. *Facemaker*, which displays only four-color CGA graphics and supports only dot-matrix printers, is not exactly at the technological forefront, but the kids will find it fun. The program is copy-protected, which means you'll need to be careful not to lose the program disk. You'll need it to start Facemaker even after you've copied the program to your hard disk.

Connections

One of the Raskin family's favorite games is to play *Facemaker* with pencil and paper. One person draws one feature of the face, and passes it on to the next person, who adds another. The faces creation can be quite hysterical.

Figure 15.2 With Headline Harry, kids play reporter as they study history.

Headline Harry and the Great Paper Race

Davidson and Associates, Inc.

Ages: Ten to adult

Skills Taught: History, geography, problem-solving

In many ways, *Headline Harry* is a variation on the *Carmen Sandiego* theme. It touches on history and geography. But while *Carmen* has a relatively simple and straightforward plot, *Headline Harry* is considerably more complex and difficult. But it is also about geography and real history instead of geography and fictional crime. Those with a true passion for history and mystery and a fairly decent background in history will love it. But it requires a considerable degree of motivation and a higher degree of parental participation than most of the other games reviewed here.

Two newspapers in town (yours and theirs) are out to scoop one another on the same story. You work for the good guy, Headline Harry, and attempt to uncover the true news before Marvin Muckraker creates some awful fictional journalism. During the play, you are presented with three news stories that each have some basis in true history. But only one is the major story you're trying to scoop. The stories are mixed together and intertwined, and your job is to separate the important story from the others.

To do this, you select a destination from a map of the US, sift through facts, interview informants, and file pieces of your story as the clues check out.

Various tools help you to uncover clues: a radio delivers related news broadcasts and music; a tape recorder plays quotes from informants; a telephone lets you contact Harry and others; a notepad lets you record the clues and then wire them in to check their accuracy. The Mac version includes actual newsreel footage as QuickTime movie clips. A briefcase lets you collect lost items of the opponents that you may encounter on the way, and from those you can glean valuable information. Of course, you are playing against time, and if you head off on the wrong trail, you may find you don't have time to file a good and accurate story.

The program uses the same First Byte digital speech technology used in other Davidson games such as *Kid Works*. With it, you can clearly hear the voices in the game. In addition to supporting speech through the regular PC speaker (although not very well), a host of other sound devices like the AdLib and SoundBlaster cards, as well as PS/1 and Tandy sound, are supported.

Although the tools and the plot are certainly engrossing, this is a complicated game, possibly more complicated than it needs to be. The news stories span history from the 1950s to 1990 and include such diverse scoops as the Beatles' appearance on *The Ed Sullivan Show*, Rosa Parks's role in desegregation of the South, the first kidney transplant, and more. The clues you enter in the notepad must be worded very precisely to be accepted.

I've watched adults play this game and grow frustrated, and the children I've used the game with don't fare much better. Still, if you have a passion for history and the diligence to separate the mundane from the newsworthy, Headline Harry will keep you happy. The graphics, sound, and action are quite good. Also, you get a sense of the period in which the historical events happened. There is a real context that is both engaging and fascinating.

> **Tip**
>
> As we went to press, The Learning Company shipped *Time Riders in American History*. Its premise is similar to *Headline Harry's*—you answer questions to solve a historical news story. The play is more clearly directed and manageable. You travel hi-tech style through Time Riders headquarters and use gadgets to uncover clues. Recommended for ages ten and older.

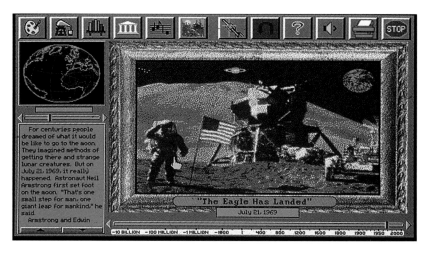

Figure 15.3 Kids travel through time and into space with *Knowledge Adventure.*

Knowledge Adventure

Knowledge Adventure, Inc.

Ages: Seven to 70

Skills Taught: History of civilization

Just like the television series, *Connections*, which aired on PBS stations a few years ago, the computer game *Knowledge Adventure* brings together history, geography, and culture in a fascinating panoply of onscreen activity. Just as each week the TV series traced inventions and innovations throughout the history of the world and created connections or links to other events, *Knowledge Adventure* helps your child make these same types of connections. One of the main ideas of the program is to illustrate how progress and innovation are often the result of certain events coming together in history.

But with *Knowledge Adventure*, instead of passively watching a television set, your child can actively control the exploration by manipulating icons on the computer screen. *Knowledge Adventure* combines text, music, and some elaborate, full-color illustrations.

The main activity screen presents your child with an attractive graphic depicting a place in time, along with a timeline and a globe. Across the top of the screen are icons representing categories of culture: art, literature, science, music, architecture, and so forth. Whether you use your mouse to click on the globe, the timeline, some element of the picture in the main screen, or an icon, you are transported to different places and events in history. Your child may use the mouse to click on a location on the globe, to zoom in close on a city on the map, or to pan outward for a view of the cosmos. Or he can click on the timeline to travel to a different era. He can also click on the elements of the pictures on screen to learn more about the adventure in front of him.

Each picture is accompanied by a text window filled with information that your child can read to learn more about the picture in front of him. The text is written in interesting, anecdotal style. And your child can click certain areas within the text to jump to a related area. So, for example, when the opening screen depicts the astronauts placing a flag on the moon, you can press the sound icon to hear "One small step for man, one giant leap for mankind," or you can click on the flag and be whisked to a story about Betsy Ross and the mystery of whether or not she really created the flag. If you want to know about the artists that lived at the same time Beethoven was composing the Ninth Symphony, you can move from Beethoven and click on the art icon.

The program prompts children to think about the connections in the events they see on screen. For instance, a child reading about Betsy Ross and the controversy over whether she really did sew that famous flag might click on the teapot displayed alongside her in the picture. That takes her to Great Wall of China. Not an obvious connection, but the Chinese did introduce the Western world to tea.

Click on the wall, and the program carries you to the Golden Gate Bridge, which, like the wall, is a masterful feat of human engineering.

Connections

Knowledge Adventure uses what its creators call a "Knowledge Engine" from which similar games can be developed. Since we looked at *Knowledge Adventure*, a new game called *Sports Adventure* has been released. Sports fans of all ages will love it. And by the time you read this book, the company will have introduced *Science Adventure*. This edition was created with the help of the late Issac Asimov, and an early peek at it proved to be very exciting.

One criticism we have of *Knowledge Adventure* is that occasionally it was difficult for children to make some of the connections, as with the teapot and China. The creators have assured us that in future versions you will be able to access a Connections button that will help you figure out why certain events are related.

When the children tire of exploring for exploration's sake, they can test their knowledge with a trivia game. The game poses questions whose answers lie somewhere in the child's journey. The faster the child gets to get the proper picture, the more points he earns. With its entertaining sound and graphics, Knowledge Adventure is the best of a new breed of software. You'll only wish there were more screens, sounds, and connections among elements.

Three Tips for Knowledge Adventurers:

1. Kids love playing the *Knowledge Adventure* quiz game against each other to see who gets the answer in the fewest clicks of the mouse. But the program makes no provisions for multiple players. Keep scores on paper for group play.

2. The *Knowledge Adventure* manual includes a Learning Guide section, with tips for parents showing how to make connections and how to vary the play. Be sure to read it before turning the manual over to your children.

3. You can't print the *Knowledge Adventure* pictures that you see in the game, but you can print the text. Many children will want to use the text as a jumping-off place for school reports. Keep crayons and paper nearby for younger children who want to illustrate the little stories they can print from the game.

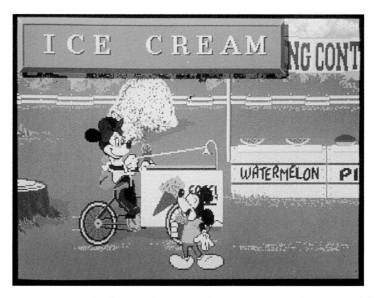

Figure 15.4 The puzzles in *Mickey's Jigsaw Puzzle* come to life.

Mickey's Jigsaw Puzzle

Walt Disney Computer Software

Ages: Five and up

Skills Taught: Traditional puzzle-solving

Imagine a book of electronic puzzles with fifteen beautifully illustrated scenes that feature Mickey Mouse characters. That's what you get with this game. But it's more than a simple do-it-once-and-put-it-away puzzle. The puzzles can be split in different ways to conform to a child's ability level. Children can play puzzles of four, nine, sixteen, 25, 36, 49, or 64 pieces using the same illustrations. To piece together the puzzle, they simply click with the mouse to grab a piece from the pile and insert it into an on-screen form that looks like a blank puzzle. When they're finished, the game rewards them by bringing the illustration to life with animated action.

Mickey's Jigsaw Puzzle teaches puzzle-making skills and manual dexterity, but there's also an interesting level of abstraction that goes on with this game. Since your child can never manipulate the puzzle pieces with his fingers the way he would with traditional puzzles, he must learn to abstractly manipulate shapes using a mouse, keyboard, or joystick. And this is an important computer skill.

Connection

GeoJigSaw from PC Globe is another program that lets you create puzzles from pictures. *GeoJigsaw* uses scenes from history: The Ice Age or Dinosaur era, for example, as well from as maps. You can divvy up pieces from these scenes to create complicated puzzles of up to 294 pieces and then let your kids race against the clock to put them back together.

PC Globe

PC Globe

Ages: Nine and up

Skills Taught: Map and atlas skills

PC Globe, from the company of the same name, is an easy-to-use, finely detailed world atlas with color maps of 177 countries. It can be used by adults as well as children and is an excellent resource for world map-lovers and children with lots of geography assignments.

Children can find maps of individual countries by entering the name of the place at a menu prompt, or by pointing and shooting (placing your cursor somewhere on the world map and clicking or hitting the Enter key).

The world map can display coalitions of countries, as well as political and economic entities, rivers, and cities. Country maps can be topographical as well as geographical, displaying physical features such as elevations, agricultural products, and major cities and boundaries.

The program includes a database that provides a wide range of information as adjuncts to the maps. Search the database to find information on population, culture, and ethnic groups for a given country. The program will also give you readings on longitudes and latitudes and will calculate the distances between points. It can even calculate currency conversion and time changes, which makes it a great item to cart along on a family trip abroad. The program supports a number of different kinds of printers, so the maps can be printed. Or, maps can be saved in the PC graphics file format, PCX, so that they can later can be imported to a graphics program or desktop publishing program and used in school reports and documents.

PC Globe, with its pull-down menus and visual displays, is incredibly easy to use. There is also a United States edition called *PC USA*. Younger students will enjoy browsing, and older ones will rise to the head of their social studies classes with the beautifully rendered maps they can create using the program.

Sparse documentation is this program's chief drawback. *PC Globe* wasn't really designed for the education market or for use in the home. It was designed for corporations and businesses that need access to geographical data. And so the information in the manual wasn't written with children in mind. Be prepared to do a little coaching, and you'll surely do a little learning as well.

Connection

After a rousing session with *Carmen Sandiego*, boot up *PC Globe* for a more in-depth look at the places you learned about in the game.

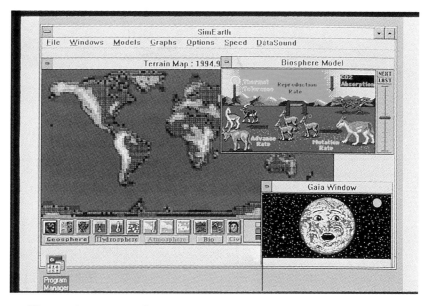

Figure 15.5 SimEarth puts your child in control of the planet.

SimEarth, SimCity, and SimAnt

Maxis Software (also distributed by Broderbund)

Ages: Twelve to adult

Skills Taught: Logic, strategy, urban planning, animal behavior

These games, which simulate city management, the ecology of the Earth, and ant behavior, respectively, are so involved and complex that they probably have no business being included in a book for children. But they are such incredibly good games that we would be remiss if we didn't mention them. *SimEarth*, *SimCity*, and *SimAnt* are definitely for the big kids of the family. Think of them as something to grow into long after *Carmen Sandiego* ceases to be a challenge.

SimCity is a simulated city that the player builds and governs. Players are given a limited number of resources to provide all of the amenities a good city should have: police, sports stadiums, and sanitation for example. Players must control population growth, pollution, taxes, unemployment and more—all the things that trouble our real urban lives. The game is immense fun, extremely educational, and can go on forever. At a minimum, after playing it for a few hours, you'll gain a newfound respect for the mayor of your city. At the maximum, you'll gain new insights on the complexity of urban problems and the strategies they require. *SimCity* is available for PC-compatibles, including a Windows version, and for Macintosh computers.

A sequel to *SimCity*, *SimEarth* allows you to play the same type of simulated game, only this time you play an omnipotent force in control of the earth. Here, you must pay careful attention to fragile ecosystems. Finally, as we went to print, Maxis introduced *SimAnt*. You guessed it! It's a charming simulation of an ant colony.

For fans of the more concrete, the recently released *A-Train* creates a simulated railroad without soldering tiny tracks.

Figure 15.6 Dr. Quandry's island offer puzzles to solve.

The Secret Island of Dr. Quandry

MECC

Ages: Ten and up

Skills taught: Logic

The action in this game revolves around Dr. Quandry, a sinister character who plots a series of challenging games on his enchanted island. The games are variations of many popular logic and puzzle-solving games: for example, the Tower of Hanoi, where you must create a balance between two sides of a scale), and a number-sequencing game.

The graphics are appealing. So is the sound, but there's not much novelty or innovation in this relative newcomer to the market. Dr. Quandry doesn't have much personality, nor does the island. Still, even though it may not be the favorite game on your shelves, the puzzles are fun, and the value for the dollar is excellent. There's lots to explore and do.

Think Quick!

The Learning Company

Ages: Seven and up

Skills Taught: Deductive Reasoning, puzzle-solving, logic

Think Quick! is a cross between a thinking kid's version of *PacMan* and an *Adventure Construction Kit.* Instead of wandering aimlessly through the game *PacMan*-style, kids move with a mission through the maze-like rooms in the Castle of Mystikar.

Mystikar's world, with its trick doors, cryptic maps, pattern-matching clues, safe hideouts, secret panels, magic elements, and hidden passageways, has a logic all its own. There is an area of the game, known as Knight's School, which is actually an interactive tutorial that guides your child through this mysterious world and readies him for battle with Mystikar's pesky Dragon and his Slimeworm henchmen. Kids attend to six or seven game clues at once as the play evolves. And they must devise some serious sequencing strategies, as they work against the clock to become a dragon-battling knight. The game features three increasingly difficult levels of play in the various games with Medieval themes. Each includes a a heavy-duty expert session that calls upon kids to summon up their best problem-solving abilities.

The peak problem-solving experience occurs when they've mastered all the games. And The Learning Company, sensitive to children's need for success, makes that an attainable goal. The games are challenging but not intimidating. Once a child has conquered each, he can head for The Castle Creator, where he is given tools to program his own *Think Quick!*-style games. This offers children a good sneak preview of what programming is all about.

Think Quick! is actually an old game. The game doesn't wow you with fancy graphics. Its four-color CGA screens offer a rather plain fare of jaggedy-looking dragons and worms. The action sequences, like the one where kids must escape from the Slime Worm's Belly, are slow. Adults may find the story theme akin to that of most Grade B science fiction flicks. But, for all its drawbacks, kids seem to adore it. Oftentimes Robin's children would rather play *ThinkQuick!* than play with the most high-tech game they own. And, without knowing it, they're playing a robust and compelling game of strategy.

Figure 15.7 The Treehouse put older children in an activity-filled setting.

The Treehouse

Broderbund Software

Ages: Six to Ten

Skills Taught: Language, dramatic arts, math, music and science concepts

Broderbund's *Playroom*, which we discussed earlier in book, is built around the notion that you can simulate a world of play for children on the PC. But *Playroom* is for young children. *Treehouse* takes up where *Playroom* left off. The game is geared for slightly older children, although youngsters as young as four or five will be able to find plenty to explore in its special world, if they've already played with *Playroom* and are ready to move on.

Treehouse presents children with a colorful screen display of a backyard treehouse, where two playful possums live and romp. The main room of the treehouse is a place full of exploration. It has a blackboard that your child can color with a set of paint tools. Clouds that are seen through the window change shape when you click on them. And everyday there's a hero or heroine who pops up on a board with text that your child can read. Visitors (other characters) pop into the treehouse, and all sorts of objects such as fruit, balloons, and bird nests fill the scene with whimsical antics. Each visitor can perform animated activities when your child summons them with a click of the mouse.

Behind seven of the Treehouse objects, your child will find full-fledged games. One features a Silly Sentence Theater, where children can write a play, using pictures, words, and graphics that answer who, what, when, and where. String them together and roll the action to watch your movie and hear the words spoken.

Connections

There are dozens of activities you can use to encourage your child to expand upon *Treehouse* activities. For example, he might create his own imaginary animal and give it a habitat and classification. He can create his own flip books using the same who-what-where structure as he learns in *Treehouse*.

The best part of the game is the musical treats. For instance, one game asks your child to match notes to tones and even produce his own tunes by using the notes in a musical notation. By clicking on different instruments, you can hear the song played as different instruments might play them. You can also learn about these instruments and how they are used in an orchestra. Once you've composed a song you can play it back using different instruments and sounds.

Another game has a science theme. You learn about animals' habitats, diets, anatomy, and their classification as you try and guess the mystery animal through a process of elimination. Finally, a road rally game teaches your child how to perform simple money transactions. Each time he lands on a square he is presented with a message that requires a monetary computation.

Tip for IBM PC-compatibles Users

Both The Silly Sentences Theater and Musical Notation games are more enjoyable if your PC is equipped with one of the many sound cards the program supports. With a sound card your child can hear her creation spoken or played back. The built-in PC speaker offers sound too, but it's not as crisp.

CHAPTER 16

ART SOFTWARE—
THE ELECTRONIC CANVAS

In a world of papier maché, fingerpaints, and modeling clay, the computer can be another important medium of expression for the budding artist. Children's graphics software offers electronic tools for drawing, painting, shape-making, and even animation. And in a world of pianos and violins, the computer gives us another medium —one where trial-and-error is encouraged and even the worst musician can achieve some musicality.

The graphics software packages reviewed below are the electronic equivalent of a box of Crayolas. Using them helps foster a child's sense of graphics, lets her sneak in a few computer skills and (something parents will appreciate) leaves no mess behind. The music packages let children interact with musical notes, and rhythms, and pitch in an experimental manner.

Compared to traditional media, the computer cultivates abstract manipulation skills. You never manipulate a computer image directly the way you do a pencil and paintbrush. Keyboards and mice run interference. Move the mouse, and a line appears on screen; click the mouse, and you flood an area with color. Similarly, you don't pluck a string or blow a horn. The music process is more abstract on the computer.

Graphics software also demands mastery of complex sequences. Your child will learn to select a color palette, a brush, and an object fill—all as part of the process of electronic painting. The software appears simple, but there's a serious hidden agenda—computer literacy and manual dexterity. And in music composition, the elements of a piece, such as pitch, rhythm, and the sound of a particular instrument, are all introduced in manageable chunks.

More pragmatically, from a parent's eye view, electronic arts and crafts software doesn't make a mess, and electronic music is relatively easy on your eardrums and those of your neighbors. Each time we watch kids blissfully clicking on an electronic palette, we count our blessings in the form of crayons that haven't been ground into carpet and paint splatters on walls that won't need scrubbing.

Here are the top children's graphics and music programs.

Figure 16.1 Cartooners makes kids into comic-book artists.

Cartooners

Electronic Arts

Ages: Three to adult, best suited for ages Nine to Sixteen

Skills Taught: Drawing cartoons in book form

This was a great idea that didn't go far. Although somewhat dated, *Cartooners* can expose children to the fine art of comic book creation. *Cartooners* takes the principles of frame-by-frame cartooning and translates them into an electronic medium. The package includes canned backgrounds, cartoon characters (mostly imaginary animal friends), props, canned music, and the ability to write your own speech balloons.

Each character gets a repertoire of movements. For example, the rabbit hops and the fox lunges. The idea of the program is to select a background scene (there are farms, forests, and even graveyards) and populate it with whatever characters and props your child chooses. Next, she selects the movements to give the characters on the screen and types their words into speech balloons.

When she's satisfied with her basic script, she clicks on the record button and records her work, frame by frame. Now all she has to do is dub in a little canned music (spooky and happy sounds, doinks and more) and she's got herself an animation—something with bunnies hopping, eyes popping, wolves gnashing their teeth, all of it recorded for posterity.

Even children who are too young to animate can play with the program in its Look mode. The Look mode provides a prerecorded show, one that the kids don't have to create. And, the program allows kids to print copies of each frame of their animation, making comic books for younger siblings to color.

ColorMe: The Computer Coloring Kit

Mindscape

Ages: Three to Seven

Skills Taught: Art

ColorMe combines a junior-sized paint system, a kid-oriented clip-art library, and some traditional arts and crafts materials into an attractive basket of goodies. You can use *ColorMe* to create sixteen-color illustrations on the screen. And, children with more utilitarian leanings can use ColorMe's accessory items to create buttons, stickers, and printed coloring books.

The icon-based paint program lets the fledgling artist wield a joystick, koala pad (a special kind of electronic drawing tablet), mouse, or keyboard to draw on screen. An ingenious giant-sized crayon icon with segments of color is the palette menu. The drawing cursor looks like a mini-crayon. And four different brush styles, ranging from a thick marker to a grainy halftone, are included. Your child can leave the Draw options after she produces an attractive line drawing and select *Fill* to spill color into closed areas in the picture.

The OOPS icon saves many a frustrated child from hysteria by allowing her to undo her previous action. And a Big Dots icon lets the deft user add some clever touches. A text tool helps your child annotate artwork with four varieties (albeit one size) of type. And the clip art is plentiful. It includes the ColorMe Kids characters at play and the near-classic Rainbow Brite characters and their milieu.

Your child selects clip art by choosing an option called Cut from Disk. The program then lists the clip-art files by name. A visual hard-copy reference guide would be a helpful addition but, unfortunately, there are no pictures in the manual to allow your child to see the art she's about to choose. It won't be visible until it comes on screen, so it may take a bit of trial and error before she gets what she wants. Once an object is selected, it can be moved, pasted, or flipped on screen. Your child can cut and paste parts of clip art images to create wild combinations. And most clip art comes in two flavors: outline form for those who prefer their own coloring schemes, and Already Been Colored for those into mass production.

The *ColorMe* accessories appeal to the traditionalist in all of us. Each *ColorMe* Kit includes adhesive-backed printer paper, colored printer paper, button makers, binders, cards and envelopes. They even include a package of eight honest-to-goodness crayons! Combine these old standbys with printed output (any IBM-graphics or Epson-compatible dot-matrix printer will do; no laser printers are supported) and the product becomes as important as any that teaches the process of drawing. Supplies can be reordered as necessary.

Despite a few shortcomings in this program (you can't size an object, can only cut and paste rectangular areas, and have no graphics primitives, such as circles and squares), *ColorMe* is a seductive way to wile away the hours.

Tip

Take a few minutes to import each of the clip art pictures into a *ColorMe* file and print the whole thing out. This gives your child a printed reference when she is looking for the perfect picture for her project.

Figure 16.2 MetroGnomes's Music simplifies music for young children.

MetroGnome's Music

The Learning Company

Ages: Four to Seven

Skills Taught: Pitch recognition, rhythm and beat, beginning note recognition

The Learning Company's approach is to put solid educational content in a colorful, playful setting. This time the content is music—pitch differentiation, sound discrimination, and rhythm awareness in particular.

The five games that make up *MetroGnome's Music* are based on the Orff approach to music, where music is taught through active sensory motor play and discovery. The Orff approach has been used successfully with very young children and does not stress traditional music-reading skills.

The game takes place in the MetroGnome's elfin world of music. Each of the five games has its own colorful setting—a mushroom house, a flower garden, a picnic blanket, and so on. Each game can be reached either by clicking on a game number or exploring the scenery and moseying over to a game.

A Hi-Lo Rescue game teaches note discrimination by asking children to press the same note that they just heard the gnome play on a tree ladder. Melody Maker lets you record a song by clicking on a xylophone like keyboard. Match a Tune is a matching game similar to a memory game. Pick and Play plays favorite nursery rhymes. Our favorite is the Take a Trip game, where you must tap out the same "time" that an elf does in order for the train to leave the station.

This is one of the best music games for very young children that we've seen, although we like the *Treehouse*'s music component better for older kids. It might have been better to begin to introduce the notes and their names. Also, remember that the game loses a bit of its captivating resonance if you don't have a sound card. Music appreciation is tough through a tinny PC speaker.

My Paint

Saddleback Graphics

Ages: Three and up

Skills Taught: Art

Our chapter on kids' paint programs in Section II discussed a program called *Kid Pix*. But another program that's a bit more akin to traditional adult-oriented paint programs is *My Paint*, which offers a well-chosen subset of adult paint program tools, combined with whimsical, brightly colored, animated menus.

Kids can draw freestyle, using tools that are very much like what you'd find in an adult paint programs. Or kids can color in predrawn pictures. *My Paint*'s icons are animated. For instance, the OOPs icon, for undoing actions you decide you didn't want to do, is a face that gently shakes its head "no-ingly" from side to side. The eraser icon is shown animatedly erasing a flower, while the brush icon is shown as a hand painting a line. When children choose a color from the twelve-color paint palette, the one they chose makes itself known by coloring the inside of a smiling face on screen.

The program doesn't have all the special effects you'll find in *Kid Pix*. It has no text tool, and there are not a lot of tools to work with. The program has many nice touches, however, including a color-cycling icon that lets you turn your drawing into a kind of cycling neon color splotch. And a special rainbow paintbrush leaves a trail of rainbow colors as your child paints with it.

If the blank slate gets boring, your child can chose from 28 predrawn pictures (additional books are available) and fill in the areas with color in a coloring-book style exercise. There's also a gift box shown on screen. It opens to reveal a magic wand. As your child moves the wand across the screen, a surprise picture book image appears. And if she clicks on the icon that looks like lips, she'll hear sound effects (albeit poor ones) emanate from the coloring book drawings.

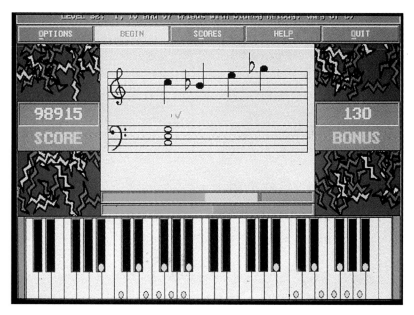

Figure 16.3 NotePlay introduces children to musical notation.

NotePlay

Ibis Software

Ages: Five to adult

Skills Taught: Music sight-reading

NotePlay combines the elements of an arcade game with music education, sight-reading in particular. The unique thing about the program is that you can use it with a MIDI keyboard, which is an external piano keyboard that you can attach to your PC. This means that you can actually play a piano through your computer.

The concept is intriguing, and whether you are a rank beginner or an accomplished musician, there is something to be learned from *NotePlay*. The 36 skill levels of exercises begin with simple "Play these three notes in treble clef," and work up to some rather complicated arrangements that require playing the bass and treble clefs simultaneously. You are introduced to passages with counterpoints, triads, and harmonic intervals.

Essentially the computer sounds out a series of notes as they are portrayed across the screen. You try and duplicate it. You have a choice of using a mouse and clicking on keys that appear in an onscreen keyboard (using the keyboard keys to simulate piano keys) or using a MIDI keyboard. Using a mouse to input the notes is rather awkward and very far removed from the reality of playing a keyboard. Using the keyboard keys to imitate a piano's keys feels bizarre (for example, you press keys a row above the other keys to make them sharp and flat.) The keyboard hookup is an innovative idea, though. And there is other music composition and music software that can also use MIDI keyboards. Apartment-dwellers may find it a real space savings to use a MIDI keyboard and a PC in lieu of a piano.

The arcade part of *NotePlay* is a bit like a combination of the old TV show games, *Beat the Clock* and *Name That Tune*. You race against the clock, and if you complete the musical phrase in the allotted time, you are rewarded with one of those old-fashioned happy faces and a bit of music.

Ibis has some other interesting titles: *RhythmPlay* asks you to mimic the computer and practice rhythms; *Play It by Ear* offers sight-reading training. *NotePlay* should have your child reading music fairly well in no time.

Picture Wizard

Computer Support Corporation

Ages: Five to adult

Skills Taught: Drawing and charting

It doesn't have the whimsy of a *KidPix*, but *Picture Wizard* is a full-featured drawing program for kids, and in the long run it is probably a more practical tool. *KidPix* is what we call a paint program; the package contains tools that let you paint the electronic canvas one pixel at a time. *Picture Wizard*, on the other hand, is a drawing program; it provides tools for drawing shapes—squares, polygons, and lines.

Picture Wizard is a scaled-down version of Computer Support Corporation's grownup drawing package, *Arts and Letters*. It provides the same basic tools as *Arts and Letters*—the ability to draw shapes, add text, and fill colored areas.

In addition to providing drawing tools and color palettes, *Picture Wizard* includes all sorts of templates for special projects. For example, there's a calendar template that whips up a calendar with the basic holidays for each month of the year. We used these monthly calendars as the backbone for our own—embellishing them with our own family's important dates and events each month.

There are also templates for mazes. You can start with *Picture Wizard*'s canned mazes and use their format to create your own. You can print banners and invitations and create paper projects, like paper-airplanes and pinwheels. A big selection of attractive clip art (professional-quality drawings) are stored on the disk as well.

Picture Wizard even has a charting module for kids. The module, which lets you input data and draw line, bar, or pie charts, provides a great introduction to charting for your children. And *Picture Wizard*'s typeface library adds a touch of class for school reports, invitations, and flyers.

Remember that you'll need Windows to use *Picture Wizard*, which means that you need a fully rigged PC in terms of memory and hard disk storage capacity. *Picture Wizard* is most handy for school-aged children. Its typeface, clip art library, and charting make it a great tool to keep around for reports.

The New Print Shop

Broderbund Software

Ages: Five through adult

Skills Taught: Design, writing, and publishing

This product might be thought of as the toaster of the computer world—it's such a handy appliance. It's an "announcement" generator for making certificates, invitations, banners, calendars, flyers, and other leaflets that herald everything from a new baby to a new tooth, from a performance to a special award. *Print Shop* is the indispensable tool for these types of family type commencements and rites of passage.

Print Shop is another example of a classic program that gets better with age. While early versions were somewhat primitive in their user interface, the latest version has easy-to-use, pop-down menus, more fonts, better graphics capabilities, and is more desktop publishing-oriented than previous versions. Over the years, printing options have also improved, with support for color printers and laser printers.

This new version of *Print Shop* has a checklist of the steps your child must follow to make her creation, for example. All she needs to do is pick the steps to create a specific kind of announcement and then make personal alterations and additions. A preview screen reflects the progress, one step at a time.

A related program that you can use with *Print Shop*, called *Print Shop Companion*, helps your child make calendars as well. It includes a Quick Print feature that lets your child write single lines of text to be printed on a printer. It also includes Name File, a utility that lets your child create a list of up to 150 names for later use.

Print Shop makes it easy to move and copy, stretch and shrink, and expand and reduce elements on the page. Your child can change colors, insert graphics, create borders, and use *Print Shop* to make giant calendars, tiny gift cards, and wide banners. She can even try publishing "big books" up to eight feet high and six feet wide. The biggest limitation is that the only way to edit text is to backspace and retype.

For those who aspire to more grown up packages, Broderbund recently introduced *Print Shop Deluxe*. With a graphical user interface, lovely clip art, and sophisticated templates, the new version is really targeted toward the small business market.

CHAPTER 17

CD-ROM SOFTWARE— THE WAVE OF THE FUTURE IS HERE NOW

Computer technology moves at a lightning pace. Traditional floppy disks are making way for a new media called CD-ROM, which stands for Compact Disc Read-Only Memory. These discs are the same as the CD-audio discs that you play music from, but they can store digital information in the form of graphics, animation, and text, in addition to sound. Many CD players include software that allows you to play audio CDs, but you can't play computer CDs in your audio CD player.

CD-ROM software often features sophisticated sound, which means children can use software titles that were previously too difficult for them. The computer can now speak to them and show them what to do, which takes away some of the pressure of reading lengthy text and documentation.

The main advantage of CD-ROM is that it's a much more efficient way of storing software than traditional floppy disks. A single CD holds the equivalent of 200–300 high-density 3.5-inch floppy disks. In other words, you can fit an entire illustrated encyclopedia and more on a CD-ROM disc. And because the electronic files that hold high-quality graphic and sound information are extremely large, CD-ROM's large storage capacity makes it an ideal way to deliver programs that can play high-fidelity CD audio, digital speech, and digital movies.

So, what's the bad part about CD-ROM discs? (You didn't expect it to be only good news, did you?) There are disadvantages:

- For the time being at least, CD-ROM is what's known as a read-only medium. That means that you can play the discs as many times as you want in order to retrieve information, but you cannot store new information on them.

- While they look like audio CDs, CD-ROM discs require that you have a special CD-ROM player. You can add one of these to your system. But it'll cost you a couple of hundred dollars, and installing the hardware on a PC-compatible requires some expertise. Mac CD-ROM players plug right into the SCSI port.

- Playing software programs from a CD-ROM disc is often a lot slower than playing from your hard disk. The CD-ROM players are not terrific at finding data that is flung all over the disc.

So, when you look up a word in the CD-ROM encyclopedia, it may take longer than it would for you to look it up manually in a printed book.

- Many, if not most, of these CDs require MPC level PCs or color-capable Macs. CD-ROMs that run under DOS tend to be just text based, without sound or graphics. Most multimedia CDs require Windows 3.1, more RAM, and VGA graphics.

CD-ROM technology is still young. But despite this fact, software titles are coming out very quickly and they are very exciting. Here are some of the most exciting that we've seen.

Amanda Stories, A Silly Noisy House, and Rodney's Wonder Window

The Voyager Company

Ages: Four to Twelve

Skills Taught: Reading appreciation

(Also available as a set of four discs)

The Amanda stories are some of the most whimsical computer literature for children that we've seen. Amanda Goodenough is a marvelous children's author, whose work has already earned her a reputation on Macintosh computers. Characters like Inigo the Cat and Your Faithful Camel star in interactive adventures for non-readers. Children click and explore their way through the story, and the plot develops based on the children's actions. All of these titles are available for the Macintosh. Amanda stories is also available for PC-compatibles.

Composer Quest

Dr T's Music Software

No age rating

Skills Taught: Music appreciation

This is sort of a *Carmen Sandiego* for learning about composers from 1600 to the present. Your child hears segments of music while viewing newspaper headlines about a particular era. Then he takes his best guess on who the composer is. You can also use this disc, without the game, simply to listen and learn about the great composers.

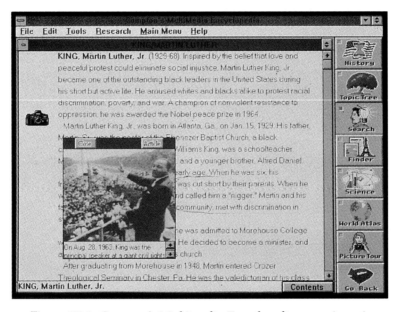

Figure 17.1 Compton's Multimedia Encyclopedia puts pizazz into reference materials.

Compton's Multimedia Encyclopedia

Britannica Software

Ages: Eight through adult

Skills Taught: Reference

Pricey at $795, *Compton's Multimedia Encyclopedia* uses recordings, photos, and graphics in every article your child accesses. The disc features more than 32,000 articles; 15,000 images, maps, and graphs; 45 animation sequences (demonstrating such actions as how the eye works); 5,000 charts and diagrams; a world atlas; a U.S. history timeline; and a dictionary.

Figure 17.2 Grandma an little Critter head for the beach in *Just Grandma and Me.*

Living Books: Just Grandma and Me, Arthur's Teacher Trouble, and The Tortoise and the Hare (available soon)

Broderbund Software

Ages: Three to Ten

Skills Taught: Reading, word-recognition, logical thinking

Just Grandma and Me is the first in a new Broderbund series called Living Books. Living Books comes in CD-ROM format and includes animation and sound. More important, Living Books are interactive, which means that your child can navigate through the books in any fashion she sees fit.

Just Grandma and Me is a story written by Mercer Mayer, one of the leading children's book authors in the country. It first appeared in traditional print. The story is about a trip to the beach, told from the child's perspective. As you click and move between items that appear on these colorful screens, all sorts of things happen: flowers open and start singing; a lifeguard does a boogie at the beach; our hero gets buried in the sand, caught in a large picnic umbrella, and more.

You have an option to read the story in a linear fashion, like a traditional book, but we found that most kids just want to poke around and have fun. The CD also includes Spanish and Japanese versions of the story. Broderbund (along with another company, Sierra Online) has been the leader in including multiple languages in the same software box. It's an important step in the right direction.

Macmillan Dictionary for Children

Macmillan New Media

No age rating

Skills Taught: Reference

This is the electronic version of the hardcover dictionary. It contains 13,000 words with photographs and illustrations accompanying the definitions. Some entries have sound and animation. All have an audio pronunciation. There are also games, including a spelling bee and Hangman.

Mammals: A Multimedia Encyclopedia

National Geographic Society

Ages: Nine through adult

Skills Taught: Reference

Mammals: A Multimedia Encyclopedia is the result of a joint venture between IBM and the National Geographic Society. The disk combines film clip-like animation, sound effects, graphics, and text to explore the habits of various mammals. Your child can click on a mammal, read about its habits, see a map of its habitat, listen to its sound and watch it in motion. A game lets you search for animals around the world.

Microsoft Bookshelf

Microsoft Corporation

No age rating

Skills Taught: Reference

This CD, though primarily for adults, provides 30 lessons that combine games, music, speech, and cultural information. You listen to phrases and try to repeat them. Kids will have fun too.

The disc features a reference library for young adults and children, which combines narration, music, animation, and graphics to augment the contents of seven different reference guides, including: the *Concise Columbia Encyclopedia*, the *American Heritage Dictionary*, *Roget's Electronic Thesaurus*, *The World Almanac and Book of Facts*, *Bartlett's Familiar Quotations*, and the *Hammond Atlas*. The entrys aren't as detailed as a printed reference, but they're great for entry-level research.

Three versions of the disc are available, one for multimedia PCs (that's the one that adds graphics, sound and animation), one that contains the straight text of these books, and one that combines Microsoft's adult word processor *Word* for Windows with *Bookshelf*. For children, the multimedia version is the best.

Mixed-Up Mother Goose

Sierra On-Line

Ages: Four to ten

Skills Taught: Pre-reading

There is a floppy disk-based version of this, but the CD-ROM version presents children with nursery rhyme characters that speak to you in both Spanish and English. The characters appear in a storybook world without the object their nursery rhymes indicate they should be carrying. When you match a nursery rhyme character with his or her missing object, you are rewarded with a rich audio rendition of the appropriate nursery rhyme. Maps guide you through this nursery rhyme land to help Mother Goose reattach the various characters and their missing paraphernalia. This rendition is an animated, musical extravaganza.

Multimedia Beethoven: The Ninth Symphony

Microsoft Corporation

Ages: Ten to adult

Skills Taught: Music reference

One of the best produced CD-ROMs to date, *Multimedia Beethoven* guides you through Beethoven's majestic Ninth Symphony. As your child listens to the Ninth on CD-audio-quality recording, she is shown what Beethoven's Vienna was like and is also offered an in-depth analysis of the movements. The tour guide teaches her to appreciate the piece with a deep understanding of its elements.

Voyager's CD Companions

Beethoven: Symphony No. 9, Stravinsky: The Rite of Spring, Schubert: "The Trout" Quintet, Richard Strauss: Three Tone Poems, Mozart: The "Dissonant" Quartet

Voyager's companion series is an in-depth, interactive appreciation of music. Each CD includes a Pocket Guide that lets you play any section of the piece, a Close Reading that gives an analysis of the music, a glossary of musical terms, the Composer's World which puts the music in the context of its time, and a Game to test your new-found musical knowledge. Its designed for adults, but good for older children.

Voyager has chosen and created wonderful illustrations to accompany the performances and even injected a bit of humor like the Trout Cookbook included with the Schubert CD. All of these discs are available for the Mac, and Beethoven is also available for PC-compatibles.

The 1992 Grolier Multimedia Encyclopedia

Distributed by The Software Toolworks

The New Grolier's Electronic Encyclopedia is available from Voyager for the Macintosh

No age rating

Skills Taught: Reference

First introduced in 1985, Grolier's had the first and one of the most popular CD-ROM-based encyclopedias on the market. In its initial incarnation it was entirely text-based, but this newest version adds multimedia features including video, animation, and sound. At

$395, the encyclopedia is less expensive than some of the other CD-ROM-based encyclopedias, and it has a larger number of listings. It includes 33,000 articles (over 10 million words) and has all the text and many of the pictures found in the 21–volume hardcover edition of *Grolier's Academic American Encyclopedia.*

There are plenty of new articles in this latest version, which cover topics such as the Persian Gulf War and HDTV. This makes it one of the most up-to-date encyclopedias available. The company also issues annual updates which you can purchase ($97 list price). Digitized video segments include NASA missions and major sports events. Animation sequences include the human body and the solar system. Audio segments feature musical compositions and famous speeches. A timeline reference allows students to explore events chronnologically, and a knowledge tree allows students to do a broad search and then narrow the focus. Schools will enjoy the fact that the encyclopedia can be used over a network. The encyclopedia contains fairly difficult passages of text and is best suited for children ages ten and older.

Our House

Context Systems

Ages: Preschool

Skills Taught: Computer and logic readiness

Featuring Bill Keane's *Family Circus* (syndicated in various magazines), this disc allows the kids to explore things inside a house to get an idea of how things work. For example, you click on a toaster and see that electric coils are behind it, or click on the washing machine or sink to find out what's behind it. Also, kids get some information on how chores were done in the past.

Playing with Language

Syracuse Language Systems

No age rating

Skills Taught: Spoken English, French, Spanish, or German

Unlike other CD-based software that attempts to teach foreign languages, this is designed for children. The foreign language is presented through interactive stories and games. Over 200 words and phrases are taught in English, Spanish, German, and French on separate discs.

Tip

Multimedia computing is exciting because it combines so many different types of input such as sound and animation. But because multimedia computing requires some very hardware- and system-intensive computing magic, you'll need to make sure your hardware is up to the task. If you are planning to buy CDs, you should carefully read the section on multimedia PCs (See Chapter 1). For instance, all of the CD-ROM discs for IBM PC-compatibles mentioned in this section, with the exception of National Geographic's *Mammals*, require Microsoft Windows and the Microsoft Multimedia Extensions.

APPENDIX

A

HARDWARE

Here is an alphabetical listing of all the hardware vendors mentioned in Section I. They are categorized according to the devices they sell: Computers, mice, and sound cards. Write to them at these addresses or call to request information. Shop around before you take the plunge. Often, you'll find these computers and devices at deeply discounted prices.

Computers

Macintosh Computers
Apple Computer, Inc.
20525 Mariani Ave.
Cupertino, CA 95014
800-776-2333; 408-996-1010

PS/1
IBM
Old Orchard Rd.
Armonk, NY 10504
800-426-2468; 914-765-1900

Magnavox HeadStart
Philips Consumer Electronics Corp.
One Philips Dr.
Knoxville, TN 37914
800-722-6224

Tandy Computers
Tandy Corp.
1800 One Tandy Center
Ft. Worth, TX 76102
817-390-3011

Mice

KidzMouse
Logitech, Inc.
6505 Kaiser Dr.
Fremont, CA 94555
800-231-7717; 510-795-8500

Microsoft Mouse
Microsoft Corp.
One Microsoft Way
Redmond, WA 98052-6399
800-426-9400; 206-882-8080

Sound Cards

The Disney Sound Source
Disney Software
500 S. Buena Vista St.
Burbank, CA 91521
818-567-5360

The Ad Lib Card
Ad Lib, Inc.
220 Grande Allee, E, Ste. 960
Quebec City, QB, CD G1R 2J1
800-463-2686; 418-529-9676

The SoundBlaster
Brown-Wa-gh Publishing
16795 Lark Ave.
Los Gatos CA 95030
408-395-3838

APPENDIX

B

SOFTWARE

Here is an alphabetical listing of all the software vendors and programs mentioned in this book, along with a recap of the skills they teach, their prices, operating requirements and, so that you can write or call for more information, the vendor's address and telephone number. The prices you see here are the vendors' recommended retail prices. You can usually find these programs at much lower discount prices in stores and catalogs.

America Online
8619 Westwood Center Dr.
Vienna, VA 22182
(800) 827-6364, (703) 448-8700

- *America Online.* This is an online service, generally more suited to adult kids than young ones. It is easy to use and features games and services for home computer users with either IBM PC-compatible computers or Macintoshes and a modem. Call for up-to-date monthly fees and the software needed to access.

Compton's New Media
2320 Camino Vida Roble
Carlsbad, CA 92009
(619) 929-2500

- Compton's *Multimedia Encyclopedia,* $595 DOS version, $695 Windows version (requires Windows 3.0 or higher with multimedia extensions), $795 Macintosh version due out in late 1992. A CD-ROM multimedia reference disk for ages eight through adult.
- *The Family Encyclopedia* $395 for Windows, $295 for DOS

Broderbund Software
500 Redwood Blvd.
Novato, CA 94948
(415) 382-4400, (800) 521-6263

- *Bank Street Writer Plus,* $79.95, IBM PC-compatible and Macintosh 128K versions only. A word processor that helps teach writing skills to ages seven to twelve.
- *Just Grandma and Me, The Living Book Series,* no suggested retail price but available in stores from $39.95 to $54.95 for Macintoshes and multimedia PCs. This CD-ROM pre-reading program for ages three to ten also teaches keyboard and computer skills.
- *Kid Pix,* $59.95 for Macintoshes and IBM PC-compatibles. This paint and drawing program for ages three to twelve features talking alphabets in English and Spanish, brushes and tools that make sounds, and a small kids mode for tykes. The Macintosh version lets kids record personal greetings and poems in their creations.
- *Kid Pix Companion* for Macintosh and IBM PC-compatibles. This enhancement to *Kid Pix* adds even more goodies, such as new brushes and rubber stamps.
- *The Playroom,* $49.95 for IBM PC-compatibles and Macintoshes. This preschool readiness program takes kids on adventures in pre-reading and math.

- *The New Print Shop*, $59.95 IBM PC-compatible version, $49.95 Apple II version. This art and desktop publishing program is for ages five to adult.

- *The New Print Shop*, Graphics Library-Sampler Edition, Party Edition, Holiday Edition, $34.95 IBM PC-compatible version, $24.95 Apple II version. This program adds nearly 100 pictures, designs, and symbols to *The Print Shop*.

- *The Treehouse*, $59.95 for Macintoshes and IBM PC-compatibles. This program for ages six to ten teaches language skills, art, math, music, and science concepts.

- *Where in Europe is Carmen Sandiego?*, $49.95 for IBM PC-compatibles and Macintoshes. This mystery game teaches map awareness and cultural appreciation to ages eight and up.

- *Where in the USA is Carmen Sandiego?*, $49.95 for IBM PC-compatibles and Macintoshes. A mystery game that teaches map awareness and American history to ages eight and up.

- *Where in the World is Carmen Sandiego?*, $49.95 for IBM PC-compatibles and Macintoshes. A mystery game that teaches world map awareness and cultural appreciation to ages eight and up.

- *Where in the World is Carmen Sandiego?*, *Deluxe Edition*, $79.95 for IBM PC-compatibles and Macintoshes. A mystery game that teaches world map awareness and cultural appreciation to ages eight and up.

- *Where in the World is Carmen Sandiego?*, *CD-ROM Deluxe Edition*, no suggested retail price but available in stores from $70 to $100. This mystery game on a CD-ROM disc teaches world map awareness and cultural appreciation to ages eight and up.

- *Where in America's Past is Carmen Sandiego?*, $49.95 for IBM PC-compatibles and Macintoshes. A mystery game that teaches history and geography to ages eight and up.

- *Where in Time is Carmen Sandiego?*, $49.95 for IBM PC-compatibles and Macintoshes. A mystery game that teaches historical awareness and cultural appreciation to ages eight and up.

CompuServe Inc. CompuServe Information Services
5000 Arlington Center Blvd.
Columbus, OH 45220
(800) 848-8199

- *CompuServe.* This is an online service, generally more suited to adult kids than young ones. It is not the easiest online service to use if you're new to computers. But it is the largest, with a wealth of options for professional as well as home computer users. It supports both IBM PC-compatibles and Macintoshes. A modem is required. Call for up-to-date monthly fees and the software needed to access it.

Computer Support Corporation
15926 Midway Road
Dallas, TX 75244
(214) 661-8960

- *Picture Wizard*, $89.95. Available for IBM PC-compatibles only. This is a drawing and charting program for ages five to adult.

Compu-Teach Educational Software
78 Olive Street
New Haven, CT 06511-6909
(800) 44-TEACH, (203) 777-7738

- *Talking Once Upon A Time*, $49.95 for IBM PC-compatibles, Macintoshes, and Apples; $59.95 for Apple II GS. This program, for ages six to ten teaches writing and thinking skills by allowing kids to compose illustrated stories.

Context Systems
333 Byberry Road
Hatboro, PA, 19040
(215) 675-5000

- *Our House*, $69.95. This CD-ROM disc for pre-schoolers requires Windows 3.0 or higher and Multimedia Extensions. A Macintosh version has been announced for late 1992.

Davidson and Associates, Inc.
P.O. Box 2961
Torrance, CA 90509
(800) 545-7677

- *Headline Harry and the Great Paper Race*, $59.95 for the 256-color version; $49.95 sixteen-color version. Available for IBM PC-compatibles only. This program for kids aged ten to adult teaches history, geography, and problem-solving.
- *Kid Works*, $49.95 for IBM PC-compatibles; *KID WORK Z*, $59.95 for Macintoshes. This publishing program teaches writing, illustration, and storytelling to ages four to ten.
- *Math Blaster Mystery*, $49.95 for IBM PC-compatibles, Macintoshes, and Apple II series. This detective program for ages six to twelve teaches math fundamentals, pre-algebra, and problem-solving skills.
- *New Math Blaster Plus!*, $49.95 for IBM PC-compatibles; $59.95 for Macintoshes or Windows. This arcade-style math game for ages six to twelve teaches math fundamentals and problem-solving skills.
- *What's My Angle?*, $49.95 for IBM PC-compatibles; $59.95 for Macintoshes. This math program for ages fourteen to adult teaches basic geometry concepts, problem-solving skills, and proofs to demonstrate how geometry applies to real-life situations.

Dr T's Music Software
124 Crescent Rd.
Needham, MA 02194
(617) 455-1454

- *Composer Quest*, $99.95. This CD-ROM disc features recordings of classical musical from the seventeenth to twentieth century, along with stories and facts about the compositions. Requires Windows 3.0 or greater and Multimedia Extensions.

EARTHQUEST, Inc.
125 University Ave.
Palo Alto, CA 94301
(415) 321-5838

• *Earthquest*, $59.95 for Macintoshes and IBM PC-compatibles. This program is a mini-encyclopedia full of charts and tables about Mother Earth, cultures, and ecology, for ages ten to adult.

• *Earthquest Explores Ecology*. $59.95, for Macintoshes only. Similar to *Earthquest* but devoted to an in-depth look at ecology, this program for ages ten to adult features a game called The Renegade Tour in which renegade vegetables run to save the planet, as well as loads of information on the Rain Forest.

• *Time Treks*, $59.95 for Macintoshes only. This world history adventure game covers the period from 3400 BC to the present, for ages ten to adult.

Electronic Arts
1450 Fashion Island Blvd.
San Mateo, CA 94404
(800) 245-4525

• *Cartooners*, $49.95. Available for IBM PC-compatibles only. This drawing and cartooning program, recommended for ages three to adult, is fun for the whole family.

First Byte
PO Box 2961
Torrance, CA 90509
(800) 545-7677

• *Eco-Saurus*, $39.95 for IBM PC-compatibles; $49.95 for Macintoshes. This dinosaur adventure game with an ecological theme builds reading and problem-solving skills in ages four to nine.

• *Spell-A-Saurus*, $44.95 for IBM PC-compatibles; $49.95 for Macintoshes. This dinosaur adventure game features digitized speech to reinforce spelling skills in ages five to twelve.

Grolier Electronic Publishing
Sherman Turnpike
Danbury, CT 06816
(203) 797-3500, (800) 356-5590

• *New Grolier Multimedia Encyclopedia*, $395 for Macintoshes, IBM PC-compatibles, and multimedia PCs. Annual updates make this CD-ROM disc, best suited for ages ten and up, one of the most up-to-date encyclopedias available.

Ibis Software
140 Second St. Suite 603
San Francisco, CA 94105
(415) 546-1917

- *NotePlay*, $49.95. Available for IBM PC-compatibles only. This music instruction program for ages five to adult supports sound cards and electronic keyboards. It builds skills in music sight-reading.

- *Play It by Ear*, $99.95 for IBM PC-compatibles only. Music students, beginning to advanced, learn to play by ear by matching tones to music shown on the computer screen.

- *RhythmPlay*, $49.95, for IBM PC-compatibles only. Beginning music students learn rhythms with an arcade-style game and an onscreen metronome in one- and two-handed rhythm exercises.

Knowledge Adventure, Inc.
4502 Dyer St.
La Crescenta, CA 91214
(800) 542-4240

- *Knowledge Adventure*, $79.95. Available for IBM PC-compatibles only. This program supports various sound cards and links cultural events in Western civilization, including art, music, and history, for ages seven to seventy.

Power Industries
Wellesley Hills, MA
(800) 395-5009

- *Delta Drawing*, $69.95

Logo Computer Systems Inc. (LCSI)
PO Box 162
Highgate Springs, VT 05460
1-800 321-LOGO

- *LogoExpress*, $99 for IBM PC-compatibles and Apple computers only. Logo-based telecommunications package.

- *LogoWriter*, $89 for IBM PC-compatibles, Macintoshes, and Apple computers. An introduction to programming for ages seven and up.

Maxis
2 Theatre Square Suite 230
Orinda, CA 94563
(800) 336-2947

- *SimAnt*, $59.95, for Macintosh Plus or above and IBM PC-compatibles. This simulation for ages twelve to adult takes you into the life of an ant colony.

- *SimCity*, $49.95 for monochrome Macintoshes, color IBM PC-compatibles (DOS), and Windows. $79.95 for color Macintosh version with Terrain Editor. This logic and strategy program challenges ages twelve through adult to manage city resources and urban conditions.

- *SimEarth*, $69.95 for Macintoshes, IBM PC-compatibles (DOS), and Windows. This logic and strategy program challenges ages twelve through adult to manage natural resources.

Macmillan New Media
124 Mt. Auburn St. Suite 324S
Cambridge MA 02138
(617) 661-2955

* *Macmillan Dictionary for Children*, $59.95. This illustrated and spoken dictionary on a CD-ROM disc requires Windows 3.0 or greater and Multimedia Extensions.

MECC (Minnesota Educational Computing Corporation)
6160 Summit Drive North
Minneapolis, MN 55430-4003
(800) 685-MECC, (612) 569-1500

* The *Secret Island of Dr. Quandry*, $49.95 for IBM PC-compatibles. This adventure game for ages ten and up builds logic skills.

Microsoft Corporation
One Microsoft Way
Redmond, WA 98052
(800) 426-9400

* *Microsoft Bookshelf*, $195. Available for IBM PC-compatibles only, separate versions for DOS and Windows. This CD-ROM disc includes a wide range of reference materials and is suitable for teens and adults. It requires Windows 3.0 or greater and the Multimedia Extensions.

* *Multimedia Beethoven: The Ninth Symphony*. $79.95. Available for IBM PC-compatibles in a Windows version only. This CD-ROM disc features a multimedia presentation of Beethoven's Ninth Symphony for teens and adults.

* *Windows*, $99 for IBM PC-compatibles only. This "environment," from which you can launch other programs, brings a Macintosh look to IBM PC-compatibles. Windows features games and utilities and provides the interactive multimedia capability you'll need for much of the new children's software and for almost all of the interactive CD-ROM discs for IBM PC-compatibles. Be sure you get Windows version 3.1 with Multimedia Extensions, so that you can reap its sound and animation strengths.

National Geographic Society Educational Services
PO Box 98018
Washington, DC 20090
(800) 368-2728

* *Mammals: A Multimedia Encyclopedia*, $149.95 for IBM PC-compatibles. A Macintosh version will be available Fall 1992; call for pricing. This CD-ROM disc is an animal reference that features sound for ages nine through adult.

OSCS Software Development Inc.
354 NE Greenwood Ave.
Suite 108
Bend, OR
(503) 389-5489

- *QuikMenu III*, $89.95; for IBM PC-compatibles only. This is a menu-builder for adults who want to set up a menu to make it easier for the kids to reach their favorite programs.

PC Dynamics
31332 Via Colinas Suite 102
Westlake Village, CA 91362
(800) 888-1741, (818) 889-1741

- *Menu Works Personal*, $39.95, *Menu Works Advanced*, $89.95; IBM PC-compatibles. This is a menu-builder for adults who want to set up a menu to make it easier for the kids to reach their favorite programs.

PC Globe
4700 S. McClintock
Tempe, AZ 85282
(602) 730-9000

- *Bushbuck Charms, Viking Ships & Dodo Eggs*, $49.95. Available for IBM PC-compatibles only. This game teaches geography using a colorful, musical, and animated global scavenger hunt. The vendor offers no age rating. However, kids seven and older will be interested. A sound card is recommended.
- *Geo Jigsaw*, $39.95 for IBM PC-compatibles only. These twelve musical and animated geographic jigsaw puzzles are for ages seven and up.
- *PC Globe*, $69.95. Available for IBM PC-compatibles only. This electronic world atlas, for ages nine and up, will interest both kids and adults with its maps and other resources for school and travel.
- *PC USA*, $69.95. Available for IBM PC-compatibles only. This electronic United States atlas, for ages nine and up, will interest both kids and adults with its number of maps and resources for school and travel.

Prodigy
44 Hamilton Avenue
White Plains, NY 10601
(800) PRODIGY

- *Prodigy*. Call for latest prices on software and monthly membership fees. Available for IBM PC-compatibles and Macintoshes. With Prodigy software and a modem to link to its multifaceted online service, everyone in the family will be entertained.

Queue, Inc.
338 Commerce Dr.
Fairfield, CT 06430
(800) 232-2224

- *Facemaker*, $29.95 for IBM PC-compatibles or Commodores; *Facemaker Golden Edition*, $39.95, for Apple or IBM PC-compatibles 5.25-inch disks, $49.95 for IBM PC-compatible 3.5-inch disks. This logic program for ages five to ten offers pre-programming skills. The programs differ only in that the Golden Edition features printing.

Saddleback Graphics
12812 Garden Grove Blvd. Unit P
Garden Grove, CA 92643
(714) 741-7093

• *My Paint*, $49.95. Available for IBM PC-compatibles and Apple IIGS. This paint pro-
  gram for ages three and up introduces drawing and color concepts and fosters creativity.

Sierra On-Line
PO Box 485
Coarsegold, CA
(800) 326-6654

• *Mixed-Up Mother Goose.* Available for IBM PC-compatibles only. $49.95 for the sixteen-
  color version; $69.95 for the CD-ROM multimedia version. A 256-color version will be
  available Summer 1992, price to be announced. This program brings illustrated and animated interactive fairy tales to disk for ages four to ten.

Simon & Schuster Software
Prentice-Hall Computer Publishing
11711 N. College Ave.
Carmel, IN 46032
(800) 428-5331, ask for Julie Otto

• *Typing Tutor 5* and *Typing Tutor 5 for Windows*, $50 each and $2 shipping and handling.
  Macintoshes and IBM PC-compatibles. Typing instruction with 15,000 word practice
  vocabulary, features typing and word games for children.

SVE
1345 W. Diversey Parkway
Chicago, IL 60614
(800) 829-1900

• *ColorMe: The Computer Coloring Kit*, $44.95 for IBM PC-compatibles, Apple II series,
  and Commodore 64/128. This paint program for children, ages three to seven, features
  drawing tools and clip art.

Syracuse Language Systems
719 E. Genesee St.
Syracuse, NY 13210
(800) 688-1937, (315) 478-6729

• *Playing with Language, $89.95.* This CD-ROM disc is available for IBM PC-compatibles
  only and requires Windows 3.0 or greater and an audio board to teach English, Spanish,
  French, or German.

The Learning Company
6493 Kaiser Drive
Fremont, CA 94555
(415) 792-2101, (800) 852-2255

- *Challenge of the Ancient Empires*, $49.95 for IBM PC-compatibles only. Problem-solving adventures in ancient civilizations await students ages ten to fifteen.
- *Math Rabbit*, $39.95 for IBM PC-compatibles and Apple II series; $59.95 for the talking Macintosh version. This program for ages three to seven builds early math and problem-solving skills.
- *MetroGnome's Music*, $49.95 for IBM PC-compatibles only. This music program for ages four to seven helps kids recognize pitch, rhythms and beats, and notes.
- *Midnight Rescue!*, $49.95. Available for IBM PC-compatibles only. This program combines reading skills with arcade action for ages seven to ten.
- *Operation Neptune*, $59.95. Available for IBM PC-compatibles only. A sea adventure game for ages seven and up, requires math and strategic calculations to win.
- *Out Numbered!*, $49.95 for IBM PC-compatibles only. This program, for children seven to fourteen, poses math word problems.
- *Reader Rabbit*, $49.95 for IBM PC-compatibles; $59.95 for the talking Macintosh, Tandy, and Apple IIGS versions; $39.95 for the Apple II series. This program presents children with an animated word factory to build early reading, spelling, and vocabulary skills for ages three to seven.
- *Reader Rabbit 2*, $59.95. Available for IBM PC-compatibles only. This program is a continuation of Reader Rabbit for ages five to eight. It teaches phonics and word recognition.
- *Spellbound*, $49.95. Available for IBM PC-compatibles only. This program for ages seven to twelve features digitized speech to help build spelling and thinking skills.
- *The Writing Center*, $89.95. Available for Macintoshes only. This is an easy-to-use word processing and publishing program for ages seven and up.
- *The Children's Writing and Publishing Center*, $69.96 IBM PC-compatibles; $59.95 Apple II series version. This is an easy-to-use word processing and publishing program for ages seven and up.
- *Think Quick!*, $49.95 for both IBM PC-compatibles and Apple II series. This adventure game builds thinking skills for ages seven and up.
- *Treasure Mountain!*, $49.95. Available for IBM PC-compatibles only. This is a fantasy exploration game that reinforces reading, thinking, math, and science skills for ages five to nine.
- *Writer Rabbit*, $49.95 for IBM PC-compatibles and Apple II series. The program, for ages seven to ten is designed to build reading and writing skills.

The Voyager Company
1351 Pacific Coast Highway
Santa Monica, CA 90401
(800) 446-2001

- *Amanda Stories:*, $59.95, *A Silly Noisy House*, $59.95, *Rodney's Wonder Window*, $59.95 for both IBM PC-compatibles and Macintoshes. These CD-ROM discs feature sound and animation in interactive stories for children ages four to twelve.

Tom Synder Productions, Inc.
90 Sherman St.
Cambridge, MA 02140
(617) 876-4433

- *Choices, Choices*, $89.95 each version. Available for Apple and IBM PC-compatibles. Two versions: On the Playground and Taking Responsibility; to teach ethics, morals, logic, and problem-solving to children in kindergarten through sixth grade.

- *Decisions, Decisions*, $119.95 each version. Available for Apples, IBM PC-compatibles, and Macintoshes. Offers ten different critical thinking problems to teach ethics and morals, logic, and problem-solving to children in grades five to twelve.

Walt Disney Computer Software
500 S. Buena Vista St.
Burbank, CA 91521
(800) 688-1520

- *Mickey's 123s*, $39.95. Available for IBM PC-compatibles only. This pre-school math program for ages three to seven introduces number concepts.

- *Mickey's ABCs*, $39.95. Available for IBM PC-compatibles only. This pre-school math program for ages three to seven introduces the alphabet.

- *Mickey's Colors and Shapes*, $39.95. Available for IBM PC-compatibles only. This pre-school math program for ages three to seven introduces colors and shapes.

- *Mickey's Crossword Puzzle Maker*, $29.95. Available for IBM PC-compatibles only. This game-making software for ages five to eleven emphasizes general reading skills, vocabulary, synonyms, and spelling.

- *Mickey's Jigsaw Puzzle*, $49.95. Available for IBM PC-compatibles only. This colorful puzzle-solving game for ages five and up builds logic skills, along with awareness of shapes and colors.

Weekly Reader Software
10 Station Pl.
Norfolk, CT 06058
(800) 327-1473

- *New Talking Stickeybear Alphabet*, $49.95, for the Apple IIGS only. This program uses speech to introduce pre-reading skills to ages two to five.

- *New Talking Stickeybear Opposites*, $49.95, for the Apple IIGS only. This program for ages two to five introduces the concept of opposites.

- *Stickeybear ABCs*, $39.95 for Apple. This program offers pre-reading skills to ages two to five.

- *Stickeybear Alphabet*, $49.95 for IBM PC-compatibles. This program requires a sound board and uses speech to introduce pre-reading skills to children ages two to five.

- *Stickybear Numbers*, $39.95 for Macintosh LC with Apple II card and IBM PC-compatibles. This program for ages three to six introduces numbers and counting.

- *Stickeybear Opposites*, $39.95 for the Macintosh LC with an Apple IIe card and Apple II series. This program for ages three to five introduces the concept of opposites.
- *Stickeybear's Reading Room*, $59.95 for Macintosh color. This program uses animation and sound to promote reading and thinking skills in both English and Spanish, for ages four to eight.
- *Stickeybear Shapes*, $39.95 for the Macintosh LC with an Apple IIe card, the Apple II series, and IBM PC-compatibles. This program for ages two to five introduces the concept of shapes.

Other Software Companies

These software companies distribute other programs appropriate for kids that we simply did not have room to cover in greater depth. You may contact them directly for information.

Claris Corp.
5201 Patrick Henry Drive
Santa Clara, CA 95092
(408) 727-8227

- *Claris Works:* $299
- *MacWrite II:* $129
- *HyperCard Development Kit:* $199
- *HyperCard Upgrade Kit:* $99

Cyan, Inc.
PO Box 28096
Spokane, WA 99228
(509) 468-0807

- *Cosmic Osmo and the World's Beyond the Mackerel:* $59.95 CD
- *Cosmic Osmo:* $47.95
- *The Manhole CD-ROM:* $34.95
- *The Manhole:* $29.95
- *Spelunx* (available through Broderbund)

Discis Knowledge Research
45 Sheppard Avenue East Suite 802
Toronto, Ontario M2N 5W9 Canada
(416) 250-6537, (800) 567-4321

- *Discis Book Library:* $69.95 to $89.95

Great Wave Software
5353 Scotts Valley Drive
Scotts Valley, CA 95066
(408) 438-1990

- *AMERICAN DISCOVERY:* $49.95
- *Concert Ware+:* $69.95
- *KidsMath:* $49.95
- *KidsTime:* $49.95, PC $29.95
- *NumberMaze:* $49.95 b&w, $69.95 color, $59.95 DOS
- *Decimal & Fraction Maze:* $69.95
- *Reading Maze:* $49.95 b&w, $69.95 color

Lego Dacta
555 Taylor Road
PO Box 1600
Enfield, CT 06083
(203) 749-2291, (800) 527-8339

- *LogoWriter Robotics:* $262
- *LEGO TC Logo Starter Pack:* $525 PC (Mac version next year)

Logo Foundation
250 West 57th Street, Suite 2603
New York, NY 10107
(212) 765-4918

Que Software
Prentice Hall Computer Publishing
11711 North College Ave.
Carmel, IN 46032
(317) 573-2500

- *Typing Tutor 5:* $49.95 Mac and PC-compatible

Scholastic, Inc.
PO Box 7502
2931 E. McCary Street
Jefferson City, MO 65102
(800) 541-5513

- *Bank Street Writer for the Macintosh:* $129.95
- *Operation Frog:* $99.95

Software Toolworks, The
60 Leveroni Ct.
Novato, CA 94949
(415) 883-3000
Tracy Egan, Public Relations

- *Mavis Beacon Teaches Typing!:* $49.95 Mac and PC-compatible
- *Mavis Beacon Teaches Typing! Version 2:* $49.95 PC, $59.95 Windows

- *World Atlas:* $89.95 Mac and PC-compatible, $149.95 MPC (CD-ROM)
- *Time Table of History:* $99.95 Mac and PC-compatible (CD-ROM)
- *The 1992 Grolier Multimedia Encyclopedia:* $395 Mac and PC-compatible (CD-ROM)
- *The Miracle Piano Teaching System:* $479.95 Mac and PC-compatible (Includes keyboard)

Terrapin Software, Inc.
400 Riverside St.
Portland, ME 04103
(207) 878-8200

- *Logo for the Macintosh:* $99.95
- *PC Logo:* $99.95

Wings for Learning
PO Box 660002
Scotts Valley, CA 95067
(800) 321-7511, (408) 438-5502

- *Storybook Theater:* $129 Mac only
- Additional Storybooks for Storybook Theater: $79 Mac only
- *A Field Trip to the Rainforest:* $99 Mac only
- *A Field Trip into the Sea:* $99 Mac only

INDEX

Ad Lib card, 291
adult programs, 54
Amanda stories, 363
Apple II coprocessor card, 15
arcade games, 51–52
arithmetic, 108, 110. *See also* math programs
art programs, 348–51, 353–56

Bank Street Writer Plus, 287
batch files, 83–84
BushBuck Charms, 324
buyers' clubs, 65–68

cables, 76
Calculator, 204–6
Calendar, 201–4
Cardfile, 135–36, 206–10
"Carmen Sandiego Day" kit, 133
Carmen Sandiego games, 118–21. *See also specific games*
    on Prodigy, 235
Carmen Sandiego game shows, 139
Carmen Sandiego novels, 140
Carpal tunnel syndrome, 30–32
Cartooners, 349–50
CD-ROM disks, 37–38, 255, 362–70
    advantages and disadvantages of, 362–63
CGA (Color Graphics Adapter), 26
chairs, 77
Challenge of the Ancient Empires, 323–24
childproofing
    your computer, 76–79
    Windows, 85–86, 90–91
*Children's Writing and Publishing Center, The/The
    Writing Center*, 166–90
    advanced features of, 184–86
    Apple II computers with, 186–88
    publishing a daily journal with, 174–84, 187
    quick tour of, 169–73
choosing a computer, 6–7
classifieds, buying a computer through the, 70
ColorMe, 350–51
color monitors, 23, 25, 40
Commodore computers, 11
Composer Quest, 363–64
Compton's Multimedia Encyclopedia, 255, 364
computer fairs, 69
computers. *See* IBM PC-compatibles; Macintoshes
copy protection, 95–96
counting programs, 108, 310–12
CPUs (Central Processing Units). *See* microprocessors
creativity tools, 53

database management, with *Cardfile*, 206–10
database programs, 135–36
density, screen, 25
desks, 77

desktop, 84
desktop publishing programs, 168, 288–89, 302
Dinosaur Discovery Kit, 32
discount stores, 65–68
DiskDoubler, 21
Disney software, 291–95
Disney Sound Source, 291–92, 294–95
display adapters, 23
    IBM PC-compatible, 27–28
    for Macintoshes, 15
displays. *See* monitors
Dodo Eggs, 324
DOS, 194–95
dot density, 25
drill-and-practice software, 53–54
drive bays, 20
Dvorak keyboard, 31

Earthquest, 327–28
Earthquest Explores Ecology, 328
ecology, 327–28
edutainment software, 50–51
EGA (Enhanced Graphics Adapter), 26
ethics, 325
expansion slots, in Macintoshes, 15

Facemaker, 328–29
Family Tree Maker, 132
fantasy games, 52–53
file compression software, 21
First Byte speech technology, 289
floppy disk drives, 19, 78
floppy disks, 19, 78
Fun Time Print Kits, 292

game port, 33
games. *See also specific programs*
    arcade, 51–52
    edutainment, 50–51
    role-playing and fantasy, 52–53
    simulations, 50
    value of, 94
garage sales, 69–70
geography programs, 324, 327, 330–31, 336–37
GeoJigSaw, 336
geometry, 317–18
graphics programs. *See* art programs; painting and
    illustration programs
gray-scale monitors, 25
Grolier's Academic American Encyclopedia, 252–54, 369

hard disks, 19–21
hardware. *See* IBM PC-compatibles; Macintoshes; *and
    specific items*
    vendors of, 372
Headline Harry, 330–31

HeadStart SX-20 CD computer, 40
Hercules cards, 23
history programs, 330–34
homebrew computer manufacturers, 28, 68–69

IBM PC-ATs, 18
IBM PC-compatible computers
    advantages of, 7–9
    components needed when buying, 10
    deciding whether to buy a Mac or, 7–12
    microprocessors for, 16–19
    monitors for, 26–29, 40
IBM PC-compatible systems, 39–40
independence, encouraging, 80–81
integrated software packages, 287–88

joysticks, 33
Just Grandma and Me, 365

keyboard, 33, 298
keyboard etiquette, 79
keyboarding skills, 108–9. *See also* touch-typing
KidPix, 80, 142–63
    activities with, 158–63
        Connect-The-Dots drawing, 159–60
        floor plans, 158–63
        group Apple II computers, 162
        illustrations for stories, 161–62
        matching game for pre-schoolers, 158–59
        paintings by twentieth-century artists, 162–63
        rebuses, 160
        Rorschach test, 159
        Rubber Stamp tool, 160–61
    Alphabet Line option, 153
    Connect-The-Dots option, 152
    eraser, 155
    introduction to, 144
    Line tool, 151
    menus and commands, 157
    Mixer Tool, 154
    Moving Van, 156–57
    Options Arrow, 149
    Oval tool, 151
    Paint Can tool, 149, 154–55
    quick tour of, 145–48
    Rectangle tool, 150
    Rubber Stamp tool, 147, 155
    Stamp Editor, 155
    Text Tool, 156
    tint option, 150
    tools in, 146–48
    Undo Guy, 154, 157
    Wacky Pencil tool, 148, 150
    Wacky Pen tool, 152
KidShell, 82
Kid Works, 288–90
KidzMouse, 32
kilobytes, 22
Knowledge Adventure, 332–34

Ladybug LOGO, 277
laser printers, 35–36
Lego LOGO, 277–78
Living Books, 365–66
logic programs. *See* problem-solving and logic programs
LogoExpress, 277
LogoWriter, 258–77
    components of a page in, 263
    introduction to, 260–62
    musical birthday cards program using, 270–74
    primitives (procedures) in, 264–66
    shape-maker in, 274–76
    starting a program in, 263
    variables in, 271

Macintosh computers (Macs), 7–16
    advantages of, 9
    basic and optional components of, 11
    deciding whether to buy an IBM PC-compatible or, 7–8
    drives on, 21
    microprocessors for, 13–16
    models of, 12–16
    SCSI ports on, 21
    software for, 8–9
    used, 16
    video systems of, 23–26
Macintosh systems, 41
Macmillan Dictionary for Children, 366
magazines, computer, 63
mailorder companies, 63–65
Mammals: A Multimedia Encyclopedia, 366
Map and atlas skills. *See* geography programs
Math Blaster!, 312–13
Math Blaster Mystery, 313
Math Blaster Plus!, 313
math programs, 310–18
Math Rabbit, 311–12
Mavis Beacon Teaches Touch Typing, 31–32
MCGA, 27
MDA (Monochrome Display Adapter), 23
megabytes (MB), 20, 22
megahertz (mhz), 18
memory, 21–23
menus, creating your own, 80–84
MetroGnome's Music, 352–53
Mickey Mouse software, 291–95
Mickey's ABCs, 292
Mickey's Colors and Shapes, 293
Mickey's Crossword Puzzle Maker, 293
Mickey's Jigsaw Puzzle, 335
Mickey's 123s, 292
microprocessors
    for IBM PC-compatibles, 16–19
    Macintosh, 13–16
Microsoft Bookshelf, 366–67
Microsoft Technical Support, 86
Midnight Rescue!, 296–97
Mixed-Up Mother Goose, 367

modems, 29, 33–34, 228–29
monitors, 23, 77
    gray-scale, 25
    for IBM PC-compatibles, 26–29, 40
    interlaced versus non-interlaced, 29
    for Macintoshes, 24–26
    multi synch, 25, 27
    size of, 24–25
monochrome monitors, 23
Motorola 680xx family of microprocessors, 13
mouse, 29–30, 32
Multi Color Graphics Array, 27
Multimedia Beethoven: The Ninth Symphony, 367–68
multimedia computers, 38–39, 370
multiprocessing, 18–19
multisync monitors, 25, 27
multitasking, 85
music programs, 341–43, 348, 352–53
music software, 53
My Paint, 353–54

National Geographic, on Prodigy, 244–51
New Grolier's Electronic Encyclopedia, The, 368–69
New Math Blaster Plus!, 312–14
Notepad, 199–200, 210–12
NotePlay, 354–55
NuBus boards, 15

online services, 226. *See also* Prodigy
Operation Neptune, 314–15
Our House, 369
Out Numbered!, 315–16

Paintbrush, 216–21
painting and illustration programs, 288–89. *See also*
    specific programs
parallel port, 33
PC Globe, 336–37
PCs. *See* IBM PC-compatible computers
Performa line of Macintoshes, 15–16
phonics, 297, 303
Picture Wizard, 355–56
pixels, 24
Playing with Language, 369–70
Playroom, The, 50, 80, 98–113
    Apple II computers in, 102–4
    exploratory games in, 104–11
        ABC book, 111–12
        the clock, 105–6
        computer, 108–9
        spinner toy, 107–8
        toy on the carpet, 106–7
    getting started with, 100–102
    introduction to, 100
PowerBooks, 13
power strip, 76
pre-programming skills, 328–29
pre-reading programs, 291–92, 301–2, 367
printers, 34–36

Print Shop, 356–57
Print Shop Companion, 357
Print Shop Deluxe, 357
problem-solving and logic programs, 322–32, 338–40
problem-solving skills, 312–16
Prodigy, 224–39
    The Club, 234–39
    electronic mail (e-mail), 234, 239
    Grolier's Academic American Encyclopedia, 252–54
    Jump command, 231
    National Geographic feature, 244–51
    online research with, 242–55
    Path command, 232
    quick tour of, 229–31
    shortcut keys, 233
    startup kits for, 228
program group, in Windows, 86–88
Program Manager, 196–98
PS/1 computer, 39–40
puzzle-solving programs, 335–36, 340

Quadra Macintoshes, 15
QuickDraw, 24

RAM (Random Access Memory), 21–23
Reader Rabbit and Reader Rabbit 2, 297–99
reading and writing software, 286–305. *See also* word
    processing programs
    on CD-ROM disks, 363, 365
rebus games, 289
reference books, on CD-ROM disks, 364–69
resolution, 23–24
RGB monitors, 26
role-playing games, 52–53

schools, computers used in, 8, 11
SCSI ports, on Macintoshes, 21
Secret Island of Dr. Quandry, The, 339
serial ports, 33
sharing behavior, 102
shopping for a computer, 58–72
    checklist for IBM PC-compatibles, 72
    credit card payment, 62
    employee purchase, 61
    returns and warranties, 66–68
    returns policy, 61
    sources for products and information
        computer fairs, 69
        discount stores and buyers clubs, 65–68
        garage sales and the classifieds, 69–70
        homebrewers, 68–69
        Macintoshes, 70–71
        magazines, 63
        mailorder companies, 63–65
        superstores, 66–67
    sources for products and information, 62–71
    tips on, 61–62
    used systems, 69–71
SimEarth, SimCity, and SimAnt, 338

simulations, 50
software. *See also specific programs and categories of programs*
    adult programs, 54
    alphabetical listing of vendors and programs, 374–86
    arcade games, 51–52
    bundled with hardware, 66
    buying, 69
    choosing, 46–49
    creativity tools, 53
    deciding which computer to buy and, 8–9
    demo disks, 59
    drill-and-practice, 53–54
    edutainment, 50–51
    role-playing and fantasy games, 52–53
    simulations, 50
sound, 36, 290–91
SoundBlaster card, 37, 291
sound cards, 37
Sound Source, 37, 291–92, 294–95
speakers, 36
Spellbound, 300–301
spelling programs, 109, 300–301
Stacker, 21
Stickeybear Numbers, 310
Stickeybear series, 301–2
storytelling programs, 302
Super Solvers Club, 296–97
surge protector, 76
System 6, 14
System 7, 13–14

Talking Once Upon a Time, 302–3
Terrapin Logo, 278
Think Quick!, 340
time, learning to tell, 105–6
Time Riders in American History, 332
Time Treks, 328
touch-typing, 79. *See also* keyboard skills
Treasure Mountain, 303–4
Treehouse, The, 341–43
Trivial Pursuit game, Carmen Sandiego, 134–35
typing. *See* keyboarding skills; touch-typing

used systems, 69–71
user groups, 68–69

VGA (Video Graphics Array) video systems, 27
video adapter boards. *See* display adapters
video systems, 23–29
    Macintosh, 23–26
Viking Ships, 324
Voyager's companion series, 368

What's My Angle?, 317–18
Where in America's Past is Carmen Sandiego?, 123
Where in the USA is Carmen Sandiego?, 47–48, 122

Where in the World is Carmen Sandiego?, 116–40, 326
    activities related to, 131–40
        almanac games and Apple II computers, 134, 136–37
        Carmen Sandiego game shows, 139
        Carmen Sandiego party, 133
        database of country information, 135–36
        dictionary activity, 135
        family ancestry, 132
        flags of the world, 136–37
        mock trial, 138
        music, 133–34
        national anthems game, 137
        Nintendo game, 140
        novels about Carmen Sandiego, 140
        places of interest, 139
        Prodigy online service, 139
        role-playing, 131–40
        spy clothes and gadgets, 138
        stamps and coins, 137–38
        Trivial Pursuit game, 134–35
    arrest warrant in, 127–28
    clues in, 125–26
    Crime Computer in, 125, 128, 130–31
    Evidence File in, 126–27, 130–31
    introduction to, 118–21
    quick tour of, 123–29
    timekeeping device in, 126–27
Where in the World is Carmen Sandiego? Deluxe Edition, 121
Where in Time is Carmen Sandiego?, 122–23
Windows, 22, 84–91, 192–221
    Calculator, 204–6
    Calendar, 201–4
    Cardfile, 206–10
    childproofing, 85–86, 90–91
    clock in, 206
    introduction to, 194–98
    moving around, 195–97
    Notepad, 199–200, 210–12
    for older children, 85–88
    Paintbrush, 216–21
    program group in, 86–88
    Program Manager, 196–98
    programs included in, 198–200
    quick tour of, 200–201
    sup programs to run under, 89–90
    Write, 212–16, 219–21
    for younger children, 88–89
Word for Windows, 287
word processing programs, 287–88. *See also Writing Center, The*
    for the Mac, 288
    Notepad, 210–12
    Write, 212–16, 219–21
Write, 212–16, 219–21
Writer Rabbit, 299
Writing to Read, 304–5